WESSEX
AVIATION
INDUSTRY

Supermarine Spitfire F22 from South Marston.

WESSEX AVIATION INDUSTRY

MIKE PHIPP

AMBERLEY

First published 2011

Amberley Publishing
The Hill, Stroud
Gloucestershire GL5 4ER

www.amberleybooks.com

British Library Cataloguing in Publication Data.
A catalogue record for this book is available from the British Library.

ISBN 978-1-4456-0046-8

Typesetting and Origination by Amberley Publishing.
Printed in Great Britain.

Contents

Airspeed Ambassador over Christchurch Priory.

Introduction

This book covers the various aircraft production companies of the Wessex area of Southern England. I have chosen this region as it is home territory to me and so of most interest. The boundaries of Wessex vary according to which author you read, but for my purpose I have chosen Dorset and Wiltshire, along with western parts of Hampshire and Berkshire. I intended to use the M4 motorway as my northern limit, but had to ignore this in order to include South Marston – most important in the Supermarine story. I hope the reader is happy with my choice. A large number of books have already been published on individual companies and aircraft. Here it has been my intention to present local information in a new format.

The layout of the book is in alphabetical order of the manufacturing sites, with a chronological listing of the companies found on each. During their lifetimes, most of the aviation companies covered in this book have seen amalgamations or takeovers. Sometimes this resulted in a change of name, but not always. In the case of Supermarine Aviation, athough the company became part of Vickers Aviation at quite an early stage, due to the many locations at which it could later be found I have refered to it as 'Supermarine' for most of the text. Early hovercrafts were developed by a number of Wessex aviation firms, and this is covered under the appropriate locations. Although not aircraft, the appropriate ministries regarded them as such until June 1972, at which time they came into their own category.

Although not an industrial area, Wessex was home to many pioneering aviation companies in the 1900s. The main reason was that many south-coast shipbuilders turned their hand to building seaplanes. The style of construction was similar in both cases. As the First World War progressed, the Admiralty saw the need for a large number of seaplanes and flying boats, and turned to the boat builders to fulfil their needs. In a number of cases, such as Hamble and Hythe, the Admiralty also provided large sheds for the construction of these aircraft. The aviation companies then had to weather the 1920s, when there were few orders to be had. The RAF Expansion Plan of the late 1930s brought work to Christchurch, Eastleigh, Hamble and Portsmouth, among others. The next expansion in the area was the Spitfire dispersal programme of 1940, which saw many new sites in the area and elsewhere. Some, such as Aldermaston and Reading, are outside the scope of this book. Mention must be made of the invaluable work of the pilots – men and women – of the Air Transport Auxiliary. During the Second World War, they delivered the new aircraft from the factories to the RAF Maintenance Units. Without their efforts, the production system would have clogged up.

The return to peace in 1945 saw the start of the jet age, which involved many firms within Wessex. Then the infamous Defence White Paper of April 1957 led to the rundown of the RAF from the 1960s. In May 1958, the Government indicated it wanted the large number of aviation companies in the country to be rationalised. This saw well-known names merge into BAC or Hawker Siddeley in 1959–60, or else give up aircraft production. Many turned to other fields of work. Slowly the industry declined, leaving it to smaller organisations to continue Wessex's aviation heritage.

When I started researching this book, I had it in mind that there were many large aircraft companies producing their own famous products. But what struck me was the amount of assistance provided by the companies for one another. Examples include Saro building Bluebirds for Blackburn and Viscount wings for Vickers; Folland building Chipmunk, Dove, Vampire and Venom wings for de Havilland; and Airspeed building Comet 1 fuselages for de Havilland. Another task of mine was deciding where an aircraft was 'built'. Spitfires were produced at various dispersed sites, Viscounts appeared from Hurn and Islanders from Bembridge. But it wasn't that simple. Although it has usually been possible to find where a completed Spitfire flew from, sometimes it has not been easy to establish where it was built. Many Viscount fuselages were built at Weybridge and transported to Hurn for final assembly with wings built by Saunders-Roe. Similarly, the Trident airliner would appear to have nothing to do with Wessex. But BEA's early Trident 1s had fuselages from Portsmouth and wings from Hamble. The early success of the Islander meant that Bembridge was unable to keep up with demand. So when a new aircraft was handed over to a customer, it could have been built in Cowes, Belgium, Romania or the Philippines. Avro was different. The company is normally regarded as a family business based in Manchester. Of the two founding brothers, one left to join the RFC in 1917 and the other sold out in 1928. Additionally, in the early days, much work was carried out at Hamble – the site being of great importance to the company. At one stage in 1920 the Manchester site almost closed, which could have resulted in Avro's major presence being in Hampshire.

When the Air Force or Navy had a requirement for a new aircraft, the Air Ministry issued a specification to the aircraft industry. The response might be from one company or a number of firms. The Air Ministry would order prototypes, usually from two companies, and these would be put through tests to confirm their suitability. In the 1920s and 1930s, landplanes would be tested at Martlesham Heath in Suffolk – home of the Aeroplane & Armament Experimental Establishment. Flying boats were tested at the Marine Aircraft Experimental Establishment, based in Felixstowe. Post-war Martlesham's work was transferred to Boscombe Down in Wiltshire. More detailed research testing was carried out at the Royal Aircraft Establishment at Farnborough from 1918 until 1994. Post-war Farnborough was also home to the once-annual SBAC Farnborough Air Shows, where new aircraft would be displayed each September. In more recent years the show has been held biennially and opened up to international participation. The names of these airfields crop up frequently throughout this book.

Civil airliners were usually built to official requirements, but most smaller projects were funded by their manufacturers. Frequently one comes across promising designs that have failed due to lack of finance. Aviation has always been a risky business for city investors, but without their backing, attempts to obtain private finance would probably be unsuccessful. This is a theme repeated throughout this book.

An organisation whose name crops up is the South East England Development Agency (SEEDA). This was a Government-funded quango set up in the 2000s with a remit to oversee economic and social development in the region. Interestingly, it acquired land at some former aviation sites in Wessex, namely East Cowes, Hythe and Lee-on-Solent. In June 2010 it was announced that SEEDA was to be closed down and that within the next two years the sites would be sold off.

The following is an account of how the south has followed the fate of rest of the country – in terms of the decline of a great UK industry.

Acknowledgements

As is the case with any historian, my information has been gathered from many publications and sources over the years. These include previous publications on aircraft companies and many aviation periodicals. The majority of photographs used are publicity photographs issued by the various companies, plus some of my own and others from my collection.

Special thanks go to a number of organisations and individuals. To Colin Cruddas for photographs from his collection; to Peter Dimmick and his 'archive team' at Solent Sky for allowing me access to the photograph collection and records; to Roly Errington for allowing me access to his father's diaries and photographs relating to his time at Airspeeds; to Dave Fagan for allowing to quote from his Hampshire and Dorset Aviation websites; and to Roy Nerou, who is responsible for the Chilton aircraft website. The map opposite was drawn by Thomas Bohm of User Design (*www.userdesign.co.uk*).

Finally, I must once again thank my wife for her time, patient proofreading and suggestions. As the book is biased towards facts and figures, this task has not been as easy as on previous occasions. I have had to promise her that the next book will be a more obviously gratifying type of history.

A Map of the Area

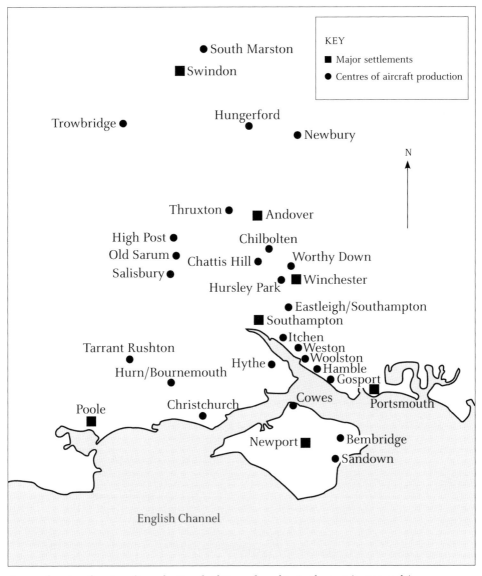

A map showing the aircraft production facilities referred to in the text (not to scale).

Bembridge

Bembridge airfield came into use in the 1920s and was listed by the Automobile Association in the early 1930s as a licensed airfield. Limited air services commenced in 1935, with a small terminal and hangar provided on the south side. The airfield was closed during the Second World War. It reopened after the war, although a hard runway was not provided until 1979.

BRITTEN-NORMAN LTD

A recurring theme of this book is that of boat builders becoming aircraft builders. The Britten-Norman name does not spring to mind with regard to this motif, however boat-building *was* the company's origin in Bembridge. In the late 1940s John Britten and Desmond Norman, both former de Havilland Aircraft apprentices, established a small yacht-building business in Bembridge, and constructed a number of successful race winners. In 1950 they decided to design their first aircraft – the BN-1F Finibee. A high-wing, single-seat ultra-light, the BN-1F was intended for home construction. With its 40 hp JAP engine the BN-1F G-ALZE proved to be underpowered and crashed during early testing in 1951. Rebuilt with a new fuselage and fitted with a more powerful 55 hp Lycoming engine, G-ALZE flew again in August, but still displayed poor flying qualities. So the partners' idea was abandoned and G-ALZE was stored in their Bembridge boathouse for many years.

The two men formed the Britten-Norman partnership in 1952 to undertake the conversion of surplus RAF Tiger Moths into crop sprayers, with Britten-Norman Ltd formed in 1953. Lack of hangar space at Bembridge initially meant that the Tiger Moths were overhauled in a church hall in the centre of Ryde. Seeking to improve aerial crop spraying, Britten-Norman developed the Micronair rotary atomiser spray equipment for Super Cubs, Tiger Moths and other crop-spraying aircraft. This increased the area covered by the pesticides. Crop Culture was formed in 1954 as an associate company to further develop 'chemical treatment by air' and their Micronair equipment was sold worldwide. Crop Culture also

Britten-Norman's entry into aviation was the BN1F Finibee ultra-light G-ALZE. It was unsuccessful and for many years was stored in a boatshed at Bembridge. Eventually it was rescued and restored; it is currently on display at Solent Sky, Southampton.

undertook aerial spraying contracts in places such as Jamaica, Nigeria and Sudan. The company became Crop Culture (Aerial) Ltd in 1956.

Returning to the light aircraft theme, Britten-Norman built a Druine Turbi two-seat ultra-light in a disused Bembridge cinema during the winter of 1956/57. It was built for use by the Popular Flying Association and, appropriately registered G-APFA, first flew on 13 May 1957. However, it proved to be another one-off.

The late 1950s saw the development of the hovercraft in Britain, and Britten-Norman had ideas for this new mode of transport. These were put into practice with the three-seat BN-1 Cushioncraft G-APYH, which undertook trials from June 1960, having been built in the small hangar on the south side of the airfield. Power was from a 175 hp Coventry Climax industrial engine. Funding was provided by the banana importer Elders & Fyffes, who saw a potential use for Cushioncraft in its Cameroon plantations. The BN-1 was only the second hovercraft to 'fly' after Saro's SR-N1 at Cowes. Initially known as the BN-1 Cushioncraft, this designation caused confusion with the earlier Finibee, so was changed to CC-1. Next came the larger Cushioncraft CC-2 in August 1961. The first was G-ARSM and was followed by two production CC-2s. All later undertook military trials, with G-ARSM used at RAE Bedford as XR814. The two production machines ended up being evaluated on land trials at Chobham from the spring of 1965. Being a more practical machine, the CC-2 enabled Britten-Norman to build up more experience. The CC-3 was a design project only, followed by the five/six-seat CC-4 in 1964. Expansion of aircraft activity at Bembridge saw the Cushioncraft work split off into a separate business in 1966, established just up the road at St Helens. The company was incorporated into British Hovercraft Corporation at Cowes in 1971.

Selling their crop-spraying equipment took Britten and Norman all over the world. This led them to realise there was a requirement for a rugged twin-engine, light-utility aircraft to serve out-of-the-way places such as West Africa. John Britten set about the design work, which resulted in the ten-seat BN2, with a mock-up built in late 1964. Still using the original hangar, a small team set about this new 'home-built' with prototype G-ATCT flown by the two directors on 13 June 1965. They flew off to the Paris Air Show four days later. The small Britten-Norman team had no way of knowing what an important aircraft they were launching. Initially it was powered by two 210 hp Continental engines, but flight-testing showed the need for more powerful 260 hp Lycoming engines. Appropriately, it was named Islander in August 1966, and the first deliveries were made to Loganair and Aurigny Air Services for 'island hopping' in August 1967. It was cheaper than American twins of a similar size, and many orders

Britten-Norman's Cushioncraft CC-1 'floating' over Bembridge airfield. This was the later stages of trials in 1961 with a dorsal fin added to improve directional stability at higher speeds.

were received from across the Atlantic, where the Islander soon found a niche market. The first for the USA was delivered by air in September 1967, followed by many more over the years. The initial price of a basic Islander was £26,000 ($62,000), with the aim being to produce one a day. A new 56,000 sq. ft factory was built on the eastern side of Bembridge airfield ('Europe's finest light aircraft factory') in 1966–67, but demand soon outstripped production. Arrangements were made in 1968 for British Hovercraft Corporation to produce the aircraft from 1970 at the former Saro works in East Cowes. The initial plan was for only the wings to be built at Cowes, but demand was such that fuselages were also built there. They were then taken by road to Bembridge for assembly. In 1968 production was running at six a month, rising to fourteen in 1969. Under an offset trade deal signed with Romania in 1968, further aircraft were built by IRMA in Bucharest from 1969. They were then flown 'green' to Bembridge for fitting out – G-AXHY was the first in September 1969. The initial contract was for 215 aircraft, but when IRMA was reorganised as Romaero in 1995, the contract was extended. Nearly half of all the Islanders produced have been built in Bucharest, with deliveries to Bembridge continuing up to 2010. One unusual test flight was by G-AVUB in May 1968, during which it landed (intentionally)

The Islanders' final assembly is underway in the new Britten-Norman hangar early in 1976. Heading the line-up is Defender version G-BDJZ, built at Gosselies and fitted out at Bembridge prior to delivery to the Indian Navy in May 1976.

An Islander in the setting envisaged by John Britten and Desmond Norman. Seen here at a jungle airstrip in Monrovia, EL-AHX is one of six Islanders delivered to Air Liberia in 1975. They operated services from the capital to remote parts of the country.

on the aircraft carrier HMS *Hermes*, which was sailing in the English Channel south of Portland. G-AWID, delivered to Thailand in October 1968, was typical of a number delivered fitted with underwing Micronair spray equipment.

The success of the Islander soon led to the development of a larger version. The first production Islander G-ATWU initially had its fuselage lengthened by 33 inches and was flown as such on 14 July 1968. Although incorporating four extra seats, it was soon realised that something larger still was required. So G-ATWU had a 7 ft 6 in extension inserted, together with a third Lycoming engine, not in the nose, as would have been expected, but, uniquely, on top of the fin. It flew on 11 September 1970 as the 'Experimental Islander Mk 3' and, as the flight was successful, it was flown to the Farnborough Air Show later in the day. It was officially named Trislander in January 1971. Capable of carrying seventeen passengers, the first production Trislander was delivered to Aurigny Air Services in June 1971. Aurigny is still operating Trislanders forty years later. The early Trislanders were rebuilt Islander fuselages – it was not until later that they had their own production line. A military version of the Islander known as the Defender was developed in 1970–71, and the camouflaged prototype G-AYTS first flew in June 1971. Fitted with a strengthened wing, it could also be fitted with underwing stores such as rockets, bombs or gun pods.

Having had its fuselage lengthened in 1968, Islander G-ATWU was further stretched in 1970 and had a third engine fitted. As the 'Experimental Islander Mk 3' it was exhibited at Farnborough in September 1970, pending the production go-ahead from Britten-Norman.

Early production Trislanders were built at Bembridge, as seen here. From 1974, production was switched to Gosselies, Belgium, with the aircraft flown to Bembridge for fitting out. At the time, Fairey SA was trying to dispose of the production rights to the Trislander.

The Trislander entered service with Aurigny Air Services of Alderney in October 1971, operating between the Channel Islands and the UK mainland. In the 1990s, three-bladed propellers were fitted to the two wing-mounted engines to help reduce noise levels.

The Defender was developed for military customers, and incorporated a strengthened wing. B-10 is one of twelve Defenders delivered to the Belgian Army in 1976. It is fitted with a small nose radar, but otherwise gives the appearance of being a standard Islander.

This warlike Defender is destined for the Mauritanian Islamic Air Force. Built as an Islander in 1975, it was converted into a Defender, despite still carrying an Islander title on its nose. 5T-MAS was delivered from Bembridge in the spring of 1976.

By 1970 Islanders were being built faster than they could be fitted out at Bembridge. As a result, a number of 'green' airframes were stored at Eastleigh, along with some fuselages from the British Hovercraft Corporation. This indicated a healthy order book, but cash-flow problems forced Britten-Norman into receivership in October 1971. Britten-Norman (Bembridge) Ltd was formed by the receiver to carry on production, pending a purchaser coming forward. In August 1972 Britten-Norman was acquired by Fairey SA of Gosselies, Belgium. The production jigs used by British Hovercraft Corporation were moved to Gosselies, along with a number of stored fuselages from Eastleigh. Fairey Britten-Norman now undertook production in Belgium, with 'green' aircraft flown to Bembridge for fitting out. At the time there was a staff of 250 at Bembridge. Problems in the USA over Trislander operating weights led to the trial fitting in the summer of 1976 of a small booster rocket under the tail engine for improved take-offs. This never went into service.

Returning to their original idea of a light aircraft, Britten and Norman designed the BN3 Nymph in 1969. A high-wing four-seater powered by a 115 hp Lycoming, the prototype G-AXFB flew from Bembridge on 17 May 1969. The Nymph was aimed at the home builder, with an anticipated price of £1,930 for a kit. An order for 100 from Australia was announced in September 1969, but the deal fell through. A downturn in the light aircraft market and preoccupation with the Islander meant that there was insufficient time to work on, and develop, the Nymph. In the summer of 1973 it was anticipated there would be a revival of the project, but this did not happen. Design studies of a much larger aircraft were undertaken in 1972, leading to the Mainlander. It resembled a Hercules-sized Trislander with power supplied by three Rolls-Royce Darts. Its rotund fuselage was capable of carrying 100 passengers and eight small cars or similar payloads. As such it could replace the Bristol Freighter and a display model saw it in British Air Ferries colours. Production would be undertaken at Gosselies and launch finance was sought in Belgium as all Fairey Britten-Norman's funds were tied up with the Islander/Trislander. In the end, the Mainlander remained a project only.

In September 1974 the Philippines placed a provisional order for 100 Islanders, part of the deal being that there would be local assembly of the aircraft. Arrangements were made for production to be undertaken by Philippine Aerospace Development Corp in Manila. This included Islanders and Defenders for the Philippine Air Force, as well as civilian sales. Some kits were shipped to Manila from Bembridge in 1976 to enable local production to get underway and, in a reversal, in 1984–86 completed aircraft were flown back to the UK for fitting

The Nymph was an attempt by Britten-Norman to enter the light aircraft industry dominated by the USA in the 1960s. First flown in May 1969, prototype G-AXFB is seen here on a test-flight over the Isle of Wight.

Above: Following a repaint, the Nymph was displayed at the Farnborough Air Show in September 1970. Kits were advertised at £2,000. Even then, it was realised that the hoped-for market was not there, mainly due to the financial downturn of the time.

Left: An ambitious plan in 1972 was the Mainlander. It was not intended for production at Bembridge, but rather with another manufacturer. However, there was insufficient demand and problems with funding. The registration refers to 'G-A Fairey Britten Norman'.

Turbine-powered aircraft were produced from the summer of 1981 in both Islander and Defender versions. This Turbine Defender is one of many used for surveillance purposes; it is fitted with a 360° optical camera on the side of its fuselage.

out and sale. Plans for a floatplane version of the Islander got as far as G-BDNP being fitted with a pair of floats at Bembridge in January 1976. The idea was given up before it could fly. In the summer of 1976, G-BDMT was modified as the Agricultural Islander and was displayed at Farnborough the following month. Instead of being fitted with Micronair equipment, G-BDMT had a large hopper under each wing for dispensing fertilisers.

Having achieved their aim, the two founding directors stood down in February 1976. John Britten set about designing the Sheriff light twin, which was later built at Sandown, and Desmond Norman formed NDN Aircraft, also at Sandown. Fairey Britten-Norman ran into cash-flow problems and was forced into receivership in August 1977. There were accounting difficulties between Bembridge and Gosselies, where Fairey were making losses. Again, production continued, pending a new buyer, which was Pilatus Aircraft of Switzerland. Pilatus officially took over in January 1979 under the name of Pilatus Britten-Norman, and injected new funds into the company. An additional hangar was built at Bembridge for aircraft completion and an 837 m concrete runway was provided in 1980. There was sufficient demand to develop a turboprop Islander, although an initial attempt with a 600 hp Lycoming-powered Turbo-Islander in the spring of 1977 proved to be a false start. With more suitable 320 hp Allison engine, Defender G-BPBN was re-engined in the spring of 1980 and flown as the Turbine Islander in August. Production aircraft appeared the following year, with the first delivered in October 1981. Trislander sales were falling off and so the final one was delivered in September 1984. Plans for continued production in Florida from 1982 using incomplete airframes came to nothing. The idea was revived in the summer of 1990, with production proposed in Australia, but again the plan came to nothing.

In the military world the development of smaller surveillance and communication equipment enabled these systems to be fitted in smaller – and cheaper – aircraft such as the Defender. Three military versions were developed in the 1980s. The CASTOR version was developed to a British MoD requirement to provide battlefield radar surveillance and was fitted with Ferranti radar in an enlarged nose. G-DLRA was the development aircraft and it first flew in May 1984. The next version was an AEW platform, which housed a Thorn EMI 360° downward-looking radar in an unsightly nose radome. Although test-flown in July 1984, G-TEMI was not fully equipped until its official launch in March 1987. No production orders were received for either version, mainly due to changing requirements. Then came the 'Multi Sensor Surveillance Aircraft', developed in conjunction with Westinghouse Corporation of the USA for use as a surveillance platform. Again this had a 360° radar in an unflattering bulbous nose, and G-TEMI was modified as the prototype G-MSSA. Two aircraft were delivered to Westinghouse in 1991–92 for trials, with two further ones remaining at Bembridge. Trials in the States showed that a larger aircraft was needed as crews were cramped due to the amount of equipment fitted in the cabin.

A number of MSSA Defenders were used from 1992 to trial a Westinghouse multi-role 360° radar – hence the unsightly bulbous nose. In the event, the Defender proved too small an airframe for comfortable operations.

The prototype Defender 4000 flew in August 1994 and was displayed at the Farnborough Air Show the following month. The lengthened fuselage provides additional working space for its crews – something that was desirable on longer sorties.

The lack of operating space in the MSSA Defender led to the BN2T Defender 4000, powered by 400 hp Allison turboprops. The Defender 4000 had a 30 inch fuselage extension over the standard aircraft and further strengthened wings. Intended for advanced surveillance duties, with a 1,000 mile range and seven-hour endurance, this new version first flew in August 1994. G-SURV was used as the demonstrator aircraft and options included underwing camera pods, torpedoes and air-to-surface missiles. The first delivery to the Irish Garda was made in September 1997, followed by various police forces and the British Army.

As part of its business rationalisation, Britten-Norman was put up for sale by Pilatus in June 1998. The following month it was acquired by investment company Biofarm Inc. and renamed Britten-Norman Ltd once again. At the time, the company had approximately 200 employees. In May 2000, the Zawawi Group of Oman formed the Britten-Norman Group, purchasing Britten-Norman from Biofarm. The Britten-Norman Group was a holding company for the various activities, with Britten-Norman Aircraft responsible for design and manufacture.

As there were a number of Trislanders still in service that needed replacing, plans were made on a number of occasions to restart production, first in the spring of 1999, when three were ordered by China Northern Airlines, then again in February 2003 and early in 2008. But on none of these occasions did Britten-Norman's plans reach fruition. In August 2005, a new subsidiary was formed – Aero Composites Ltd. Early work included the assembly of the Cirrus range of SR20 and SR22 light aircraft for European customers. However, after a couple of years, Cirrus arranged for new aircraft to be flown across the Atlantic from their Minnesota base.

In May 2010, Britten-Norman announced that Defenders would be built at a new site at Lee-on-Solent airfield instead of in Romania. This was due to the rising costs of production in what was now an EU country. The facilities at Lee-on-Solent were on part of the airfield purchased by SEEDA in March 2006. Production of Islanders continues at Bembridge, although now at a price of $989,950. In the twenty-first century, Britten-Norman still receives limited orders for Islanders, but now concentrates on 'sophisticated mission systems integration' in existing military airframes. This sees the fitment of updated avionics, surveillance and ISTAR.

June 2010 marked forty-five years since the prototype BN2 flew. Despite the many financial ups and downs over these years, the Britten-Norman Group remains the only British manufacturer left producing factory-built aircraft, the total currently standing at 1,250.

Chattis Hill

There was an RFC airfield at Chattis Hill, to the west of Stockbridge and to the north of Chattis Hill House, towards the end of the First World War. Upon the return to peace, it was soon abandoned.

VICKERS-SUPERMARINE

As part of Supermarine's 1940 dispersal plan, various sites were selected for continued Spitfire production. Chattis Hill was chosen as a final assembly site for Spitfires built in small factories around the Salisbury area. A two-bay assembly hangar was erected at the end of 1940 to the north of the original airfield. However, Supermarine decided not to use the original site, but selected a new flying area just to the west on the opposite side of the secondary road, which passed the airfield. From the spring of 1941, lorries arrived with major Spitfire assemblies, which were erected in the new hangar. Originally, the new Spitfires were to be flight-tested at High Post, but the large numbers produced resulted in Chattis Hill also being used for this purpose from the spring of 1941. Prior to delivery to the RAF, they would be parked among the trees that surrounded the hangar, and were therefore camouflaged from possible Luftwaffe attacks. Initially Spitfire Vs were produced, followed by PRIVs from December 1942, FVIIIs from the spring 1943, and then PRXIs. A few Griffon-powered FXIIs were also produced in the spring of 1943, followed by larger numbers of FXIVs in 1944 and PRXIXs in 1945. In all, over 1,250 Spitfires were completed at Chattis Hill. Seafire IICs were produced from August 1942, having originally been ordered as Spitfire Vs.

With the return to peace there was no further use for Chattis Hill; Spitfires were now delivered from Eastleigh or South Marston. However, Supermarine continued to use the site until 31 May 1948, when the company moved out to its Chilbolten site.

In 1940, Supermarine's Spitfire assembly hangar was built between existing trees to provide camouflage. Major parts were received from sites around Salisbury for final assembly. Spitfire Vs are seen here awaiting test-flying or delivery to the RAF.

Even with the end of the Second World War in sight, large numbers of Spitfires were still assembled at Chattis Hill. In 1945, these included a number of PRXIX aircraft; this one was still in RAF service in the 1970s.

Chilbolten

To the south of Andover, Chilbolten was initially a grass airfield established for the RAF during the Second World War. It was developed with hard runways in 1943 and was used by the USAAF over the D-Day period. It then reverted to the RAF, who moved out in 1946.

In 1964–67, a large radio telescope was built by the Space Research Council at the runway intersection point. Currently known as the Chilbolten Facility for Atmospheric and Radio Research, the telescope is a prominent feature of the local landscape.

VICKERS-SUPERMARINE

Due to the post-war unsuitability of High Post airfield for flight-testing, Supermarine transferred its base to Chilbolten in the spring of 1947. A former RAF hangar was taken over and a second, larger one was erected adjacent to it. Initial testing at Chilbolten was on Spitfires, Seafires and Spitefuls, along with the Attacker prototypes. Although no construction work was undertaken by Supermarine, modification work was carried out as necessary on the aircraft undertaking trials.

The prototype Attackers TS409 and TS413 undertook early flight trials from Boscombe Down in 1947, and from Chilbolten later in the same year. The third prototype, TS416, arrived equipped to naval standards. A dummy carrier deck was installed in the summer of 1947 for landing trials, prior to full-scale carrier trials by TS416 in October. On 27 February 1948, TS409, piloted by Mike Lithgow, set a 565 mph closed-circuit air-speed record. Following the loss of TS416 in 1948, TS409 was rebuilt in 1949 to full naval standards. Attacker development trials continued in the early 1950s, with the Supermarine 322 R1815 used as a chase aircraft. The Attacker's speed proved to be little improved over that of the Seafang. In August 1948, the prototype Seagull PA143 arrived from Itchen for land-based trials, returning as necessary to Southampton Water for water-based ones. VV106, the prototype Supermarine 510 and forerunner of the Swift,

Left: Supermarine 392 Attacker prototype TS409 shows off its wing shape, which was similar to that of the Spiteful. After initial testing at High Post, flight trials moved to Chilbolten in 1947. Chilbolten remained Supermarine's flight-test base for ten years.

Below: Prototype Attacker TS409 in February 1948 after Chief Test Pilot Mike Lithgow (third from left) had broken the closed-circuit air-speed record. The Attacker was the only jet fighter fitted with a tail wheel to enter operational service.

The next stage of Supermarine's fighter development was the fitting of the Attacker with swept wings and tailplane. VV106 emerged as the Supermarine 510 and undertook flight trials from Chilbolten in 1949. As can be seen, it still retains a tail wheel.

Similar to VV106, VV119 was the Supermarine 528, which incorporated a redesigned nose and air intake. Flight trials with both aircraft showed the limitations of being fitted with a tail wheel, so it was back to the drawing board for the designers.

Supermarine 528 prototype VV119 was rebuilt in 1949 as the 535 with a lengthened nose and a more suitable nose-wheel undercarriage. As such, it represented the Swift prototype but still retained its original tail wheel for safety purposes.

WJ960 emerged as the Supermarine 541 – a pre-production Swift. Flight trials at Chilbolten commenced in the summer of 1951, and the aircraft was joined by WJ965 the following summer. Both were fitted with Rolls-Royce Avon engines, as were the production Swifts.

arrived in January 1949, followed by VV119 in March 1950. Although fitted with swept flying surfaces, both strangely retained the tail wheel undercarriage of the Attacker. VV119 was soon rebuilt with a nose wheel and flew again in March 1950. VV106 was navalised with a hook in September 1950 and undertook trials in December on board HMS *Illustrious*. 'Rocket-assisted take-off' gear had to be fitted for take-offs, and general handling was considered poor, not aided by the jet fighter being fitted with a tail wheel.

The pre-production Swift WJ960 first flew from Boscombe Down on 1 August 1951 and appeared at Chilbolten in the autumn. The second aircraft WJ965 flew from Boscombe Down on 18 July 1952 and first exceeded the sound barrier during a flight on 26 February 1953. The first two production Swifts WK194 and WK195 arrived from Hursley Park in the summer of 1952 for assembly and flight-testing in the late autumn. WK198, one of the early Swifts from the South Marston production line, was modified at Chilbolten as the prototype F4, fitted with reheat, and flown in May 1953. In the summer it was prepared for a successful attempt on the world speed record, attaining a speed of 737 mph over Libya in September. Swift test-flying from Chilbolten was marked by a number of forced landings following engine failure or flameout. Luckily they resulted in little damage to the aircraft or test pilots.

In the mid-1950s the various fighter prototypes that led to the Scimitar appeared at Chilbolten. These had been built at Hursley Park and were the Supermarine 508 (VX133), Supermarine 529 (VX136) and Supermarine 525 (VX138). They were followed by the Scimitar prototypes WT854, WT859 and WW134. Since they were larger aircraft, most test-flying was now undertaken at Boscombe Down or Wisley, reducing the need for Chilbolten. Supermarine moved out to Vickers-Armstrongs' Flight Test Centre at Wisley in 1957.

Originally the fifth production Swift F1, WK198 was soon modified as the first F4 version and was flight-tested from May 1953. It was flown by Mike Lithgow in September, and held the world air-speed record, albeit only for a few days.

The straight-wing Supermarine 508 was part of the development, via the swept-wing Supermarine 535, that eventually led to the Scimitar naval fighter. Prototype 508 VX133 is seen here outside the flight hangars at Chilbolten in 1953.

Supermarine 508 VX133 undertakes flight trials from Chilbolten. As can be seen, it is a bulky single-seat aircraft with large, straight wings and a 'V' tail. Disappointingly, the tail did not show any improvement over the standard layout.

FOLLAND AIRCRAFT CO.

Having entered the field of jet fighter construction at Hamble in 1953, Folland needed an airfield to test its new prototypes. As with Supermarine, a former RAF hangar at Chilbolten was taken over for use by Folland's flight development unit. No aircraft construction work was undertaken, just minor modifications to aircraft passing through.

The prototype Midge G-39-1 arrived from Boscombe Down at the end of August 1954 and was displayed at the Farnborough Air Show a few days later. Piloted by Sqn Ldr 'Teddy' Tennant, the Midge broke the sound barrier in the autumn. The Midge was tested by Indian and Swiss pilots – the Indians being at Chilbolten to assess the Swift. G-39-1 crashed on 29 September 1955 while being flown by a Swiss Air Force pilot. The prototype Gnat G-39-2 arrived on 18 July 1955 at the conclusion of its maiden flight from Boscombe Down. The development batch of Gnat F1s undertook trials from Chilbolten from May 1956, and Indian aircraft were trialled from August 1957. The prototype Gnat Trainer

The Midge lightweight fighter G-39-1 arrived at Chilbolten shortly after its first flight from Boscombe Down on 11 August 1954. Its compact nature is plain to see, and it received favourable reports from various test pilots.

Folland's flight-test hangar at Chilbolten in 1958. No construction was undertaken in the hangar, only modifications to test aircraft. In the background are a number of early Gnats, while in the foreground are the Meteors, which were used for ejector-seat trials.

followed in the summer of 1959, first flying on 31 August. Folland also used Boscombe Down for flight-testing the Gnat. Other work undertaken by Folland at Chilbolten included the development of the Saab/Folland lightweight ejector seat, with trials undertaken using two Meteor T7s, WA690 and WF877. The first live ejection was made in December 1955 and the seats were later fitted in production Gnats. Its first use in anger was on 31 July 1956, when 'Teddy' Tennant had to eject from the Gnat prototype. Canberra VN813 arrived in June 1953 for the installation of a de Havilland Spectre rocket in its rear fuselage, plus a closed-circuit TV system to monitor its firing. WJ755 followed in the spring of 1957 for a similar modification.

Folland became part of Hawker Siddeley Aviation in the autumn of 1959. By then most of the Gnat development flying had been completed and the first few Gnat T1s had arrived. Production flight-testing of these was switched to Hawker's airfield at Dunsfold in the spring of 1961, with the Chilbolten site closing down the following year. XM706 was the last Gnat to fly out of Chilbolten in January 1962.

Christchurch

Pleasure-flying was carried out from a farmer's field to the east of the town in the late 1920s. The site was expanded in the 1930s, its use being approved by the Automobile Association. Limited airline services were operated from the grass airfield from 1934 until the outbreak of the Second World War. These services were advertised as being from Bournemouth Airport. Private flying returned at the end of the war, with the airfield closing in the mid-1960s.

AIRSPEED LTD (1934)

Airspeed's main factory was at Portsmouth, where it had been established in the spring of 1933. Following the company's Envoy airliner, it received RAF orders for a developed version known as the Oxford. In the late 1930s, a site on the north-east side of Christchurch Airfield had been acquired for the erection of a 'shadow' aircraft production factory. While the factory was under construction in 1940, Airspeed was asked by the Ministry of Aircraft Production if it would run the factory and produce vital wartime aircraft. The directors agreed and, under the management of Capt. T. Laing, arrangements were made for Oxford trainers to be produced at Christchurch to take some of the load off Portsmouth. Workers were transferred from Portsmouth at the end of 1940 and the first Oxford X6520 was completed in March 1941, coinciding with the factory's official opening. Airspeed organised subcontracting work around small factories in Christchurch, including Portsmouth Aviation at Purewell. 300 Mk Is and 250 Mk IIs were built at Christchurch, with the final one, LB538, delivered in February 1943. Although ordered by the RAF, many of the early Christchurch-built aircraft did not see home service but were delivered to Commonwealth training schools in Canada, New Zealand, Rhodesia and South Africa.

In 1941, the Airspeed Design Team, then housed at Salisbury Hall near Hatfield, produced the AS51 to meet a requirement for an all-wood assault glider. Four prototypes of what became the Horsa were ordered, with the first two built at Salisbury Hall, St Albans, and flown from Fairey's Great West Aerodrome.

The size of the Airspeed factory can be seen in this late-1940s view. Beyond the factory is the eastern end of Christchurch airfield, with Mudeford and Hengistbury Head in the distance. What appear to be paved runways are in fact well-mown grass strips.

With the opening of the Christchurch shadow factory in March 1941, Airspeed was able to increase production of the Oxford trainer. 550 were produced at Christchurch, including many for Commonwealth air forces.

The third and fourth prototypes, DG604 and DG609, were completed and flown from Christchurch early in 1942 – towed aloft by a Whitley. Initially, in 1941, 400 were ordered for the RAF, with many more to follow. As Airspeed's main Portsmouth factory was busy with Oxfords, the majority of Horsas were built by outside companies with woodworking skills, such as furniture makers Harris Lebus (2,700+ built) or companies geared to mass production, including Austin Motors (365 built). Christchurch was the only aircraft factory with capacity to produce Horsas, with the first HS101 appearing in the summer of 1942. The initial aircraft produced by Harris Lebus and Austin Motors were brought to Christchurch for flight-testing. The AS58 Horsa II flew in 1943 and was fitted with a hinged opening nose to ease the loading and unloading of small army vehicles. Whitley tugs were used to fly the completed Horsas from Christchurch to RAF Maintenance Units around the country. Other work undertaken by Airspeed in 1943 was the upgrade of 160 Seafire IICs prior to entering service with the RN. The Horsa played a major role in the D-Day landings of June 1944, including delivering the first troops to Pegasus Bridge. In the autumn a number

Christchurch was the only aircraft factory to produce Horsas. The aircraft's wooden construction enabled large numbers to be built by non-aviation firms such as Harris Lebus, a furniture maker of Tottenham. Airspeed built 695 of the total ordered – 3,727.

The Horsa was invaluable to the Allies during the D-Day operations of June 1944. Seen here in a Normandy field, the tail of a Horsa I has been blown off for ease of access. Production commenced in the summer of 1942 and continued until 1945.

were towed back by a Whitley from Normandy for repair, with others returning by sea. There had been plans in 1943 for Mosquitoes to be built at Christchurch, but production did not get underway until 1945. The first order was for 300 FBVIs and B35s, but only twelve had flown by VE Day, whereupon the order was reduced to fifty. In fact the first half-dozen FBVIs were completed at Portsmouth. Wartime production by Airspeed amounted to 550 Oxfords, 695 Horsas and six Mosquitoes.

Airspeed moved its design team to Christchurch in September 1944, with a new drawing office and technical block built the following year. Arthur Hagg moved from de Havilland at Hatfield to take charge of the design work. Upon the return to peace, further Mosquito orders were placed with Airspeed, with production of B35s continuing until February 1948. Other work included the provision of Consul parts for the main Portsmouth factory and of Vampire parts for de Havilland at Hatfield. In the late 1940s, the RAF still saw a possible need for assault glider operations. As well as seeking a new design, a number of Horsas were taken from storage for refurbishment. This resulted in sixty Horsas returning to Christchurch for overhaul in 1948–49, after which they were towed away by a resident Halifax.

With its spare capacity, Airspeed undertook production of the de Havilland Mosquito bomber, but they were too late to see action in the war. Although the Mosquito was no longer really needed by the RAF, production continued until February 1948.

The initial Mosquito bombers appeared in wartime camouflage, but by the end of the production run they appeared in all-over silver. Many were delivered directly into storage at RAF Maintenance Units, with a number later converted into target tugs.

In addition to undertaking Horsa production during the war, a number returned to Christchurch in 1947–48 for rebuilding by Airspeed. At the time, the RAF foresaw a need for assault gliders in future operations. Note the post-war roundels on the Horsa.

Airspeed's main post-war project was the AS57 airliner, design work having commenced in the summer of 1944, with a mock-up displayed in the autumn of 1945. Named the Ambassador, it was an elegant, high-wing airliner powered by two Bristol Centaurus piston engines. The design met the requirements of the wartime Brabazon Committee for a British airliner for European services. The requirement also saw the development of the turboprop Vickers Viscount. Two Ambassador prototypes (G-AGUA and G-AGUB) were ordered in September 1945 by the Ministry of Aircraft Production, who allocated serials VP216–48 to possible production aircraft. In the event, these were never ordered. In addition, a military transport version – the AS60 Ayrshire – was proposed for an RAF specification. This had a modified rear fuselage that incorporated clam-shell doors for direct loading of equipment and vehicles. Ten were provisionally ordered in October 1946, but in the following spring the Ministry announced that the Ayrshire would not be required by the RAF. Preliminary design work on the Ambassador was undertaken at Portsmouth, but Christchurch was selected for the main design office and production of the airliner – described in the spring of 1946 as 'a 28–36 seat Transcontinental airliner'. When there were concerns over the development of the Rolls-Royce Dart engines, which were to power the Viscount, Airspeed

Airspeed's post-war claim to fame was its elegant Ambassador airliner. Development was protracted, with consideration given to both piston and turboprop power. Prototype G-AGUA flew in July 1947 and is seen here on an early test flight.

Early in the Ambassador's development, there was strong interest in a military freighter version known as the Ayrshire. The Ambassador prototype was registered G-AGUA in September 1945, at which time this model of Ayrshire G-AGUB appeared.

came up with the AS59 Ambassador II design, powered by four Napier Naiads turboprops, in case production of the Viscount did not proceed. In the event, problems with the Dart engines were overcome and they were then considered for the proposed Ambassador II. Also under consideration by Airspeed was the use of two Bristol Proteuses, which were under development for the Bristol 175. From 1 January 1948, along with Portsmouth, the Christchurch factory became part of the Airspeed Division of de Havilland Aircraft. Airspeed now described itself as 'in association with de Havilland Enterprise'.

Airspeed initially foresaw a delay in the development of turboprop engines and, although the second prototype Ambassador was originally planned to be powered by Naiads, Airspeed decided to stay with the piston engine. The prototype Ambassador G-AGUA, powered by two Bristol Centaurus engines, was built in the experimental shop in the spring of 1947, and made its maiden flight on 10 July. The second prototype, now reregistered G-AKRD, flew on 26 August 1948, and in September BEA placed an order for twenty of its 'Future Mainliner'. During test-flying, the prototypes seemed to suffer more than their fair share of forced landings, but they seemed to help prove the airliners' rugged construction. In 1950 there was talk of Christchurch airfield closing and Airspeed moving Ambassador production to nearby Hurn, but this was not to be. BEA's first aircraft G-AMAD flew on 12 January 1951, with the final one delivered in the spring of 1953. The purchase price for BEA's aircraft was £165,000 each, but by September 1951 Airspeed were quoting £225,000. With its high-set wing, the Ambassador soon proved to have passenger appeal, and was well known as the Elizabethan Class in BEA service. In spite of this, the Ambassador only remained in service for six years as it was eclipsed by the turbo-prop Viscount. However, it then continued in use with the likes of Autair, BKS and Dan-Air.

Airspeed spent considerable time and effort developing the Ambassador. Despite the company's sales efforts, there was only the one order, from BEA, whose aircraft are seen here under construction in 1951.

Seen outside Airspeed's flight shed is pre-production Ambassador G-ALFR. The full take-over of Airspeed by de Havilland in July 1951 brought an end to further Ambassadors. The hangars were required by de Havilland for fighter production.

Airspeed was given the task by de Havilland of developing the Vampire Trainer. Based on the earlier night-fighter version, prototype G-5-7 flew in November 1950. After successful trials, the RAF placed its first order just under a year later.

In June 1950, Airspeed was give the task by de Havilland at Hatfield of developing the Vampire Trainer, and the prototype was constructed in the summer. Of de Havilland's classic twin-boom design, the advance trainer was developed from the Vampire night-fighter with a modified and improved cockpit layout. As such, it had side-by-side seating, as opposed to the tandem-seat Meteor Trainer then in use with the RAF. Powered by a 3,500 lb thrust DH Goblin jet engine, it retained the fighter's four cannons and underwing hard points. The prototype was displayed at the Farnborough SBAC Show in September 1950, although it was unflown at the time. Its first flight as G-5-7 was on 15 November, and it was delivered to the RAF as WW456 for trials the following March. This prototype was followed by two more, for evaluation by the Royal Navy.

DE HAVILLAND AIRCRAFT CO.

In July 1951, Airspeed was fully absorbed into de Havilland Aircraft, whose title now appeared on the factory façade. Major Hereward de Havilland, who had arrived at Christchurch in 1949, was appointed as general manager. In September 1951, de Havilland announced that it would not be developing the Ambassador further, as additional expenditure was not expected to result in further orders. In reality, de Havilland needed extra production capacity for Vampire Trainers and Venoms. The Hampshire Planning Authority announced in April 1952 that it wanted a ban on jet-flying from Christchurch – local residents having made a number of complaints. De Havilland had to go to the Minister of Local Government in order to get the ruling overturned, as it would have seriously affected business.

The RAF placed an initial order for 143 Vampire T11s in October 1951, followed by fifty-three T22s for the Royal Navy in February 1952 The first production aircraft WZ414 flew in January 1952, followed by the first for the Navy XA100 early in 1953. Initial service use saw the need for improved canopy glazing, and this was introduced from the spring of 1953, along with a larger fin area. The Vampire Trainer was ordered by many foreign air forces (e.g. New Zealand, Norway, South Africa and Sweden) as the T55, with the first, for New Zealand, delivered in the spring of 1952. The final overseas delivery from Christchurch was to Sweden in July 1953, with production for the RAF and RN continuing until May 1955. Initially, test-flying was undertaken from nearby Hurn as Christchurch still only possessed a grass runway, however in the summer of 1954 a concrete runway was at last provided. Vampire production was also undertaken at Chester and Hatfield.

On behalf of Hatfield, Christchurch undertook most of the design work for the Sea Venom naval fighter early in 1952, and built the third prototype, which flew

Initial RAF use of the Vampire T11 showed the need for an improved view from the cockpit and better directional control. XD520 shows the clear cockpit canopy introduced early in 1953, along with the revised fin and rudder.

on 16 July. The initial FAW20 variant, WM500 – which was for the Navy – flew in March 1953 and was followed by the improved FAW21 and FAW22. Thirty-nine were produced for the Australian Navy between January 1955 and January 1956. Three of the late production RN aircraft were modified in the autumn of 1958 to undertake early Firestreak missile trials with the Navy. Christchurch was also involved in the Venom night fighter, with the third prototype, WV928, built and flown on 22 February 1953. Nineteen production aircraft followed, but the majority of the RAF's order was completed at Chester. In the spring of 1954 the Christchurch workforce totalled 2,600 and the factory covered 372,000 sq. ft.

The de Havilland design team had worked on the DH116 as a Sea Venom replacement in 1952. However, it was felt that the requirement could be better suited by reviving the DH110, which had been built to a 1949 RAF specification. This was still the typical de Havilland twin-boom design, powered by two Rolls-Royce Avons. After trials at Hatfield with the modified second prototype, the Christchurch Design Office, under W. Tamblin, was tasked with bringing it up

49

To ease capacity at Hatfield and Chester, de Havilland's Christchurch site undertook production of Venoms and Sea Venoms between the spring of 1953 and January 1956. Despite Christchurch's limitations, test-flying was undertaken from the site's grass runway.

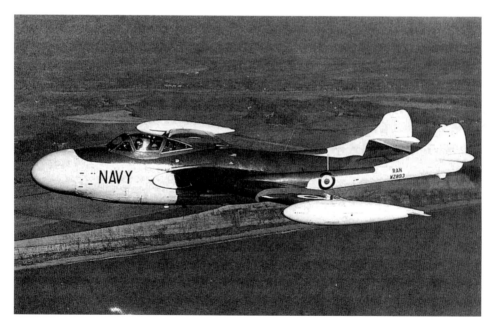

The Australian Navy ordered thirty-nine Sea Venoms and they were built at Christchurch in 1955–56. Crews were trained in Britain prior to the Sea Venoms being delivered 'down under' by aircraft carrier HMS *Melbourne*.

Venom Night Fighters were produced at Christchurch between 1953 and 1955. WX787 was the third production NF3, and it flew in September 1953. The fighters only saw limited squadron service with the RAF.

to naval production standard. Although the shape remained much the same, an 80 per cent redesign of the RAF version had to be undertaken. A naval prototype, known as the DH110 Mk 20X, was ordered in February 1954 to be built at Christchurch, and it flew as XF828 in June 1955.

Initial plans for gun armament were revised and the 110 was the first naval fighter to be armed with missiles only, in this case four Firestreaks. The Navy initially ordered seventy-five aircraft in February 1955 (although there had been talk of 400 being required), with the first, XJ474, flying in March 1957. By this time the 110 had been officially named Sea Vixen, de Havilland having originally proposed the Vixen name back in 1949 for the RAF aircraft. In the mid-1950s, the Navy favoured naming the fighter Pirate to compliment the forthcoming Blackburn Buccaneer strike bomber. In the event, de Havilland won the day. The aircraft were initially designated FAW21 by the Navy, but this was changed to FAW1 soon after production was underway. It was de Havilland's intention that only the pre-production batch of twenty-one Sea Vixens would be built at

De Havilland's design and development staff gather around the first production Sea Vixen XJ474 for a photo call in the spring of 1957. Aircraft appeared from the Christchurch production line for the next five years.

Christchurch; full production would be undertaken at the Chester site. These plans were changed and work continued at Christchurch. Production test-flying was undertaken from Hurn, where the longer runway was a safety factor, and first deliveries were made to the Royal Navy in November 1957.

Changes were coming to Christchurch as part of the Government's desire for Britain's aircraft industry to contract and in 1960 de Havilland became part of Hawker Siddeley Aviation. In the summer of 1961, Christchurch Council informed de Havilland that at some future date they intended to redevelop the airfield for housing. De Havilland responded that they needed the 20 acre factory site for continued Sea Vixen production, pointing out that the lease ran until December 1978.

A new version of the Sea Vixen with higher-powered Rolls-Royce RB108 engines was proposed in the early 1960s. In the event, the Avons were retained, but additional fuel was carried in extended overwing booms. Hawker Siddeley announced in November 1961 that it was necessary to redistribute work around

XJ488 was one of the development batch of Sea Vixens flown from Christchurch in 1959. Here it is shown later in its life while undergoing flight refuelling trials from Boscombe Down in 1966. Sea Vixen production switched to Chester in 1962.

their other sites and Sea Vixen production was being switched to Chester as originally planned in the spring of 1957. The Government welcomed this rationalisation decision. Redundancies commenced in January 1962 and the factory closed in July. Early in 1962, Sea Vixens XN684 and XN685 were partially completed as the new FAW2 version, and were flown to Hatfield for further development. They were followed by Christchurch's final FAW1 XN710 in August 1962. Post-war production at Christchurch totalled 122 Mosquitoes, twenty-three Ambassadors, 242 Vampire Trainers, eight-eight Venoms, eighty Sea Venoms and 118 Sea Vixens.

BEAGLE AIRCRAFT LTD

With the departure of de Havilland, attempts were made to find a new aircraft company to take its place. This was despite the fact that Christchurch Council

Shortly before de Havilland moved out, development of the Sea Vixen FAW2 was underway. Two development aircraft were built, but production for the Navy was undertaken at Chester. Additional fuel tanks were housed in overwing booms.

When it was announced that de Havilland was to close, there were attempts to get Beagle Aircraft to move in to produce their B206 executive twin. The efforts came to nothing, as Beagle said the site was too large.

had already stated that it wanted the airfield land for housing development. In January 1962, Beagle Aircraft indicated an interest in taking over the site for production of their B206 executive twin, whose prototype had flown at Shoreham the previous August. The Government stepped in again, saying that Beagle's takeover would be the best use of the factory and workers. In the event Beagle decided in April 1962 that the factory was too large for its requirements, and in due course production of the B206 was undertaken at the former Auster factory at Rearsby.

Beagle finally arrived in Christchurch in 1971, but not for aircraft production. The original Beagle company went out of business in 1969, following which local aerospace engineers C. F. Taylor bought the Beagle name and subcontracting work. This was moved to Taylor's Christchurch factory in Stony Lane with the premises renamed Beagle Aircraft (1969) Ltd. In 1988, this reverted to Beagle Aircraft Ltd, and the company continues its subcontract work for various aerospace companies.

Cowes

The banks of the River Medina at Cowes housed a number of well-known boat-building firms that expanded into aircraft construction in the 1910s. A grass airfield, West Medina Aerodrome (later Somerton) just to the west of the town was brought into use by Samuel White & Co. in 1915 for production test-flying of its landplane products. It was also used by Saunders for flight-testing its Avro 504s. In 1925, the airfield changed hands from Samuel White to Saunders, which continued to use it for test-flying in the 1930s. Spartan Aircraft's subsidiary company Spartan Air Lines operated services from Cowes to Southampton and Croydon in the mid-1930s. During the Second World War, Somerton was used by Saro for Walrus production test-flying. The airfield was no longer required by Saro after 1946, but there was still private flying in the early 1950s.

J. SAMUEL WHITE & CO. LTD ('WIGHT')

J. Samuel White & Co. was a well-established East Cowes firm of ship builders and was renowned for its small-to-medium-sized naval craft. In 1912, the company set up an aircraft division in its Gridiron shed, producing various biplanes under the Wight title (not White) to the design of Howard T. Wright. First to emerge was a hydro-biplane, which was displayed unflown at the Olympia Aero Show in February 1913 under the Samuel White name. It was along the lines of contemporary Farman aircraft, but with an improved wing aerofoil. Two crew members were carried in an open nacelle ahead of a 160 hp Gnome pusher engine. The type, which retrospectively was known as the Wight No. 1, was also noticeable for its two lengthy floats. After various accidents, it was rebuilt as No. 2 and flown in August 1913, by which time it was referred to as a seaplane and not hydro-aircraft. In due course it passed to the Navy.

Encouraged by the trials, there followed an enlarged Wight version with a 200 hp Salmson Canton-Unne engine and a span of 63 ft. It was displayed at the Olympia Show in March 1914 and flown the following month. By now the Wight name had been introduced – the design being the Wight Pusher Seaplane.

The Wight No. 2 Navyplane in a photograph clearly showing its layout. The crew of two are housed in the open cockpit situated in front of the pusher engine, with plenty of struts holding the floats in place. The type was developed as the Pusher Navyplane for the RNAS.

Three were ordered by the RNAS as the Pusher Navyplane and were first flown in April 1914. Three were also ordered by the German Navy, but were transferred to the RNAS on the outbreak of war. The Pusher Navyplane was followed by the Improved Navyplane AI, with seven ordered by the RNAS for North Sea patrols. Of these, No. 177 was modified into the AII, with four ordered. The new type was also referred to as the Admiralty Type 177, based on the prototype's serial number. The AI saw limited service in the Dardanelles in the spring of 1915, when it operated from HMS *Ark Royal*. To allow for future expansion, Samuel White acquired additional premises across the Medina at West Cowes.

The Wight Seaplane/Admiralty Type 840 was a torpedo bomber biplane with twin floats, powered by a 225 hp Sunbeam engine and first produced in 1914. Fifty-four were built in 1915–16, and again the type number referred to the serials of the first production batch – 835–40. At least thirty-two were built by Beardmores at Dalmuir in Scotland and Porteholme of Huntingdon in 1915, due to lack of capacity at Cowes. Early deliveries were to the RNAS at Helensburgh. The Wight Twin was a large twin-engined landplane torpedo bomber. One was ordered by the French, first flying from Somerton in July 1915, but it crashed during trials by its French pilot at Eastchurch in September. It was followed by the Wight Twin Seaplane with serials 1450/1 ordered by the RNAS as torpedo bombers. First flown in 1916, the type proved underpowered with its 200 hp

Canton-Unne engines and did not enter production. Along with most aviation firms at the time, Wights were not too worried about names for their products and the generic 'Wight Seaplane' seemed to cover everything. The name was first used in advertising in February 1914 and was still being used in May 1918.

The RNAS was using a large number of Short 184 floatplanes, and to increase numbers swiftly placed additional orders with various other manufactures. These included Wight, which built 110 in 1915–17, although the later ones were cancelled. Based on the 184, the Wight Landplane Bomber biplane prototype N501, powered by a Rolls-Royce Eagle, was built in 1916. Five were ordered for the RNAS, but, following the fatal crash of the first machine at Somerton during its second flight on 7 September 1916, it was decided to proceed with a seaplane version instead – the Wight Converted Seaplane. Fifty were ordered by the RNAS for patrol duties. The first, 9846, was a converted Landplane Bomber. Flown in 1917, only thirty-seven had been completed by the end of the war, most being powered by 260 hp Sunbeam Maori engines due to a shortage of Eagles, as used in the landplane. The Converted Seaplane's claim to fame was that in August 1917 it was the first British aircraft to sink a U-boat.

There then followed a number of designs that were either unsuccessful or too late for the war. Wight Seaplane trainers 8321 and 8322 were built, but the type did not enter production. Wights tried its hand at a landplane fighter with the diminutive Quadruplane N546, which had a wingspan of 19 ft. Flown in mid-1916 and powered by a 110 hp Clerget rotary engine, the fighter proved unsatisfactory. It was fitted with redesigned wings on two subsequent occasions, but there was no improvement in its performance. Construction of the large Wight ADI Seaplane/Admiralty Type 1000 torpedo bomber was delayed and the prototype serial 1000 did not fly until 1917. Again the type number related to the military serial. Seven were ordered for the RNAS, but only four were completed and they were probably never delivered. The Wight Baby seaplane fighter was powered by a 100 hp Gnome rotary engine. Prototype 9100 flew in 1917, followed by 9097 and 9098, which again proved unsuccessful. There was reference to the large AD Type 1500 three-engined bomber with a span of 115 ft. However, this never reached the construction stage.

October 1918 saw a change of management within J. Samuel White and, combined with the ending of the war, this brought about the end of aircraft construction. During the war the company had also maintained it programme of warship construction – destroyers and MTBs for the Navy. The East Cowes works later passed to Saunders-Roe. In the mid-1950s, J. Samuel White was still building seaplane tenders. The shipyard closed in 1963.

S. E. SAUNDERS LTD

Sam Saunders was a well-established boat builder who moved to Cowes in 1901. He formed S. E. Saunders Ltd in May 1908 to continue his boat-building activities, but in 1909 moved into 'aero-navigation' at new premises at Folly Works further upstream. By 1910 the company had expanded its premises at Columbine Yard, East Cowes, and specialised in fast marine craft and racing boats. In 1912 it collaborated with T. O. M. Sopwith to build the Bat Boat flying boat, whose hull was based on Saunders' racing boat construction methods. The hull was built by Saunders and delivered to Sopwith for completion of the aircraft, which was tested on the Medina early in 1913. It was the first flying boat to be built in Europe and was delivered as 118 to the RNAS in 1913 for bomb-dropping trials. The Folly Works were involved in a number of early flying boats, and other companies sought Saunders' assistance with regard to hull construction. So the Bat Boat was followed by a small flying boat to the design of Perry Beadle & Co. that was exhibited at Olympia in March 1914. The engine was mounted in the forward fuselage, with chain drive to the two propellers. Then followed a flying boat for White & Thompson for a proposed 'Circuit of Britain Air Race'. For their boat-building business, Saunders had developed the Consuta method of mahogany ply hull construction. This proved to be very strong and was easily adapted for flying boats. To provide further capital Vickers purchased 50 per cent of Saunders Ltd shares in June 1914.

In June 1915 Saunders received a contract from Avro to build fifty Avro 504As, which was soon adapted to cover a further 150 504As and 504Js. Additional premises adjacent to Columbine were acquired at Marshfield Road for production of the 504s, which were test-flown from a field near the Folly Works or else from West Medina. As one of a large number of subcontractors, Saunders received an order from the Admiralty for thirty Short 184 floatplanes which were built at the Folly Works as from February 1916. A follow up order for a further fifty was then received. Saunders built extra works known as the Solent Works at West Cowes in 1916, so that flying boat hulls for the RNAS could be built. These included FBAs for Gosport Aviation, followed by twenty-four complete Norman Thompson NT2B flying boats in 1916, commencing serial N2500, but not all were delivered. These were small, two-seat trainers, erected in the Columbine Works. More successful were the 100 Felixstowe F2As built from November 1917, N4080 onwards, although a further fifty F5s were cancelled at end of the First World War. During production of the F2As, Saunders was able to improve the rear hull design, which was incorporated into later production aircraft. N178 was an F5 fitted with an experimental 'hollo-bottom' hull. The one-off Saunders T1 twin-seat naval biplane fighter X14 was a private venture from chief designer

H. H. Thomas and was flown in 1918. It undertook military trials, but no orders were received. In March 1918, Vickers became a majority shareholder in S. E. Saunders Ltd, with Vickers directors elected to the board. One result of this tie-up was that Vickers at Weybridge now made use of Consuta construction, such as in their Vimy Commercial airliners. Saunders' ship-building business was sold off in October 1918.

With the return to peace, Saunders advertised in August 1919 that it designed and constructed military and commercial seaplanes and flying boats. Its first post-war product was the twin-engined Kittiwake of 1920, built to an Air Ministry commercial amphibian requirement. Designed to carry seven passengers, the hull was based on Saunders' Consuta construction methods, with the wings containing a number of novel features, including variable camber. The sole Kittiwake G-EAUD was due to take part in Air Ministry trials held at Martlesham Heath at the end of September. However, part of its wing fell off during its first flight, and in the ensuing forced landing on the Solent it hit some rocks and could not be repaired in time. Later it continued test-flying from Cowes for a further year, during which control problems were revealed. In 1920, Saunders built the hulls of three Vickers Valentia twin-engined flying boats, with the wings and tails completed by Vickers. Powered by two Rolls-Royce Condors, this was a large machine with a span of 112 ft, known as the Vickers-Saunders Valentia BS1. Construction was slow with the aircraft appearing in March 1921, March 1922 and February 1923. Collaboration with Vickers also saw the completion of hulls for Viking amphibians, which were erected at Weybridge. A falling market saw Vickers sell out to Sam Saunders in March 1921. Lack of work saw the boatyard and aircraft works temporarily closed in April. This was a low period of aircraft business at Cowes, although some overhaul work was undertaken, including DH9As for the RAF.

A 'new' Saunders era followed with the setting up of its own aircraft design department. The company's first design was the large A3 Valkyrie general-purpose flying boat. The Air Ministry ordered prototype N186 in February 1925. First flying in the spring of 1926, N186 was powered by three Rolls-Royce Condors, had a span of 97 ft and offered its crew spacious accommodation. Subsequent military trials at Felixstowe showed up the disadvantage of wooden hulls, which became waterlogged, although it took part in the RAF Scandinavian Cruise in August 1927. Next came the A4 Medina, a twin-engined, ten-seat biplane flying boat for commercial use. Prototype G-EBMG flew in November 1926 and undertook trials for the Air Council, but no orders were received. Again its wooden hull proved troublesome.

There were then two departures from Saro's flying boat designs. In 1928, the company received a contract from RAE Farnborough to build the Isacco

Helicogyre No. 3 on behalf of its designer – Vittorio Isacco. This helicopter's fuselage was similar to the Ciervas of the day, but each of its four-bladed rotors had a small Bristol Cherub engine at the tip to provide rotation – a novel idea today, but this was the infant days of helicopter development. The layout did not work when tested at Cowes in the spring of 1929 or when delivered to Farnborough as K1171 the following year. Next came the Saro A10 Interceptor all-metal multi-gun biplane fighter in 1928. Originally built as a private venture, it received Air Ministry backing in the summer of 1927. The Interceptor flew from Somerton on 27 January 1929 registered as L2, but proved to be a one-off. Military trials at Martlesham Heath later in the year confirmed the fighter's lack of directional control and problems in attaining an anticipated top speed of 200 mph. Saunders Ltd was seeking new capital, in addition to which Sam Saunders was now less active in the company. This resulted in the arrival of former Avro directors led by A. V. Roe, who invested in a reorganised Saunders-Roe Ltd in November 1928.

Probably against its better judgement, Saunders built this Isacco Helicogyre on behalf of its designer in 1928. At the end of each rotor blade can be seen a Bristol Cherub engine. The Helicogyre refused to take off at Cowes or at RAE Farnborough.

Saunders was well-known for the seaplanes it built at Cowes. However, in 1928, the company designed and built a land-based fighter – the A10 Interceptor. It appeared at a time of upheaval within the company and did not enter production.

SPARTAN AIRCRAFT LTD

Spartan Aircraft was formed on 1 April 1930 to take over the business of Simmonds Aircraft Ltd of Weston. New production facilities and offices were established at Saunders-Roe's Columbine site, plus a flight-test hangar at Somerton. The first design to appear was the Spartan Arrow two-seat biplane, the prototype having flown from Weston in May 1930, after which production switched to Cowes. It was priced at £675 and fitted with a Gipsy or Hermes engine. Production continued until 1933, by which time fifteen Arrows had been built. G-ABBE was tested as a floatplane in 1930, followed by G-ABMK in June 1931. With the reorganisations, Mr Simmonds resigned as director of Spartan Aircraft to become an MP in May 1931, with Saro's directors taking his place.

In parallel with the Arrow, Spartan built the Spartan Three Seater biplane. This was basically an updated Simmonds Spartan powered by a 115 hp Cirrus Hermes, with G-ABAZ flying in the spring of 1930. Selling for £790, the type proved popular with pleasure-flight operators and twenty-six were built between 1930 and 1934, all but one being sold in the home market. The final batch of seven was known as Three Seater II, in which the rear cockpit was enlarged to carry the two passengers. G-ABTR was converted in 1933 to have an enclosed rear cockpit (although the pilot still sat in the open), and served with Spartan Air Lines.

Spartan Aircraft moved production of its Spartan Arrow from Weston on the mainland to East Cowes in 1931. This enabled it to establish closer ties with Saunders-Roe. This 1932-built Arrow G-ABWP remains active at the present time.

To extend its appeal, the Spartan Arrow could be fitted with a variety of engines. However G-ABST was a one-off fitted with an experimental Napier Javelin engine in 1932; it was used as a flying test bed by Napier & Son.

63

Spartan's next project was vastly different, the company having been acquired by Saro in February 1931. Saro and Edgar Percival had been involved in a developing a wooden mail plane in 1931, but Percival later sold his interest. Development continued on what was now designated the Saro A24 Mailplane. Production of the three Gipsy III-engined aircraft passed from Saro to Spartan in 1932, resulting in the aircraft now being referred to as the Spartan Mailplane. It was first flown from Somerton as G-ABLI on 1 June 1931. Temporarily fitted with a twin-finned tailplane and two cramped seats in the cabin, it made a flight to India and back in June 1932. Spartan saw no future for the Mailplane, but developed a three-engined, metal-fuselage, six-seat feeder airliner version – the Cruiser I, which retained the Gipsy III engines. Worked on by Saro's designers, this retained the same basic layout but was fitted with an enlarged cabin area. G-ABTY flew in May 1932 and was demonstrated at Hendon and Heston in June and August, followed by a European sales tour in October. Airline interest was shown and Spartan developed the Cruiser II with Gipsy Major engines. This had an improved cabin for six passengers, a revised cockpit window layout, and a price of £3,950. G-ACBM, the first production aircraft, flew in February 1933. Orders were received from Czechoslovakia, Iraq and Yugoslavia, as well

Spartan produced the Cruiser airliner from 1932 and achieved a number of export sales. This Cruiser II has just arrived in Cairo in April 1934 following its purchase by Misr Airwork for use on services around Egypt.

A number of Cruisers were operated by associate company Spartan Air Lines on services from Cowes. G-ACVT is a late-production Cruiser II, delivered in the summer of 1934 and seen here visiting Croydon.

as from home customers. These included the newly formed Spartan Air Lines, which inaugurated services between Cowes and Heston on 1 April 1933. The airline had been established in February as a subsidiary of the aircraft company. Spartan agreed that licensed production of the Cruiser could be undertaken in Yugoslavia. However, only one Cruiser II was completed, and this crashed after just over a year's service. The twelfth and final Cruiser II was delivered from Cowes in December 1934. Then followed three Cruiser IIIs, which were developed especially for Spartan Air Lines. This variant had a completely redesigned fuselage housing eight passengers, almost resembling a new type. The first, G-ACYK, flew at the beginning of 1935 and entered service in April.

Following the purchase of Spartan by Saro in 1931, the companies had effectively merged by the beginning of 1933, although they continued to use the Spartan Aircraft name. With the redevelopment of the Columbine site in 1934–35, Spartan moved production to Somerton. Really this only covered the three Cruiser IIIs, with the final one flown in May 1935, the occasion marking the end of Spartan's aircraft products. However, the Spartan Aircraft name was still in use by Saro in the summer of 1936.

SAUNDERS-ROE LTD ('SARO')

In October 1928, Alliott Verdon Roe (co-founder of Avro) sold his Avro shares to Sir John Siddeley, Chairman of Armstrong Siddeley. In November, together with John Lord and Harry Broadsmith (both former Avro directors), he purchased a majority shareholding in S. E. Saunders for £42,500. The following year, A. V.

Roe was knighted for his services to aviation. These changes saw the introduction of a new 'Saro' logo, although for a while the firm continued as S. E. Saunders Ltd, changing to Saunders-Roe Ltd in July 1929. At the time Saunders described itself as 'designers and constructors of all descriptions of aircraft – wood and metal'. Up to now the company had relied on wood, but the Air Ministry now favoured metal hulls, so this brought about a change for the design team, now headed by Henry Knowler. Their A7 Severn of 1930 was a large reconnaissance flying boat that had a metal hull and was powered by three Bristol Jupiter IXs. Ordered in April 1928 and first flown in July 1930, the prototype N240 undertook military trials at Felixstowe, but no orders were placed. One noteworthy feat was the Severn making the first non-stop flight from Gibraltar to Mount Batten, Plymouth, in 1931 while attached to 209 Squadron. Although primarily a military design, Saunders also worked on the design of a luxury civil version for twenty-one passengers. Then followed the A14, which was the designation of a metal hull produced for fitting to a Supermarine Southampton flying boat. The hull had a square box shape compared to the earlier rounded, wooden designs. It was ordered in April 1928, and Saro delivered the hull to Felixstowe to be fitted with the wings and tail of a standard Southampton. As N251, it flew in the spring of 1930 and was used for trial purposes in comparison with existing Southamptons. The metal hulls of the A7 and A14 showed improvements over the previous wooden ones, although there was still some weakness in their structures.

The reformed company found commercial success with a series of smaller amphibians – the Cutty Sark, Cloud and Windhover. Using the experience of the metal-hulled A14, Saro first produced the four-seat A17 Cutty Sark twin-engined amphibian. Prototype G-AAIP flew on 4 July 1929 and was followed by twelve production aircraft. These were powered by a variety of engines and were built with Alclad corrugated plated fuselages, with plywood wings based on contemporary Avro practice. G-AAIP was initially built as a flying boat but was soon converted into an amphibian. S1575 was delivered to the RAF at Calshot in December 1930 as a trainer and another was fitted with a single Lynx engine in 1932 to the order of a Japanese pilot for a proposed Transpacific flight. Three others were operated by Air Service Training at Hamble as trainers. The Cutty Sark was followed by the A19 Cloud, which was basically an enlarged Cutty Sark capable of carrying eight passengers. Again, it had an Alclad hull with wooden wings and could be fitted with a variety of engines. The prototype flew on 15 July 1930 as L4 before being reregistered G-ABCJ. Saro built an initial batch of five, with G-ABHG flown by the Hon. A. E. Guinness as his 'VIP' aircraft from 1931. Sales were slow, but the situation was saved when K2681 was bought by the Air Ministry in 1930 for trials, resulting in an order in 1932 for sixteen Serval-engined Clouds, with strengthened hulls, for the RAF. The first entered

After re-organisation in 1928, Saro produced a number of successful small amphibians. First was the Cutty Sark, which is seen here on roll-out in July 1929. Built as a flying boat with Cirrus Hermes engines, G-AAIP was later modified into an amphibian with Gipsy II engines.

The Cloud was a larger version of the Cutty Sark. Prototype L4 is seen here on the Medina at West Cowes in the summer of 1930 with its engineers, awaiting its next test flight. Initial limited civilian sales were boosted by an RAF order for sixteen aircraft.

67

The Cloud was another Saro design that could be powered by a variety of engines. G-ABHG was used as an executive transport by the Hon A. E. Guinness for flights between his homes in Hampshire and Ireland. Note the additional aerofoil above the engines.

service as an amphibian navigation/pilot trainer at Calshot in August 1933; the final one was delivered in June 1935. The design was amended yet again as the A21 Windhover, basically an enlarged Cutty Sark with three Gipsy engines and a cabin seating six passengers. The wings were built at the Folly Works, with final assembly in the Solent Works. However only two were produced – ZK-ABW in October 1930 and G-ABJP in 1931. Piloted by the Hon. Mrs Victor Bruce, the latter was used in 1932 for an attempt 'to stay in the air for a month', during which time the Windhover would be refuelled from two Bristol Fighter tankers. After two false starts, the record attempt commenced on 9 August, but had to be cut short after only fifty-four hours – still a worthy British record at the time. G-ABJP ended its days on cross-Channel services with Jersey Airways.

In January 1931, Whitehall Securities became the major shareholder in Saunders-Roe. Whitehall was an investment corporation with wide-ranging interests, including aviation construction and airline operations. It was already the major shareholder in Spartan Aircraft, and so a close working relationship was established between Saro and Saunders.

Under an agreement with Blackburn Aircraft, Saro built its Bluebird IV biplanes from the summer of 1929. Blackburn had built earlier series Bluebirds, but due to pressing military orders only completed three Bluebird IVs. Blackburn-built G-AACB was fitted with floats at Cowes in the summer of 1929 for the Norwegian Air Force, but was not delivered. Newly built G-AAIRs appeared from Cowes towards the end of 1929, with fifty-five completed up to the end of production in May 1931. Wings were built by Boulton & Paul at Norwich, with the aircraft assembled in the Solent Works and flown from Somerton. Many were delivered to National Flying Services at Hanworth as trainers. Saro was entrusted with the construction of the prototype Seagrave Meteor twin-engined monoplane G-AAXP in 1930; it made its first flight on 28 May. The design was then taken over by Blackburn, who initially arranged for

Seen here awaiting delivery, the prototype Saro Cloud was sold to Canada at the end of 1931. Clouds were powered by a variety of engines – these are Wright Whirlwinds. One VIP aircraft was fitted with three Pratt & Whitney Wasps.

production Blackburn Seagraves, described as luxury four-seat cabin monoplanes, to be built by Saro. Military contracts for Clouds meant that Saro had insufficient capacity, so three further Seagraves were built by Blackburn at Brough.

Based on the experience of the Saunders A7 Severn and A14 metal hull, the next design from Saro was the larger all-metal A27 general-purpose flying boat for the RAF. Built to Air Ministry Specification R24/31 and powered by two Bristol Pegasus engines, the prototype K3560 flew from Cowes in January 1934, and later received the type name London. Saro had already realised that its existing premises at West Cowes were too small for production of the London. So a large assembly building – the Columbine Works – was constructed by Boulton & Paul on the existing Columbine site at East Cowes. Proclaiming the Saunders-Roe name on its façade, the impressive 50,000 sq. ft structure had a span of 200 ft, with the main doors providing a 150 ft-wide entrance. The new factory was completed in October 1935 and brought into use the following January, joining the existing Solent Works in East Cowes. The Londons were produced in the new factory and the first was delivered to the RAF in the early summer of 1936. Their wings were built by Boulton Paul, initially at Norwich, then at the company's new Wolverhampton site from 1936. The initial ten Londons were Mk Is with 690 hp Bristol Pegasus III engines, but these were superseded by the Mk II with 850 hp Pegasus X engines – the final one of forty-eight being delivered in May 1938. Crew accommodation enabled them to live on board and included a kitchen and an officers' wardroom. As a result, the London proved popular with RAF crews, and remained in service until June 1940.

A 1933 Air Ministry requirement for a long-range patrol flying boat resulted in submissions from both Saro and Shorts, with a prototype ordered from each company. The requirement issued to Saro specified that the flying boat was to be fitted with a Stieger Mono-Spar wing, which was designed for safety

The first 'large' Saro flying boat design to enter production was the London. Although it was dated by the time the type was delivered to the RAF in the summer of 1936, the London was well-liked by its crews for its flying characteristics and spaciousness.

and weight saving. For flight-testing, Cloud K2681 was rebuilt with a Mono-Spar wing and flown in the summer of 1934. Powered by four Bristol Pegasus engines, construction of the A33 proceeded slowly, with K4773 not rolled out until October 1938; it flew on 14 October. The 95 ft wing was not attached to the fuselage but was supported on strong struts attached to large sponsons. Regrettably, the A33 did not last long. While taxiing at high speed on 25 October, K4773 bounced three times after hitting a wave, resulting in the crumpling of its starboard wing. This was put down to structural failure – perhaps the Mono-Spar design strength was not as expected. The aircraft returned to the hangar but was never repaired, as Saro now had other work in hand. An anticipated order for eleven A33s was cancelled, the Short design having already emerged as the highly successful Sunderland.

Following its Consuta style of construction, Saunders-Roe had further developed aircraft quality plywood by the late 1930s. In a separate site at Cowes, they now produced 'Saro Aircraft Plywood', which was used in such types as the Anson, the DH86, and various Miles designs. By 1939 the company was producing 40 per cent of all the UK's aircraft plywood requirements. In the 1920s and 1930s, the company had continued to build high-speed launches. In 1937 this work was split off into Saunders Shipyard Ltd at a site further up the Medina from Cowes.

Despite the problems of the A33, Saro stayed with large flying boat designs. The S36 Lerwick was a twin-engined reconnaissance flying boat that resembled a scaled-down Sunderland and was powered by Bristol Hercules. It was built to an 1936 Air Ministry specification, and there was no prototype. An initial order for ten, later increased to twenty-one, was placed in June 1937. L7248, the first,

The Saro A33 prototype was produced as a long-range patrol flying boat in competition with the Short Sunderland. The A33 only made a few flights before it was severely damaged, at which stage Saro decided not to proceed with the project.

flew in November 1938 and, although much redesign work was needed on the hull shape and tail fin, the Lerwick was pressed into RAF service in the autumn of 1939. Soon revealing its poor flying qualities, the Lerwick did not live up to expectations and no further aircraft were ordered. In fact there were suggestions that Sunderlands should be built by Saro instead. The final Lerwick L7268 was delivered in May 1941, but the type was withdrawn from service in September 1942. The public were unaware of the problems, with the Lerwick being described in April 1941 as the 'fastest flying-boat in service and undertaking excellent work as a reconnaissance bomber'. This was wartime PR in action. In anticipation of Lerwick work, Saro had taken over a large hangar at Eastleigh towards the end of 1937. In the event it was used for component production. Also in anticipation of additional orders, Saro built the Medina hangar adjacent to the Columbine hangar in 1939. However, no further large flying boats were to be produced by Saro in the 1940s.

Saro studied various large commercial flying boat designs in the late 1930s, with a September 1936 advertisement featuring a double-deck passenger flying boat. Henry Knowler was in favour of large, long-range 'ocean aircraft' (not 'flying boats') capable of flying between Southampton and New York, and potentially

The Lerwick was produced to satisfy the RAF's need for additional patrol flying boats. The design soon showed up a number of shortcomings that made it unsuitable for service. Orders were cancelled and the Lerwick only served the RAF for eighteen months.

also replacing the Short C-Class on other routes. Knowler said that flying boats were needed as land planes of the day were unable to handle the necessary capacity. As part of their proposed S38 development, Saro built the A37 Shrimp in 1939 as a small-scale flying research aircraft. Although powered by four 95 hp Niagara engines, these gave a false impression of the Shrimp's size – its span was only 50 ft. First flown from Cowes in October 1939 as G-AFZS, there was little need for the Shrimp, as the S38 project did not go ahead. After initial trials, the Shrimp was stored until August 1940 and then flown to Beaumaris in Anglesey for further trials. The position of Cowes on the south coast led to the need to move some of the work away from possible enemy attacks. In September 1940 the design office was moved to Beaumaris, where it was soon joined by the flight-test department. Hangars were erected there and Saro were responsible for handling Catalina flying boats received from America for the RAF.

With no follow-up orders for the Lerwick, Saro was left with spare production capacity early in the Second World War. This was soon resolved when the company was instructed to build a Walrus air-sea rescue amphibian on behalf of Supermarine. Under the thinking of the time, the existing aircraft built by Supermarine at Itchen had metal hulls. It was realised that scarce metal could be

From this angle, it looks like a large aircraft, but the four-engined Saro A37 only had a wing span of 50 feet. Flying in the summer of 1939, it was built to investigate the aerodynamics of the proposed S38 flying boat of the late 1930s.

saved if wood was used, so the wooden-hulled Mk II was developed. Production of this version was undertaken by Saro at East Cowes, with an initial contract signed in January 1940 and X1045 first flown in May. 461 were built by Saro for the Royal Navy and RAF (compared to 285 by Supermarine); the final one, HD936, departed Cowes in January 1944. Although originally designed for the Royal Navy, wartime service saw many used by the RAF for air-sea rescue duties. Quite a large number were built at a wartime site that Saro had at Addlestone in Surrey, which remained in use until January 1944. As a replacement for the Walrus, Supermarine designed the Sea Otter, with the prototype flying in 1938. Lack of production capacity meant that Supermarine were unable to build the Sea Otter itself. An order was placed with Blackburn Aircraft in 1940, but they were unable to proceed. So another order was placed with Saro in 1942. The first of 250 Sea Otter Is for the Royal Navy, JM738, flew from Cowes in January 1943 and production was undertaken alongside the Walrus. A further forty ASRIIs were built for the RAF. The final one was delivered in July 1946; a further batch of fifty was cancelled.

Early in the war, the Solent Works were undertaking repair work on the likes of Londons, Stranraers and Walruses. During a bombing raid on 4/5 May 1942, the works were completely destroyed, along with most of the hangars at Somerton. The works were never rebuilt, and the site was cleared for the storage of flying boats prior to delivery. A replacement hangar was erected to the west of Cowes, near to Somerton airfield, for the overhaul of Walrus and Sea Otters,

With spare capacity at the beginning of the war, Saro undertook the production of Walrus amphibians on behalf of Supermarine. Whereas the Walrus originally had a metal hull, Saro developed the wooden-hulled Mk II to save scarce metal for other uses.

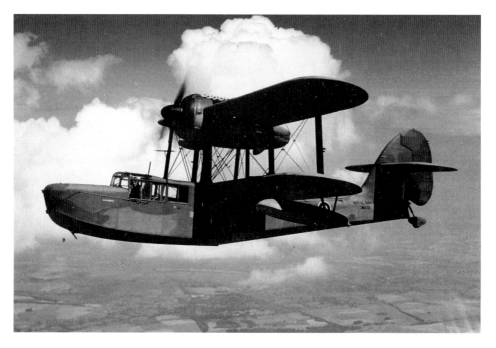

As well as the Supermarine Walrus, Saro undertook production of its replacement, the Sea Otter. Although the prototype had flown prior to the Second World War, delays meant it did not enter Navy service until spring 1943.

which were still test-flown from Somerton. In the spring of 1946, four surplus Walrus Is were overhauled as G-AHFL–FO for use as whale-spotters with United Whalers.

While at Beaumaris, the design office under Henry Knowler worked on two different flying boat projects. In December 1943, they submitted the initial design of the SR44 jet-powered fighter. By the time the design office returned to Cowes at the end of the war, this had developed into the SR A1, with three prototypes ordered by the Ministry of Aircraft Production in April 1944. The SR A1 was the world's first jet-propelled flying boat fighter, and was powered by two Metropolitan-Vickers Beryl engines. It was also the first production aircraft to be fitted with a Martin-Baker ejection seat. Intended to serve in the Far East in the fight against the Japanese, the end of the war saw the prime need for the SR A1 disappear. Prototype construction proceeded at East Cowes, with TG263 flying on 16 July 1947. TG267 and TG271 followed in 1948, but both were lost in accidents the following summer. Maximum speed was 515 mph, which was similar to the Sea Hawk carrier-borne fighter being developed for the Royal Navy. Trials with TG263 continued until 1950, but no production orders were received. Saro hoped that the outbreak of the Korean War might renew interest in the

Produced to a wartime requirement for a waterborne fighter, the SR A1 did not fly until July 1947. At high speed it produced plenty of spray on take-off, as shown here by TG263 in the Solent. Luckily, there were fewer yachts around Cowes in 1947 than in the present day.

The final SR A1, TG271, only had a short flying life. It crash-landed in the Solent on 12 August 1949. The second aircraft crashed five weeks later while at MAEE Felixstowe. By then there was no longer a requirement for a flying boat fighter.

In connection with promoting its latest fighter designs, Saro displayed the SR A1 at the Festival of Britain in June 1951. Here, G-12-1 floats on the River Thames, with the Festival Hall and Skylon behind. It is currently displayed at Solent Sky in Southampton.

Following the SR A1, Saro produced a number of designs for a swept-wing, water-based fighter around the time of the Korean War in 1951. This was the P122, which was powered by a Sapphire jet. There was no interest from the RAF or Navy.

fighter, but the Ministry cancelled further work in December 1950. Saro made a final attempt to attract interest in the SR A1 by flying it to the Festival of Britain in June 1951, having already promoted an improved design of supersonic waterborne fighter.

The other design worked on during the Second World War was for another large flying boat. A 1941 Air Ministry specification was for a long-range reconnaissance flying boat; both Saro and Shorts submitted similar designs. In March 1942 the Ministry of Aircraft Production instructed the two firms to collaborate on the Short design, resulting in the Short/Saro Shetland. Shorts built the hull and tail, Saro the wings at Beaumaris, with final erection by Shorts at Rochester. The first prototype flew in December 1944, but by then there was no longer an RAF reconnaissance requirement, so the second prototype was completed as a transport at the end of 1947. Again, there was no RAF or civil requirement for such a large flying boat. Meanwhile, in June 1943, Saro had produced its 'Case for the Flying Boat' document. This preceded the design of a large six-engined flying boat, anticipating that such an aircraft would be needed post-war for Transatlantic services. The Government's Brabazon Committee had issued requirements for post-war landplanes, but the 'Case for the Flying Boat' resulted in interest taken in Saro's design. Even before the end of the war, Saro were proposing a complete package – flying boat and Water Drome. This was a huge, covered dock area for flying boats that enabled passengers to disembark in comfort. Goodness knows what the cost would have been.

Based on their S38 and Shetland work, Saro worked on their new flying boat design, resulting in the SR45, with BOAC showing interest in January 1946. In May, three turbo-prop-powered SR45s were ordered by the Ministry of Supply, ostensibly for BOAC. There were to be many delays during the construction of these 100-seat transoceanic flying boats, which later received the name Princess. A change of power plant from six Clydes to coupled Tweeds, with a consequent wing redesign, did not help, and in fact the Princess finally emerged with ten Bristol Proteus turboprops. It was a massive 140 ton aircraft with a span of 220 ft (the Bristol Brabazon landplane was 230 ft). In the spring of 1948, the Princess's future was very much in doubt, but the Ministry of Supply agreed to continue funding as interest was shown by British South American Airways for services to South America. The first Princess G-ALUN was moved out of the Columbine Works in October 1951 for final completion, which included fitting the fin, engines and outer wings. This was because there was insufficient space within the works. G-ALUN first flew on 22 August 1952 and was displayed at the Farnborough Air Show the following month. There were problems with the Princess's Twin Proteus engines, and Bristol needed to spend development time on its own Britannia airliner, which had standard Proteuses. In March 1952, the Ministry announced that only G-ALUN would fly and the other two Princesses would be stored, pending the availability of improved engines. By now BOAC had lost interest in flying boats, having introduced Comet jets into service in May 1952. Saro seemed to be a lone voice in the world trying to promote the values of the flying boat, having formed Princess Air Transport Co. to possibly operate the aircraft. This company was 75 per cent owned by Saro and 25 per cent by Airwork, but could do nothing to save the Princess. As late as 1953 Saro was still placing advertisements extolling the value of flying boats, but no one else was interested. Airline passengers were now looking for speed, not luxury. The second and third Princesses were structurally completed by the end of 1952, with G-ALUO moved out of the works in August. Further work was halted in January 1953, when they were both cocooned and towed to Calshot for storage, pending the availability of suitable engines. There followed a variety of plans for their future use, but all came to nothing. G-ALUN last flew in June 1954, following which it was also cocooned and stored on the site of the old Solent Works. This marked the end of flying boat construction by Saro. Interestingly, Saro was visited by Sandringham G-AKCO in the spring of 1954, being moored alongside the Princess until its departure to Australia in October. In April 1967, the still-cocooned G-ALUN was towed to the slipway of the former Supermarine Itchen factory and scrapped. G-ALUO and G-ALUP were scrapped at Calshot. Estimated costs for producing the three Princesses were £2.8 million in 1946, £10 million in 1950 and £12 million by 1953. As a follow-on, in the late 1940s Knowler had designed the P135 Duchess flying boat powered by six DH Ghost jet engines; a model of it was displayed at Farnborough in September 1950. With a span of 135 ft 6 in, the Duchess was planned to carry seventy-four passengers over a range of 1,500–2,000 miles. A later version was powered by Rolls-Royce Avon engines. The RAF showed interest in the P162 version for maritime reconnaissance, with design work continuing until 1955, when thoughts of further flying boats was given up.

Subcontract work undertaken by Saro in the 1950s at East Cowes and Eastleigh included producing Vickers Valiant bomber cockpits; Vickers Viscount airliner

The Columbine hangar at East Cowes was massive when built, but it is dwarfed by the size of the Princess flying boat. All three fuselages were built inside the hangar at the same time, then they were taken outside for the fitment of tails, wings and engines.

Saro's post-war 'glory' was the Princess. Due to its size, it was rolled out of the Columbine works in October 1951 without its outer wings or engines. These were fitted in the open during the following winter – with covers provided to shelter the workers.

An August 1952 view outside the Columbine works. Princess G-ALUN floats on the Medina while G-ALUO has its fin and rudder fitted. Although it was no longer airworthy, the SR A1 was included in this Saro publicity photograph.

The majestic Saro Princess off the south coast of the Isle of Wight in 1953. Only one of the three aircraft built took to the air – the other two were cocooned upon completion and placed in storage at Calshot. Stately, luxury air travel was no longer in vogue.

Even though construction of the Princess had only just begun, Saro was already working on a jet-powered replacement – the P135 Duchess. The initial 1949 design was powered by six Ghost engines, but these were replaced by Avons in later versions.

As well as flying boats, Saro produced this design for a large transport helicopter in the summer of 1952, but the P514 Rotorcoach progressed no further that this model.

wings; Supermarine Swift, DH Vampire and Venom wings; and DH Comet 1 and 2 parts.

The next aircraft to emerge from the Columbine Works saw a complete change of direction for Saro – a jet- and rocket-propelled fighter. The Air Ministry considered this type of fighter necessary for intercepting anticipated high-flying Russian bombers. Saro submitted its initial proposal in response to a February 1952 specification, and the design was revised prior to a May 1953 order for prototypes XD145, XD151 and XD153. A small delta-winged aircraft, the SR53, had a DH Spectre rocket motor fitted below the Viper jet engine in its rear fuselage. Normally, a Viper would be considered too low-powered for a fighter, but the thrust of the Spectre negated this. Firestreak missiles were fitted to each wing tip. Progress was delayed due to problems de Havilland Engines was having in developing the Spectre rocket. It was also realised by the autumn of 1954 that larger radar would be needed to make the fighter fully effective. As a result, the design was enlarged as the SR177, and the SR53 would be a proof-of-concept aircraft. As there was no suitable airfield on the Isle of Wight, Saro initially planned to carry out SR53 flight trials from Hurn, and established the necessary facilities there in 1955. A change of plan saw XD145 taken by road from Cowes to Boscombe Down in June 1956. However, it was not until 16 May 1957 that XD145 first flew, followed by XD151 on 18 December, the third prototype having already been cancelled.

Interest in the Mach 2.35 production version, the SR177, was shown by both the RAF and Navy, with twenty-seven prototype and pre-production aircraft provisionally ordered in September 1955. These were to be powered by an 8,000 lb DH Gyron Junior jet plus a Spectre rocket engine. In 1955, design work was undertaken on a further development – the P187. This would be powered by two massive DH Gyron jet engines, plus four Spectre rockets. Due to its involvement with the engines, de Havilland Holdings acquired a majority

A further change of direction for Saro brought about the SR53 mixed power fighter. Built in the Columbine works, prototype XD145 basks in the sunshine at Boscombe Down shortly before its first flight in the summer of 1957.

The SR53 at full power on take-off, with the Spectre clearly working. The latter provided the boost that enabled the SR53 to reach operational height, after which the Viper would have been sufficient to return the aircraft to base. Armament was to be two Firestreak missiles.

shareholding in Saro in 1956, which now became the Saunders-Roe Division of de Havilland Group. With limited capacity at East Cowes, consideration was given to production being undertaken by Armstrong Whitworth Aircraft at Coventry. The West German Air Force was also interested in operating the SR177 and it was planned that licensed production would be undertaken in Germany. The infamous Government Defence White Paper of April 1957 saw the need for manned fighters done away with, and so the RAF's planned SR177s were cancelled. The naval version was cancelled in August, but Saro was still hopeful of proceeding, with the Ministry confirming in August that five prototypes would be required in anticipation of a German order. Production had commenced, but in the end the Germans decided they did not want to be the prime customer and so the SR177 was finally cancelled on Christmas Eve 1957. Saro's design team of the 1950s worked on civil airliners (from eleven to 200 seats), autogyros and VIP jets, including one based on the SR177 capable of Mach 1.8. A wide variety, for what might have been regarded as a flying boat design team.

Cowes saw another turnaround in the type of aircraft being built there. Following Saro's takeover of Cierva Helicopters in 1951, the company's Helicopter Division was established at Eastleigh. Saro continued development of the Skeeter light helicopter with the design improved under the designation Saro P501. After preliminary Army evaluation in the summer of 1956, the Skeeter was ordered as the AOP10 for further trials, with four built at Cowes in 1957 and flown from Eastleigh. The main production batch of AOP12s was ordered in May 1956, followed in 1957 by an order for the German Army (six) and Navy (four). Initially priced at £28,200, further Army orders took their total to sixty-four. Production was undertaken at East Cowes in 1958–60, with the airframes shipped to Eastleigh for final assembly and flight-testing. Work on a Skeeter replacement started in 1957, resulting in the P531. Design work was undertaken at Cowes, but development was carried out at Eastleigh.

The late 1950s saw Saro move into the new field of hovercraft design. Following testing of models by inventor Christopher Cockerell on the island, Saro received a contract from the National Research & Development Corporation to design and build a full-size hovercraft to develop the idea further. The Ministry of Supply took an interest in 1956, classifying the project as 'Secret'. This also included Cockerell, who was reminded by the Ministry in the spring of 1958 to keep quiet about the development of his invention. The SR-N1 (Saunders-Roe – Nautical One) was built at Cowes in 1959 and launched on 11 June. The early trials were successful, leading to the SR-N1 undertaking an English Channel crossing from Calais to Dover in July, wearing aircraft-style registration G-12-4. In September, it made its first public appearance at the Farnborough Air Show, carrying twenty Royal Marines on its hull.

When Saro took over Cierva Helicopters in 1951, it inherited the design of the Skeeter lightweight helicopter. Much development work was needed before the type was ready for service. This Skeeter 6 was built at Cowes and undertook military trials in 1955.

Saunders-Roe began working on hovercraft in the late 1950s. At the request of the NRDC it built an experimental craft to Christopher Cockerell's design. This was the SR N1 of 1959, seen here later in its life with Westland titles.

The military showed interest in the later SRN2, and ordered an enlarged version as the SRN3. This was delivered to the IHTU at Lee-on-Solent in the summer of 1964 and is seen here kicking up plenty of spray near to its base in the Solent.

WESTLAND AIRCRAFT LTD

The reorganisation of Britain's aircraft industry in 1959 saw Westland Aircraft taking over Saro with its helicopter and hovercraft work in August. However, the Saunders-Roe name remained, with the Columbine hangar now proclaiming 'Westland Aircraft Ltd – Saunders-Roe Division'. Westland was mainly interested in the potential of the P531 helicopter. Hovercraft development continued, leading to the larger SRN2 sixty-eight-seat machine in January 1962, which had more practical use. Registered G-12-5, it undertook experimental passenger services between Weston-super-Mare and Penarth in the summer of 1963 and between Southsea and Ryde in 1963–64. The SRN2 design was enlarged into the SRN3 in November 1963 for military trials with the Interservices Hovercraft Trials Unit at Lee-on-Solent, and delivered as XS655 in June 1964. The huge car-carrying, 400 passenger cross-Channel SRN4 followed in December 1967; six were built. The initial version carried 254 passengers and thirty cars, but an

The SRN4 was built at Cowes in 1967 and is seen here outside the Columbine hangar. Four were operated by Seaspeed on cross-Channel services from the summer of 1968, with two further aircraft operated by Hoverlloyd. Note the lettering style above the hangar door.

enlarged version carried 418 passengers and sixty cars. It entered service with Seaspeed in August 1968 and continued until travellers' needs were better served by the opening of the Channel Tunnel.

For Saro's designers it was then back to a small-sized hovercraft – the SRN5 in April 1964, which carried eighteen passengers. Soon lengthened into the thirty-eight-passenger SRN6, it became the first hovercraft to enter large-scale production, and operated cross-Solent and cross-Channel services. Two SRN5s, XT492 and XT493, were delivered to the IHTU in the summer of 1964; they were known as the Warden. XT493 was later rebuilt as a SRN6 Winchester, with further new-built SRN6s delivered for joint-service use from 1965. In conjunction with Bell Aerospace, the SRN5 was sold to the US Navy, who used it for operational service in Vietnam. The SRN6 also saw military service in Iraq and with the Iranian Navy. A total of sixty-eight SRN5s and SRN6s were built.

Work with rocket motors in connection with the SR53 led to a new line of work in collaboration with RAE Farnborough. In July 1955, Saunders-Roe

The SRN5 was the first hovercraft to enter production; it first appeared in the spring of 1964. To provide further capacity, it was easily lengthened into the SRN6, which doubled the number of passengers. Note the British Hovercraft Corporation titles.

received a 'Super Priority' order to proceed with the development of the Black Knight single-stage research rocket. Powered by an Armstrong Siddeley Gamma rocket motor, these were built in the Columbine Works with the rocket engines tested at High Down, near Freshwater, from April 1957. The first launch of a Black Knight was from Woomera in September 1958. Work continued following Westland's takeover in 1959, and there was a total of twenty-two launches until November 1965. Based on the Black Knight experience, Saunders-Roe then built the Black Arrow three-stage rocket-powered satellite launcher, with the first test from Woomera made in July 1969. After four successful launches, the programme was cancelled by the Government in 1972.

BRITISH HOVERCRAFT CORPORATION LTD

The British Hovercraft Corporation was formed on 1 March 1966 to further the hovercraft development work of Saunders-Roe and Vickers, with Westland Aircraft having a 90 per cent shareholding and NRDC 10 per cent. The Columbine

In the late 1970s, British Hovercraft Corporation undertook the restoration of Supermarine S6A racer N248 on behalf of Southampton Council. It was then moved back across the Solent and is currently on display at Solent Sky.

The Columbine site in Westland's days, for some reason looking rather deserted. The works hangar was built in 1936 and the original house was retained as administration offices. The hangar door bears the Jubilee Union Flag, which was painted in 1977.

Works were now branded 'british hovercraft corporation' (the lower-case letters deliberate), which was later amended to 'British Hovercraft'. The corporation was taken over fully by Westland in October 1970.

Development and production of the SRN6 continued in the late 1960s. With designation changed to BH to denote British Hovercraft, the BH7 military variant appeared in October 1969 and there were sales to the Royal Navy and the Iranian Navy. XW255 appeared in the summer of 1970 and was delivered to IHTU in March 1971 as the Wellington class. The BH7 marked the end of major hovercraft work at the Cowes site. From September 1979 the Navy classified their hovercrafts as ships, not aircraft.

To keep the workforce at Cowes busy, BHC obtained a contract from Britten-Norman in March 1968 to build Islanders, and the completed airframes were delivered by road to Bembridge for fitting out. This work continued until July 1972 when the receivers were appointed by Britten-Norman. By then, 363 had been delivered by BHC, plus a number of kits. A new landmark appeared in East Cowes in 1977. The Columbine Works door was painted as a massive Union Flag to mark Queen Elizabeth's Silver Jubilee.

GKN AEROSPACE

In November 1984, the Columbine site became Westland Aerospace, then GKN Westland Aerospace when GKN took over the company in 1994. Much subcontract work was undertaken for other aerospace companies – Shorts, de Havilland Canada and Lockheed, as well as Westland itself. Later the title changed to GKN Aerospace.

In 2006, forty acres of GKN's North Works were purchased by SEEDA for inclusion in the Cowes maritime business centre redevelopment plan. As part of Cowes Waterfront Initiative, the Columbine hangar now forms part of Venture Quays. The remainder of the site continues to be used by GKN Aerospace.

Eastleigh (Southampton)

Eastleigh airfield was originally developed as an Aircraft Acceptance Park for the RFC in 1917. As such it was provided with a number of hangars, which then passed to the US Navy when they arrived in 1918. The airfield closed in 1920 and the hangars were used for migrant accommodation. Purchased by Southampton Corporation, the site was redeveloped as a municipal airport, which was officially opened in November 1932. The RAF arrived in the summer of 1935 and established four FAA Squadrons on 1 October. The airfield was transferred to the Admiralty in 1940. It was re-established post-war as Eastleigh Airport, and major investment in the 1980s saw the emergence of the rebranded Southampton Airport.

SUPERMARINE AVIATION

Supermarine was a well-established manufacturer of seaplanes. With the development of Eastleigh Airport in 1932, Supermarine moved into two of the First World War hangars, which it would use as a flight-test base. This was for amphibian and land-based aircraft built at their Hythe and Woolston sites, including the prototype Seagull V in the summer of 1933. February 1934 saw the first flight of the new F7/30 fighter K2890, which had to be returned to Woolston for modifications. The first production Walrus K5772 appeared in March 1936, but the site's claim to fame was the first flight of Spitfire prototype K5054 by Mutt Summers on 5 March 1936. After initial testing, it departed to Martlesham Heath for official trials. Most of the test-flying was undertaken by Jeff Quill, with designer R. J. Mitchell visiting whenever his health allowed. Supermarine and Vickers held a press demonstration day on 18 June 1936 when a Wellesley, a Walrus, the Spitfire prototype and the brand-new Wellington prototype were displayed. The first production Spitfire K9787 arrived by road from Woolston in May 1938 for final assembly. It first flew on 14 May before departure to Martlesham Heath for further trials. The sixth production aircraft K9792 was the first to be delivered to the RAF at Duxford on 29 July. Eastleigh was now responsible for final assembly and flight-testing of the new fighter. The initial

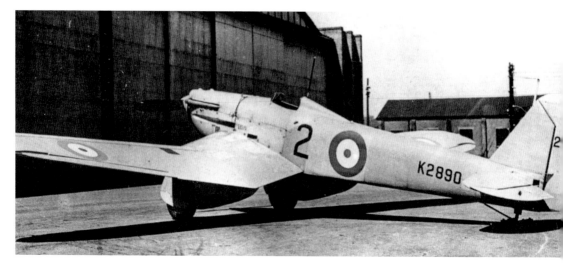

The unsuccessful Supermarine F7/30, a day- and night-fighter, between the hangars at Eastleigh in 1934. Test-flying revealed a number of problems with the aircraft, so Mitchell and his design team started work on a brand new aircraft – the Supermarine 300.

Supermarine's and Vickers' Press Day at Eastleigh in June 1936. On display are Spitfire prototype K5054, a Walrus, a Wellesley and the Wellington prototype. At the time Supermarine described the Spitfire as 'the World's fastest fighter'.

Walruses built at Woolston and Hythe were test-flown from Eastleigh in the late 1930s and the early days of the Second World War. K5780 is an early production aircraft from Woolston and is seen here at Eastleigh in the summer of 1936.

RAF order was for 310 Spitfires, and to cope with this large number Supermarine erected a twin-bay flight-test hangar on the south side of the airfield. Additional space was created by covering in the area between two of Supermarine's original hangars. Initial Spitfire supplies from subcontractors were erratic – in June 1938 there were twenty-five fuselages from Woolston, but only four sets of wings from the subcontractors. Over the following months, such problems were resolved. In the spring of 1939, Spitfire K9834 was modified at Eastleigh for an attempt on the air-speed record; it was fitted with an uprated Merlin and clipped wings. Flown as N17 the attempt did not proceed, as the Messerschmitt Me209 broke the record in April. The last of the RAF's initial batch of Spitfires flew in September 1939. By then, Supermarine had received Spitfire orders from many countries, e.g. Estonia, Greece, Portugal, and Switzerland, but these were cancelled upon the outbreak of the Second World War. However, one was delivered to France and two to Turkey in 1939–40. Just over 1,500 IAs and IBs were assembled at Eastleigh between March 1937 and March 1941. The Spitfire III prototype N3297 first flew in March 1940, although the second prototype did not arrive until June 1941.

The destruction of Supermarine's Woolston and Itchen production factories in September 1940 initially saw a drop-off in final assembly work at Eastleigh. However, major parts soon started arriving from other production facilities, which Supermarine had already set up around Southampton. So lorries arrived from garages and small factories with Spitfire assemblies, with the Spitfire Vs superseding the Is by the end of the year. Early versions of PR Spitfires appeared in May 1941. From 1941, production flight-testing was moved a few miles north to Worthy Down, which was considered a safer airfield, given the possibility of enemy attacks.

Spitfire I X4942 was modified as the prototype VI and flown in July 1942. This was followed by production VIs in 1942–43; VIIIs from November 1942 until June 1943 (this was the first major Griffon powered version); IX from June 1942 onwards; XIVs from late 1944; and XVIIIs from June 1945 – too late for war

Final assembly of Spitfire Is at Eastleigh early in 1939, by which time two new assembly hangars were in use by Supermarine. There had been delays with initial deliveries of the fighter to the RAF, but these had been resolved by the end of 1938.

K9822 being prepared for flight-testing in December 1938. At this stage the fighters still carried their serial numbers under their wings. Supermarine's price for one of these early Spitfires was £8,783; in 1948, a Seafire FR47 cost £8,900.

Early production Spitfire Is – assembled at Eastleigh – are here operating from Hornchurch early in 1940, in service with 65 Squadron. These aircraft were originally fitted with two-bladed propellers, but after a few months these were replaced with three-bladed ones.

Spitfire VIIs were assembled at Eastleigh from June 1943. This version was fitted with an improved Merlin engine, which was then used in the successful Spitfire IX. MD184 is seen on the airfield in May 1944, prior to delivery.

Spitfire PRXIX PS853 was one of many of that variant built in the Southampton area during the later stages of the war. It was initially used for development trials before delivery to the RAF, with whom it still serves under the ownership of the Battle of Britain Memorial Flight.

With the return to peace in the summer of 1945, Supermarine refurbished surplus Walruses for overseas users. Seen here at Eastleigh is one of six delivered to the Argentine Navy in 1949. Some civil conversions were used from Antarctic whaling ships as whale-spotters.

service. By the spring of 1944, newer marks of PR Spitfires began to be received for final assembly – PRXs in the spring of 1944 and PRXIXs from May 1945. During the war, Walruses and Sea Otters built by Saro at Cowes were flown to Eastleigh for delivery to the RAF and RN. Surplus Walruses were overhauled in the summer of 1944 prior to delivery to RNZAF.

Spitfire work slowed down following the return to peace. In 1947, any remaining flight-test work was moved to Chilbolton, with Eastleigh working on conversions and overhauls. In June and July 1950, twenty F22s were refurbished for Egypt and delivered from Eastleigh. Four Spitfire F24s arrived by road from South Marston early in 1949 for completion and delivery to the RAF. These were the final Spitfires completed with VN496 departing in April. Along with the Itchen works, a number of Walruses and Sea Otters were overhauled for foreign air forces in 1946–47. These including eight Sea Otters for the Danish Navy. Supermarine announced a four-seat civilian Sea Otter in the autumn of 1946; demonstrator G-AIDM appeared in 1947. It was purchase by Shell for survey work in Venezuela early in 1948, but was the only civilian one produced by Supermarine. A number of Spitfire IXs were converted into two-seat trainers in 1948–51. Overseas air force customers were India (ten), Netherlands (six) and Eire (six). G-ALJM was Supermarine's Tr IX demonstrator, in use from October 1949. Privately owned Spitfire V G-AISU was overhauled in the spring of 1950. In later years it was purchased by Supermarine and flown for display purposes with its RAF markings – AB910 'QJ-J'.

Swift wings were built for the South Marston production line in the early and mid-1950s, followed by Scimitar wings. The prototype Supermarine 545 Swift replacement was constructed at Hursley Park in 1955 and moved to Eastleigh for completion at the end of the year. It would then have moved to Boscombe Down for its maiden flight in the spring of 1956, but before that could happen the project was cancelled. Supermarine closed its Eastleigh site in 1957; one of the First World War hangars was taken over by Folland and the flight-test hangar

The one-off Kay Gyroplane was built by Oddie, Bradbury & Cull in the winter of 1934/35. It is seen here at Eastleigh prior to its first flight, for which it was taken to Perth, Scotland; it received the registration G-ACVA. It is currently on display at the National Museum of Scotland.

was occupied by Ford Motors. The remaining First World War hangars were used for extending the airport's terminal area, and were eventually demolished in December 1988 as part of the airport's redevelopment.

ODDIE, BRADBURY & CULL LTD

Formed by Messrs Oddie, Bradbury and Cull, OBC moved into one of the First World War hangars in 1934 and undertook subcontract work for other manufactures, including rotor blades for Cierva. It built the prototype Kay Gyroplane G-ACVA, but this was taken to Perth for its first flight in February 1935. Work on the second Gyroplane, G-ACVB, was not completed. The business became a limited company in July 1935 and undertook aircraft engineering and manufacture. In the spring of 1938, Oddie, Bradbury & Cull received instructions to construct five Cierva C40 autogyros for the RAF. British Aircraft Manufacturing at Hanworth was initially going to build the C40s on behalf of Cierva, but the work passed to Oddie, Bradbury & Cull when British Aircraft went out of business. L7590 was the first to be delivered in October 1938. The Kay Gyroplane G-ACVA had returned to Eastleigh for attention by the end of 1938, and was demonstrated to the Air Minister in January 1939.

Upon the outbreak of the Second World War, Oddie, Bradbury & Cull became a Civilian Repair Organisation, and also undertook subcontract work on the

Folland 43/37 engine testbed aircraft. The company built wings for all twelve and assembled P1774 and P1775 in 1940 prior to delivery by road to Folland at Staverton. Other work included production of the 'Oddie Fastener', which was used in many aircraft types. In 1951, Oddie, Bradbury & Cull moved from the airport to new premises in Portswood Road where it continued to supply parts to the aircraft industry.

FOSTER WIKNER AIRCRAFT CO.

Australian Geoffrey Wikner arrived in England in May 1934 and, along with V. Foster, formed the Foster Wikner Aircraft Co. in 1936 to build the FW1 Wicko. This was a high-wing, two-seat light aircraft capable of aerobatics with a top speed of 140 mph. Prototype G-AENU was built at Bromley-by-Bow, London, and, powered by an 85 hp modified Ford V8 car engine, it flew from Stapleford in September 1936. In the spring of 1937 the company took over one of Eastleigh's

Foster Wikner arrived at Eastleigh in 1937 to undertake production of the Wicko light aircraft. Sales proved slow and only a few aircraft had been completed by the outbreak of war. G-AFJB proved resilient and still flies today.

hangars, which offered more space. From here, G-AEZZ first flew in August as the FW3 Wicko with a 150 hp Cirrus engine. It was then fitted with a 130 hp Gipsy Major and, as the GM1 Wicko, entered limited production until the outbreak of the Second World War with a sale price of £895. It was advertised as the 'finest aircraft for training Civil Air Guard pilots' but there were no such sales – nine having been produced up to the summer of 1939. A number were then used by the RAF as the Warferry, which was equipped with a third seat. Foster Wikner continued in business during the war, undertaking subcontract work for other aviation companies. After the war, in the spring of 1946, Geoffrey Wikner flew home to Australia in a converted Halifax bomber.

CUNLIFFE-OWEN AIRCRAFT LTD

On 9 August 1937, millionaire Sir Hugo Cunliffe-Owen formed BAO Ltd for the construction of aircraft and ancillary work. It took over one of the First World War hangars, changing its name on 11 May 1938 to Cunliffe-Owen Aircraft. Sir Hugo was already Chairman of British American Tobacco, who provided finance for the fledgling Cunliffe-Owen Aircraft.

In April 1937, Sir Hugo had announced his intention to enter a New York–Paris air race that August with an 'All British Clyde Clipper'. This was a version of the American Burnelli UB-14 'Flying Wing' airliner, which was being built by Scottish Aircraft & Engineering at its new factory at Willesden. An elaborate mock-up of the British Burnelli Flying Wing was completed by the beginning of 1937, but little further work was undertaken before Scottish Aircraft went into receivership in July. This meant that Sir Hugo was unable to enter the race. However, he was so taken by the merits of the UB-14 that he formed BAO to continue the work started by Scottish Aircraft.

Prior to production commencing at Eastleigh, the prototype UB-14 was shipped across from America in the summer of 1937 with the intention of undertaking demonstrations in Great Britain and Europe. Red tape meant that it got no further than Southampton Docks; it was eventually taken on to Holland. It finally reached Eastleigh in January 1938, by which time work had commenced on the Cunliffe-Owen OA-I – a redesigned and re-engined version of the UB-14. Construction of the all-metal, stressed-skin aircraft was undertaken in the company's original hangar. Meanwhile, in May 1938, work commenced on a large factory on the south side of the airport for production of additional aircraft. Costing £150,000, the 3½ acre site was close to Supermarine's flight-test hangar. Initial plans showed the eventual need for 2,000 workers. The prototype OA-I Flying Wing was registered G-AFMB and flown for the first time on 12 January 1939, which just preceded the official

The First World War hangar initially used by Cunliffe-Owen Aircraft when the company set up business at Eastleigh in 1937. The hangar was used for construction of the Burnelli-inspired OA-1 Flying Wing in 1938, later becoming part of the airport's terminal.

opening of the new factory. Press coverage of the event referred to it as the British Burnelli, not the OA-I. The OA-I carried 15–20 passengers and was powered by two Bristol Perseus engines. Details were announced of the similar-looking OA-II eighteen-seater, which appeared in Cunliffe-Owen advertisements of the time, where the company was described as 'Designers and Constructors of Flying Wing Type Aircraft'. The OA-I undertook trials at Martlesham Heath in the summer of 1939, but its performance did not come up to expectations. Further trials were undertaken in September for the Air Ministry, which was looking for possible new transport aircraft. Due to the outbreak of war, no production of the OA-I was undertaken. G-AFMB was eventually acquired by the Air Ministry, which passed it on to the Free French Air Force.

Cunliffe-Owen had also formed an association with Lockheed Aircraft of California, and in September 1938 assembled the first of a number of Lockheed 14s for British Airways. These airliners arrived by sea, with two Lockheed 12As assembled in the spring of 1939. One was G-AFTL, for Sydney Cotton, who used

The modern-looking Cunliffe-Owen factory that was built in 1938 and officially opened in January 1939. The airport is to the left and Supermarine's flight-test hangar is top left. The factory still exists today, as part of Ford's Transit assembly plant.

The one and only Cunliffe-Owen OA1, based on the American Burnelli design, flying over Southampton Docks in 1939. No orders were received. Cunliffe-Owen's factory space later proved valuable for wartime fighter assembly and production.

Cunliffe-Owen's vast new hangar area was used for the assembly of American-built aircraft arriving for service with the RAF. Seen here are some of the many Curtiss Tomahawks handled, most of which would have arrived at Southampton Docks.

it for 'reconnaissance' flights over Germany. These were followed in the summer of 1939 by the first of a large number of Hudsons for the RAF. In 1941, Cunliffe-Owen completed an airstrip at nearby Marwell Park, which proved a better location for test-flying since it was outside the Southampton barrage balloon area. At least twenty small hangars were provided to house the aircraft.

With spare production capacity at the outbreak of the Second World War, Cunliffe-Owen were chosen in 1939 to build 200 Hawker Tornado fighters, but these were cancelled in July 1941, along with the Vulture engine. The Vulture did not come up to expectations and so Hawker proceeded with the Sabre-engined Typhoon instead. Cunliffe-Owen's factory was badly damaged in a bombing attack on 11 September 1940. In addition to its rebuilding, there was a major extension to the factory space in 1941. At this time, major parts were made for Supermarine Walruses (for Saro at Cowes) and Bristol Blenheim IVs. Many American aircraft destined for the RAF were assembled by Cunliffe-Owen on arrival in the UK – Airacobras, Baltimores, Bostons, Havocs, Mohawks, Lightnings, Marauders,

Large numbers of Bell Airacobras were also assembled by Cunliffe-Owen. However, they did not prove suitable for RAF use and so there was a problem of what to do with them. After storage, the majority were delivered to Russia.

Tomahawks and Venturas. The Airacobra was not a success in RAF service, and a large number of those assembled in the spring of 1942 were stored at nearby Marwell Park, then packed again and dispatched to Russia. There was a worse problem with the Lightning – only AF105–07 reached Cunliffe-Owen and the majority remained in America. Trials with the initial three showed that the fighter was unsuitable for RAF operations, and so the order was cancelled.

From the end of 1942, Cunliffe-Owen converted 118 Spitfire VBs into fixed-wing Seafire IBs; the work was shared with AST at Hamble. With space still available, the company was awarded a contract in January 1943 on behalf of Supermarine to build large numbers of Seafires. (They were also built by Westland Aircraft at Yeovil). 250 folding-wing Seafire IIIs were ordered in January 1943, followed by later contracts for a further 100. The first, NN333, was delivered to the Navy in December 1943, and the last was delivered in November 1944. 150 Griffon-engined Seafire XVs were ordered in July 1943. PR338, the first, was delivered in March 1945, the last in January 1946. Twenty Seafire XVIIs were ordered in February 1944 – this version having the teardrop canopy of the later Spitfires.

The large factory space available to Cunliffe-Owen was used from the end of 1942 for work on Seafires. Initially, the company undertook conversion of Spitfires into Seafire IBs. As seen here, it went on to produce Seafire IIIs from the following year.

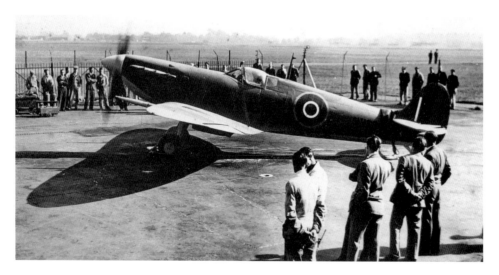

Directors and workers look on as Cunliffe-Owen's first Seafire III undertakes engine runs in November 1943. 250 of this mark were built over the next twelve months, followed by Seafire XVs and XVIIs – production of which continued after the war.

TODAYS PROJECT..

TOMORROWS ACHIEVEMENT

Despite its involvement with the assembly of American-built fighters for the RAF, the Cunliffe-Owen team had time in 1942 to come up with this design for a post-war, long-range airliner. There is a resemblance to the later Airspeed Ambassador.

Seafire production by Cunliffe-Owen totalled over 500; orders for others were cancelled. On behalf of Supermarine, the company built the prototype Spitfire F22 SX549 in the summer of 1944; it flew in November. Cunliffe-Owen also built the prototype Seafire F45s LA442 and LA444 and then converted Seafire F45 TM383 into the prototype F46.

Other wartime work saw Hudson reconnaissance aircraft modified for air–sea rescue duties with underwing radar aerials added. The first airborne lifeboat was fitted under a Hudson III in 1943 for trials and other conversions followed. Cunliffe-Owen also operated a Hudson repair facility at Macmerry, East Lothian. From the spring of 1943 new Halifax II bombers were received for the installation of H2S radar and conversion for RAF Coastal Command duties as GRIIs. Towards the end of 1944, Halifax Vs were converted for a meteorological role. Early 1944 saw overhaul work on RAF Typhoons in the build-up to D-Day. Despite wartime pressures, a summer 1943 Cunliffe-Owen advertisement showed a model of a proposed modern-looking, four-engined, twin-fin airliner. It did not progress further than the drawing board.

A post-war view of Cunliffe-Owen's factory. The 1939 site was greatly extended by a large assembly hangar (left) and a further production area was added in 1941 (top). The parked Lancasters are awaiting conversion to the ASR role.

With the return to peace, Cunliffe-Owen undertook work for Cierva. This included the overhaul of former RAF Cierva C30s for civilian owners. More importantly, the company constructed the two W11 Air Horse prototypes for Cierva. The RAF decided to replace its ASR Hudsons IIIs with Lancasters and these were converted by Cunliffe-Owen. In 1946, Cunliffe-Owen worked on ASR3s and GR3s for Coastal Command. Cunliffe-Owen proceeded with the design of a 10/12-seat feederliner powered by two 550 hp Alvis Leonides engines – the COA19 Concordia. This was to 'meet worldwide needs of regional and feeder-line operators'. The prototype was built in the winter of 1946/47 and, registered as Y-0222, it first flew on 19 May 1947. Production commenced on an initial batch of six, but only the first production aircraft G-AKBE flew, as on 18 November the company announced that it was abandoning the project, which included two trial aircraft for BEA and a VIP version for India. The reason was the poor worldwide economic conditions at the time, a lack of capital within the company, and little interest following a European sales tour. Four weeks later, Sir Hugo died. This marked the end of Cunliffe-Owen, as they gave up aircraft work. The completed

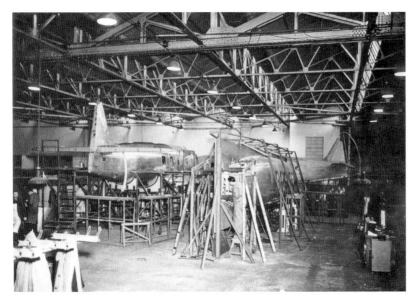

Cunliffe-Owen made an attempt to enter the civil market with the practical-looking Concordia feederliner. Here are the mock-up (rear) and first two aircraft under construction early in 1947. By the end of the year, the project had been cancelled.

The Concordia prototype Y-0222 first flew in May 1947, but only one production aircraft was completed and flown. Having invested heavily in the project and lacking further capital, Cunliffe-Owen was forced out of business by early 1948.

A view of the Concordia, presumably at the time of its roll-out in 1947. No special ceremony in those days – just people power. Unfortunately it was built for a market that did not exist, surplus Dakotas and Dragon Rapides being available at cheap prices.

and un-completed aircraft were put up for sale by tender at the end of May 1948, and all remaining aircraft were scrapped. This was unfortunate for Cierva, as Cunliffe-Owen were building the prototype Cierva W11 Air Horse helicopters.

Cunliffe-Owen's factory passed to Briggs Motor Bodies, which was associated with the Ford Motor Company. In addition to its prime aim of providing Fords with body panels, during the war Briggs had produced aircraft and engine components. In the late 1940s, the company was involved with jet engines and in 1951 the Ministry of Supply included Briggs in its 'super priority production' plan to provide 'hot end' parts for Rolls-Royce Avons, Armstrong Siddeley Sapphires and Double Mambas. This involved combustion chamber pots, exhaust cones and reheat jet pipes. The Eastleigh factory helped Briggs fulfil the increased orders, with the company being absorbed into Ford Motor in the spring of 1953. The factory was later used for the production of Ford Transit vans.

FOLLAND AIRCRAFT LTD

Folland's initial connection with Eastleigh was in 1940, when Oddie, Bradbury & Cull undertook work on its 43/37 testbed aircraft. The company built the wooden wings and completed the first two aircraft. Folland was using space at Eastleigh in the early 1950s for subcontract work. When Supermarine moved out of Eastleigh in 1957, Folland took over some of its hangar space for the production of Gnat fighter fuselages. This was to ease the workload at the main Hamble factory, which now concentrated on Gnat Trainers. Gnat fuselages destined for Finland and India were produced at Eastleigh until the mid-1960s.

To supplement factory space at Hamble, Folland took over one of Supermarine's hangars in 1957 for construction of Gnats for Finland and India. As with Hamble-built aircraft, test-flying was undertaken from Chilbolten – Eastleigh only had a grass runway.

CIERVA AUTOGIRO CO.

Although Cierva C30s and C40s had been seen at Eastleigh in the late 1930s and the war, they had been handled by either Oddie, Bradbury & Cull or Cunliffe-Owen. It wasn't until the spring of 1946 that Cierva Autogiro moved in, with Alan Marsh as its general manager and chief test pilot. During the war, Cierva was based at Thames Ditton, having been purchased by James Weir in 1944. The director of Weir Aircraft, he had previously been closely associated with Cierva at Hamble in the 1920s. Post-war expansion plans saw the need for larger premises, hence the move to Eastleigh. Cierva set up a licence agreement with Cunliffe-Owen over the use of its premises. The company brought with it a number of ex-RAF autogiros for overhaul. There were limited sales of these autogiros, with G-ACUU used as demonstrator. In 1946–47, overhaul work was also undertaken on Hoverfly Is. Flight trials continued with the experimental Cierva W9 helicopter PX-203 (note Weir Aircraft's 'W' prefix), which had first

When Cierva arrived at Eastleigh it brought a number of C30 autogyros for overhaul. Due to lack of hangar space, the work was undertaken by Cunliffe-Owen. G-ACUU was the demonstrator C30, but there was now little interest in autogyros.

Cierva also brought with it the design of the W11 helicopter. A mock-up of this large machine was built by Cunliffe-Owen in 1946, but a major redesign of the helicopter had to be undertaken before the prototype was built.

flown in October 1944 from Thames Ditton. It was an advanced design for the time, with an Alouette-style cockpit for three and a tube-like rear fuselage carrying the engine exhaust to the rear efflux to counter torque. Following two crashes, it was rebuilt at Eastleigh in the spring of 1947 and fitted with dual control. It crashed again in January 1948 and on this occasion was not rebuilt.

The main project Cierva brought with them was the W11 heavy-lift helicopter, of which details had originally been announced in July 1945. It was a very large machine, powered by a 1,600 hp Merlin engine and capable of carrying a 5,000 lb payload, It received the name Air Horse in 1946. Pest Control became interested

The Air Horse undertook much development flying from Eastleigh in 1949–50. The complex structure to support the rotors can be clearly seen. Initially appearing as G-ALCV, the W11 was repainted in military markings before its first flight in December 1948.

in the autumn of 1945 for its use in worldwide 'pest destruction', resulting in a prototype being ordered by the Ministry of Supply in July, with a second added early in 1947. Due to Pest Control's interest, the W11 soon became known as the Spraying Mantis. Because of lack of space, Cierva arranged for Cunliffe-Owen to build a mock-up of the W11 design in the spring of 1946. This had two rotors either side of the front fuselage and one to the rear – at the time, the fuselage had an open framework. Following model testing in the summer of 1946, the rotor layout was changed with one in front, and two to the rear, of a new box-like fuselage. This was capable of holding a 3 ton payload and also housed the Merlin engine. As a comparison, the W11's fuselage was 65 ft long whereas a present-day Chinook's is 51 ft. Crop-spraying equipment would be attached to the outriggers, which supported the rotors. The Cierva W12, a smaller version of the W11, was announced in September 1947. Fitted with fourteen seats and powered by two Alvis Leonides engines fitted outside the fuselage, two prototypes were reportedly under construction. However, it would appear that this was not

In 1947, Cierva worked on the design of the W12, which was of the same general layout to the W11, but smaller. Both passenger and freight versions were proposed. The bulge behind the cockpit partly covers one of the Alvis Leonides engines.

the case. For the civil market, Cierva proposed the larger W11T, powered by two Merlins outside the fuselage and carrying 30–36 passengers or freight. A model was displayed at Farnborough in September 1949. The prototype W11s were built by Cunliffe-Owen, with the unflown first prototype displayed as G-ALCV at the Farnborough Air Show in September 1948. After ground-testing at Eastleigh, it first flew as VZ-724 on 8 December. At the time it was the world's largest helicopter. Cierva had to take full responsibility for the project following the demise of Cunliffe-Owen in November 1948. Pest Control had lost interest in the W11 by 1950, mainly due to its large size, but the Ministry of Supply was still firmly behind the project. The second prototype appeared as WA-555 early in 1950; its civil registration of G-ALCW was not used. Before WA-555 took to the air, VZ-724 crashed on 13 June 1950 after its front rotor failed, killing the test crew of three. WA-555 was then used for ground tests and tethered flying in 1950–51, as part of the investigation into the crash of VZ-724.

A further Cierva helicopter design, the W14 Skeeter, also appeared in prototype form at Farnborough in September 1948 as G-AJCJ. It returned to undertake its first flight at Eastleigh on 8 October. Originally known as the Spectre until March 1948, this lightweight, two-seat helicopter was powered by a new British flat-four engine – the 108 hp Jameson. Intended for training duties or private ownership, it had an anticipated sale price of £2,000. Early trials revealed problems, including insufficient power and lack of robustness in the airframe. So it was greatly redesigned as the Skeeter II G-ALUF, which was shown at the following Farnborough Air Show and first flew on 15 October 1949 with a 145 hp Gipsy Major engine. The Air Ministry showed interest for its use in the

Cierva designed the Skeeter as a training or private-owner light helicopter and it was flown in October 1948. However, trials of the Skeeter I revealed ground resonance problems plus a lack of power. So it was back to the drawing board to design the Skeeter II.

AOP role by the Army and Navy. Unfortunately, the new version suffered ground resonance problems during early trials, and eventually broke up during a test in June 1950. Despite this, three Skeeter 3s were ordered by the Ministry of Supply for trials as WF112–14.

Despite Ministry of Supply backing, the Air Horse programme proved too much of a financial strain for Cierva, resulting in the company being taken over by Saro in January 1951 as its Helicopter Division.

SAUNDERS-ROE ('SARO')

Saro's arrival at Eastleigh following its takeover of Cierva on 22 January 1951 was not its first involvement with Eastleigh. In 1937, Saro had taken over premises with the intention of producing parts for Lerwick flying boats under construction at Cowes. In the event, they were used for subcontract work following cancellation of the Lerwick. This continued during the Second World War, including Walrus parts, followed by Sea Otter parts, for Cowes. Lack of work on the return to peace saw the hangar pass to Rollason Aircraft in 1946.

In January 1951, Cierva was taken over by Saro, who continued to work on the Skeeter helicopter. WF112 was one of three Skeeter 3s built for military evaluation in 1952, but the helicopter was still beset by ground resonance problems.

Saro formed a new Helicopter Division and, as Rollasons moved out in June 1951, were soon able to move back into their former hangar. The Saro site also undertook work on the SRA1 and Princess, as well as building 760 sets of Vampire wings and tailplanes for de Havilland at Christchurch (under subcontract from Folland). They built Swift and Scimitar parts for Supermarine and 420 Viscount wing sets for Vickers-Armstrongs at Weybridge and Hurn between 1952 and 1959. Saro continued testing Air Horse WA-555 until the end of 1953, when it was finally grounded. Very little flying was undertaken, most trials being on the ground.

Development work continued on the redesignated P501 Skeeter, with WF112 and WF113 assembled in 1952–53 for service trials. Initially powered by a Gipsy Major engine, WF112 later received a 180 hp Blackburn Bombardier. An optimistic 1953 advertisement promoted the Skeeter 'for naval communication' and WF114, also with a Bombardier, appeared with Royal Navy titles. However, the Skeeter's trials proved disappointing as it still suffered from ground resonance problems. In 1953 the Ministry of Supply withdrew its support due to the development problems, leaving Saro to proceed alone as a private venture. In 1953 Saro produced a small pulse jet engine for fitting to the tip of each rotor. Its 45 lb of thrust was suitable for all lightweight helicopters such as the Skeeter, with a second version of 120 lb also produced. In the event, it was a Napier tip rocket that was finally air-tested on G-ANMI in 1956. Saro built further development Skeeters, with Mk 5 G-AMTZ/XG303 demonstrating that the various problems had finally been solved. So a pre-production batch of Skeeters was ordered in May 1955 as AOP10s XK479–82. Powered by 215 hp Gipsy Major engines, they were built at East Cowes in 1957, assembled at Eastleigh, and delivered to Middle Wallop for trials. These four were followed by the production version, the AOP12, which was again built at East Cowes and assembled at Eastleigh from the spring of 1958. As well as the British Army, they were also produced for the German Army and Navy. A civil demonstrator, G-APOI, was flown in September 1958, but this version was not developed. The final Skeeter was delivered to the Army from Eastleigh in July 1960.

Skeeter 6 trials aircraft G-ANMJ outside Saro's hangar in 1955. This large hangar had been built in 1938 for use by Imperial Airways. As such, it provided Saro with plenty of space. The second Imperial hangar was used by the Hampshire Aeroplane Club.

Skeeter activity inside Saro's hangar in the spring of 1958. The main sections were built at East Cowes and transported to Eastleigh for assembly. A civil demonstrator is in the foreground and centre rear is the P531 mock-up, with the two prototypes just visible left, rear.

Production Skeeter AOP12 XL809 awaiting delivery to the Army in April 1960. Although small and underpowered, the Skeeter gave the Army valuable experience of helicopter operations pending introduction of the more suitable Scout.

Even before the production Skeeters had been delivered from Eastleigh, Saro's designers at East Cowes were working on a developed version. This emerged at the end of 1957 as the P531 turbine-powered, general-purpose, five-seat helicopter, with a mock-up completed at Eastleigh. The initial G-APNU and G-APNV were built as a private venture at Eastleigh, with G-APNU first flying on 20 July 1958. Further prototypes were flown, showing improvements over G-APNU and G-APNV and powered by a variety of turbine engines (Blackburn Nimbus and Turmo; DH Gnome). Interest was shown by both the Navy and the Army, and the design was further refined for both users. P531-0s XN332–34 were ordered in March 1959 for trials with the Navy later in the year, with an enlarged P531-2 produced for the Army. An evaluation batch of eight powered by Blackburn Nimbus engines was built at Eastleigh in the spring of 1960, with XP165 flying in August.

In the spring of 1958 the Hiller XROE-1 mini helicopter was demonstrated in Europe with the hope of obtaining NATO orders. It had won a US Marines

For P531 sea trials, a special landing platform was fitted on the stern of frigate HMS *Undaunted*. Based at Portland with 700x and 771 squadrons, XN334 is seen here on the platform in the summer of 1960. Production Wasps were built by Westland at Hayes.

competition and Hiller arranged for Saro to build ten XROE-1 Rotorcycles. These were single-seat, fully foldable, ultra-light helicopters. The first was flown at Eastleigh in October 1959, and five were delivered to the US Marines for further trials. The others were intended for Helicop Air of Paris, but no orders had materialised by the end of 1961, so the XROE-1 project was passed to Sud Helicopters in France, who displayed one at the 1963 Paris Air Show.

In August 1959, Saro's helicopter division was taken over by Westland Helicopters and became Westland Helicopters, Saunders-Roe Division. Development of the P531 continued, with the name Wasp chosen by Westland, although the service trials versions were still refered to as P531s. Then the name Sprite was selected for the Army version, with the Navy version being the Wasp. The first Army aircraft was displayed at Farnborough 1960 as the Sprite, but by the spring of 1961 the name had changed to Scout. Originally, the Gnome-powered Wasp had been promoted as a civil helicopter, but no civil versions were produced. As part of Britain's aircraft industry consolidation process,

The caption to this 1959 publicity photo describes G-APVL as a P531 Wasp. This was due to Westland's indecision as to the type's definitive name. Fitted with a skid undercarriage, G-APVL was a development aircraft for the Army's Scouts.

Westland also took over Fairey Aircraft in May 1960. As a result, operations at Eastleigh were run down, with production Wasps and Scouts built at Fairey's Hayes site from 1961. Eastleigh was involved in building the forward fuselage section of Wessex HC2's for Yeovil in 1960 before eventual closure of the site in the spring of 1962. Their main hangar was demolished in June 1989.

HAMPSHIRE AEROPLANE CLUB

Run by Viv Bellamy, the club has been formed at Hamble in March 1926, moving to Eastleigh in October 1932. In the late 1950s the club planned to build six Currie Wot biplanes with an anticipated sale price of £600. This was a pre-war design of a Mr Currie, who now worked for the club. Capable of being fitted with a variety of engines, the single-seat biplane had a span of 22 ft but only two were completed at Eastleigh – G-APNT flying on 11 September 1958 and G-APWT on 20 October 1959. In the winter of 1958/59, G-APNT was fitted with floats at Hamble, but not flight-tested. The floats were then fitted to G-APWT at the end of 1959, but the biplane would not take off. In January 1960, G-APNT was fitted

The Hampshire Aeroplane Club entered aircraft production in 1958 with the construction of two Currie Wots. Both G-APNT and G-APWT are displayed outside the Clubhouse in 1959 – Saro's helicopter assembly hangar is seen behind.

The Currie Wot was a neat 1930s single-seat biplane design, two having originally been built in 1938. G-APNT is seen here later in its life and fitted with a more powerful engine. Kits and plans of the Currie Wot were available for home construction.

Spurred on by the building of the Currie Wots, the Hampshire Aeroplane Club set about the design and construction of a twin-engined, touring aircraft of all-wood construction – the BH1 Halcyon. This artist's impression shows the aircraft accommodating four people.

Construction of the Halcyon proceeded in 1961, reaching the stage of engine runs by the end of the year. There was still much work to be done when G-ARIO was severely damaged early in 1962, bringing an end to the project.

with a 70 hp Rover turbine engine. The unofficial names 'Wet Wot' and 'Turbo Wot' were used for these modifications. The Aeroplane Club then built the four-seat, twin-engined BH1 Halcyon in 1960–61 to the design of Ray Hilborne (BH1 = Bellamy Hilborne). The incomplete prototype G-ARIO was damaged in taxiing trials in February 1962 and so the project was abandoned. The club intended to complete the building of Knight Twister aerobatic biplanes G-APXZ and G-ARGJ in 1962. Their fuselages had been built in the Bristol area and then moved to Eastleigh in January 1962. But the wings and tails were never built, and so the idea was abandoned. Two film replicas were then built by the club. Firstly a Roe IV Triplane replica G-ARSG was built for *Those Magnificent Men in Their Flying Machines* and flown in July 1964, then in the following year Pfalz DIII replica G-ATIJ was built for the *The Blue Max*. This marked the end of aircraft construction, with the club closing in December 1966.

Gosport

There was no airfield at Gosport connected with aircraft construction; the location was another example of boat builders turning to aircraft building. The later RAF airfield was a separate site.

GOSPORT AIRCRAFT CO.

In 1916, the well-known local ship-building firm of Camper & Nicholsons moved into the aviation business with the formation of Gosport Aircraft Co. The directors of the two companies were the same and additional construction facilities were provided on the banks of Portsmouth Harbour. Sixty FBA Type B training flying boats were ordered for the RNAS, with N2680 first flown in December 1917. The flying boats were delivered to Lee on Solent, but only half had been completed by the end of the war. Gosport also received orders for Felixstowe F2A and F3 flying boats, with construction of their hulls undertaken by Camper & Nicholsons. Lack of space meant that a new shed was erected at Camper & Nicholsons' Northam yard on the River Itchen at Southampton (opposite Pemberton-Billing) for erection of the Felixstowes, but again many were cancelled with the ending of the war. Fifty Felixstowe F5s were also due to be built at Northam, but only ten were completed before the order was cancelled. The hull of Fairey Atalanta II N118 was completed at Gosport in the spring of 1919 – it was reputedly the largest flying boat hull in the world at the time. It was transported to Phoenix Aircraft at Bradford to be fitted with its wings and tail.

With the return to peace, Gosport Aircraft tried to branch out into the civil market. It advertised itself as 'builders of flying boats for the Air Ministry, commercial and pleasure use'. In February 1919 it opened an office in New York and in July announced a range of six types of flying boat. Two were based on the Felixstowe F5 and the others were new designs, ranging from the single-seat Shrimp sports plane to the 103 ft-span, twin-engined Fire Fighter. In August 1919, John Porte joined the company as chief designer, having gained fame designing flying boats while with the RNAS at Felixstowe, later gaining the title of 'Father of

One of the flying boat designs announced by Gosport Aircraft in July 1919 was that of a patrol boat. Aimed at an anticipated 'Colonial Requirement' for a fast patrol or police boat, the twin-seat design was estimated to cruise at 60 mph for six hours.

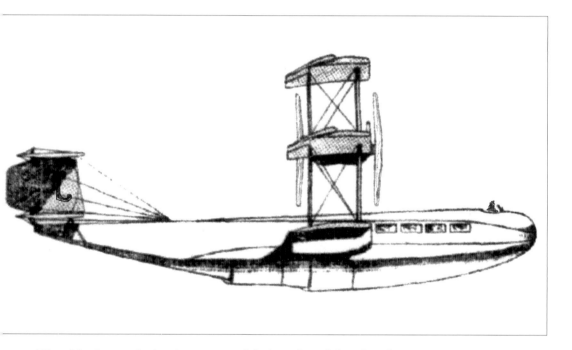

When John Porte arrived at Gosport Aircraft he brought with him the Felixstowe Fury, a triplane reconnaissance design. He further developed this as the Gosport G9 cargo design, but his death in October 1919 soon led to the folding of the company.

the British flying boat'. The intention was to develop and sell surplus Felixstowe F5s. Gosport Aircraft converted F5 N4634 as a civil demonstrator 'Gosport Flying Boat' G-EAIK in August 1919. It flew to the Dutch Air Exhibition at Amsterdam at the beginning of the month, taking five hours for the flight. As a follow-up, the Gosport G9 long-range, triplane cargo flying boat was planned. It was based on the Felixstowe Fury, which Porte had designed while at Felixstowe. Engines were to be three Rolls-Royce Condors, but Porte's death from tuberculosis in October meant that it was not built. Undaunted by this setback, in December Gosport Aircraft announced its range of G5 flying boats, which had been proposed by Porte, but lack of finance and a decline in interest in flying boats meant no orders were forthcoming. Gosport Aircraft was wound up by Camper & Nicholsons by the autumn of 1920, with the works used for ship-building.

Hamble

As with many Wessex locations, Hamble's prolific aviation industry was a development of boat builders turning to aviation. This commenced with seaplane construction at Hamble Point from 1912. The original Hamble South grass airfield was opened in 1916, but the later airfield at Hamble North was not opened until 1926. It was used by Avro, Fairey, Supermarine and Simmonds, but was never provided with a hard runway. Hamble South closed as an airfield in 1933, and Hamble North in April 1986.

HAMBLE RIVER, LUKE & CO.

Two local firms – Hamble River Engineering and Luke Brothers – formed Hamble River, Luke & Co. in 1912. In May, the new company built a hangar at Hamble Point, which, at the time, was a bleak spit of land between the Hamble River and Southampton Water. Known as the Hydro-Aeroplane Station, the hangar was to house two Henry Farman 'hydro planes', which were being demonstrated along the south coast in July. Following the visit of the Farmans, Hamble River, Luke & Co. decided to develop its own seaplane at the end of 1913. Known as the HL1, it was exhibited at the Olympia Show in March 1914, although it had not flown. It was similar in shape to the biplane Wight Seaplane being built at Cowes – it had a streamlined fuselage nacelle for the crew of two, with a 150 hp NAG pusher engine. In March 1914, the company reported that several HL1s with 160 hp Gnome engines were under construction, but none appear to have been completed. The sole HL1 (serial 105) eventually passed to the RNAS, but Hamble Luke gave up ideas of aircraft construction. Its works were put up for auction early in June 1915 and were eventually taken over by Fairey Aviation.

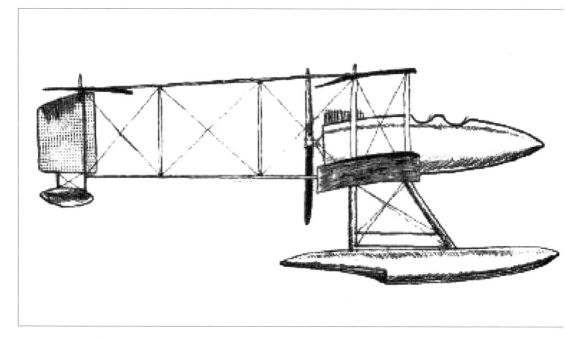

A sketch of the Hamble River, Luke & Co. HL1 of 1914. After a display at Olympia Exhibition, production of the type was planned. An initial batch of six was announced, but the works had closed by the following year.

FAIREY AVIATION CO.

Fairey Aviation was established in July 1915 and its name will always be associated with naval aircraft. Through his contacts, Richard Fairey, the chairman and initial designer, soon received an order to build twelve Short 827 seaplanes. Initially Fairey leased factory premises at Hayes, Middlesex, to build the 827s, but they took over the former Hamble River, Luke & Co. premises from 1916, with a new slipway giving access to the River Hamble for flight-testing. Hayes built the fuselages and Hamble the wings and floats. Westland Aircraft of Yeovil also made use of the Fairey factory. It built twelve Short 184s for the RNAS and the first arrived from Yeovil by rail at Hamble in January 1916 for flight-testing. The 184s were followed from July by twenty Short 166s. Following the Short 827s, Fairey built its own design for the RNAS – the Campania seaplane. The first production aircraft, N1000, arrived from Hayes in February 1917 and was flown on 16 February. Powered by a Rolls-Royce Eagle engine, the type was named after HMS *Campania*, which had been fitted with a 200 ft flight deck so that aircraft could land on board – not on the sea. Fifty production aircraft, commencing N1000, were built at Hayes and test-flown from Hamble. This was

A view inside the Fairey factory in 1916. This was the former River Hamble, Luke & Co. hangar. Short 827 seaplane fuselages have arrived from Hayes and are being fitted with locally built wings and tailplanes.

A Westland-built Short 184 on Fairey's slipway in 1916 about to be launched onto the River Hamble. The aircraft were transported from Yeovil by rail, assembled in Fairey's hangar, and then flight-tested prior to delivery to the RNAS.

to be a route followed by many Fairey products – built at Hayes and transported to Hamble for test-flying.

In 1917, a Sopwith Baby fighter was rebuilt at Hayes and fitted with improved wings and a 110 hp Clerget engine, becoming the prototype Hamble Baby floatplane 8134. First flown from Hamble, it was followed by fifty production aircraft (from N1320). The Baby was also built by Parnall & Sons as both floatplane and landplane. In 1917, Fairey built two experimental N2 patrol seaplanes, which had differently styled wings. Trials of the aircraft – serials N9 and N10 – were carried out at Hamble and by the end of the year they were being referred to as Fairey IIIs. So started the line of one of Fairey's most famous aircraft. Re-engined with a 450 hp Napier Lion and fitted with shorter wings, N10 was registered G-EALQ in 1919 for use in the Schneider Trophy Race, held at Bournemouth in September. The following year it was converted into an amphibian and ended up in use as a 'hack' at Hamble. The majority of Fairey IIIAs were built at Hayes, with testing undertaken from Hamble. The first seaplane version – the IIIB – flew from Hamble on 8 August 1918 and sixty were ordered (from N2230). Many of these were produced as the improved IIIC version, with the first N2255 flying at Hamble in July 1918. The Fairey IIID spotter reconnaissance seaplane followed and proved successful in service. The first production aircraft N9450 flew in August 1920 and was tested as floatplane at Hamble the following year, with over 200 built at Hayes. The seaplane versions were flown from Hamble and the landplanes from Northolt. Six were built for the Australian Navy, with the first – described as 'Fairey Long-Distance Seaplane' – handed over at Hamble in August 1921. The Portuguese Navy ordered a total of eleven, and the first, *Lusitania*, was handed over on 4 January 1922. This was used in an unsuccessful Transatlantic flight from Portugal to Brazil in March–April 1922, but was forced down off the Brazilian coast due to lack of fuel. Two were delivered by air to the Swedish Air Force in June 1924 and four for the Netherlands Navy were delivered in May 1925. In October 1924, non-military IIID floatplane G-EBKE was tested from Southampton Water prior to shipping to British Guiana for flying-ambulance duties.

In 1918, the Admiralty placed an order with Fairey for three large, four-engined, long-range flying boats to Specification N4. Construction was spread around the aircraft industry, with the wings and tail of one – N129 *Titania* – built at Hayes and the hull by Fyffes of Clyde. These arrived at Hamble in 1920 for erection and testing. However, the trials, which were due to commence in the spring of 1921, were cancelled. N129 was stored until moved by road to the Isle of Grain, from where it eventually flew in 1925. The hulls of the second and third were respectively built by May Harden & May at Hythe and Gosport Aviation at Gosport The protracted development time meant the need for the N4 flying boat had disappeared.

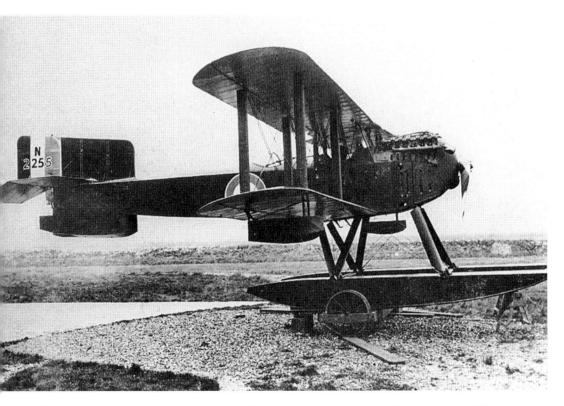

The Fairey III proved a successful design and large numbers of various marks were delivered from Hamble to the RNAS from 1918 onwards. They remained in service until the mid-1930s. N2255 is an early IIIC fitted with floats

Above left: A number of versions of the Fairey III were seen at Hamble in the 1920s. Although mostly fitted with standard undercarriages, many were float-equipped, as is this IIIF mounted on an RN cruiser's catapult. Normally the Fairey IIIs operated from carriers.

Above right: Fairey IIIs first appeared at Hamble towards the end of the First World War, and were produced in large numbers for the RNAS. Export versions in 1921 include this IIIC ANA.3 – one of a batch of six for the Australian Navy.

The Fairey Flycatcher fighter was well liked by its naval pilots. Flycatchers were built at Hayes in the mid-1920s but many float-equipped aircraft, as seen here, were initially tested at Hamble before delivery to the Fleet.

The Pintail was a fighter reconnaissance seaplane/amphibian designed to an Air Ministry specification. Prototypes N133–35 were ordered in 1920 with the first flown on 7 July 1920. All were slightly different and, although there were no home orders, three Pintail IVs were sold to the Japanese Navy in the summer of 1924. The Pintail was followed by the Flycatcher biplane fighter, with three prototypes, which could be equipped with wheels, floats or as amphibians, ordered in March 1922. Prototype N163 was flown as a landplane from Hamble airfield on 28 November 1922, and was later delivered to Martlesham Heath for testing. N164 was a floatplane, first flown on 5 May 1923, followed by the amphibian version, N165. A Flycatcher II followed, with prototype N216 flying on 4 October 1926, following which production was undertaken at Hayes with floatplane versions tested from Hamble. The Flycatcher was successful in its role and well-liked by its crews; about 200 were built. The one-off Fremantle long-range reconnaissance biplane N173 was built at Hayes in 1924 and was first flown at Hamble on 28 November. It was a large floatplane powered by a Rolls-Royce Condor engine and was capable of carrying seven passengers. Ordered in October 1923, it had been the Air Ministry's plan to undertake a round-the-world flight with the Fremantle, but had been beaten to the post by a flight of

Fairey Aviation was well-known for the wide range of naval aircraft it produced over the years. This view of Flycatcher replica S1287 over Southampton Water is meant to recall the 'carefree' flying days of the 1920s.

Douglas aircraft in September 1924. So, after further testing at Hamble, N173 was delivered to RAE Felixstowe in June 1925 for development work.

The Fairey III line ended with the IIIF, produced for both the RAF and FAA. Prototype N198 initially flew from Northolt as a landplane on 19 March 1926 before being sent to Hamble. Here it was fitted with floats, flown again on 20 April, and delivered to MAEE Felixstowe. Production floatplane versions were delivered from Hamble from 1927, including six for the Argentine Navy at the end of 1928, five for Chile, ten for Greece, and two for New Zealand. A 1929 advertisement highlighted the adaptability of the IIIF – its variety of engines plus options of wheel or float undercarriage. A developed version of the IIIF was the Fairey Gordon for the RAF. Twenty were sold to the Brazilian Navy, with five floatplane versions being flight-tested at Hamble. For the FAA, the IIIF was developed as the Seal and followed the usual practice. The prototype S1325 was flown on 27 November 1931 as a landplane and then from Hamble as a floatplane on 29 September 1932. As the majority of production aircraft for the

Fairey's Swordfish claim to fame was that it was obsolete before it entered service in 1936, but remained in service throughout the war. Hamble was used by the prototype undertaking floatplane trials, followed by similar production versions in the late 1930s.

FAA were delivered with wheels, only a few of the floatplane versions appeared at Hamble.

The one-off S9/30 fleet reconnaissance biplane S1706 flew as a landplane on 22 February 1934 and then as a floatplane at Hamble on 15 January 1935. Instead of being fitted with the usual twin floats, the S9/30 had a single main float with small stabilising floats under each wing and was a step between the IIIF and Swordfish. S1706 ended up with MAEE Felixstowe. Further development to Specification S15/33 led to the TSRII (Torpedo-Spotter-Reconnaissance) K4190, which first flew on 17 April 1934, and later moved to Hamble, where it was flown with floats on 10 November. When ordered into production in the spring of 1935, the type received the name Swordfish – surely the best known of Fairey's aircraft. The third production aircraft, K5662, was tested as a floatplane, but only a small number of production aircraft were equipped with floats from new and so were not seen very often at Hamble. The Seafox light reconnaissance floatplane was developed and built at Hamble, the prototype K4304 first flying on 27 May 1936. The second prototype, K4305, was flown as a landplane from Hamble airfield on 5 November. It was powered by a Napier Rapier engine, and the biplane's pilot still sat in the open, although the observer sat behind in an

The Seafox was a naval reconnaissance aircraft, with production undertaken in 1937–38. Of sturdy construction, they were capable of being catapult-launched. The Seafox was the final major type of aircraft to be built by Fairey at Hamble.

enclosed cockpit. The Seafox was capable of being catapult-launched from Royal Navy capital warships, and served in all parts of the world. Its claim to fame was that it was a Seafox crew that spotted the German battleship *Graf Spee* in 1939. The first of sixty-four production floatplanes flew on 23 April 1937, and production occupied the entire Hamble factory. The Seafox proved to be the last in the line of naval biplanes from Fairey.

By the early 1930s, Fairey realised that the site at Hamble Point was now so full that there was no room for further expansion. So to cater for increased production, Fairey took over a factory at Heaton Chapel, Stockport, in the autumn of 1935. This led to a decline in aviation work at Hamble, although the site played its part in the Second World War, mainly with the overhaul of Swordfish and Albacores. However, the site produced a large number of high-speed launches and motor torpedo boats for the Royal Navy and RAF.

Post-war, Fairey no longer needed Hamble for mass aircraft production. The factory at Stockport, along with Hayes, was able to cope with production of Barracudas and Fireflies. Fairey tried to enter the light aircraft market through its associate company in Belgium – Tipsy. The Belgium-built Tipsy M OO-POM was tested in the UK as G-6-1 in 1947–48 (the registration G-AKSX was allocated in

A Fairey Primer trainer flying over Southampton Docks in 1949. Two Primers were built at Hamble in 1948 for RAF trials for a new elementary trainer to replace the Tiger Moth. The order went to the competing de Havilland Chipmunk.

In the 1950s, Fairey still undertook overhaul work on Fireflies. This included the conversion of five Mk Is as target tugs for the Indian Navy. However, the majority of the Hamble site was now in use by Fairey Marine for boatbuilding.

It is hard to believe that these are the former Luke hangars at Hamble Point. Used for aircraft production by Fairey Aviation, they later passed to Fairey Marine. Re-clad by recent owners, this is their current state within the Hamble boatbuilding complex.

February 1948 but not carried). As a result, Fairey decided to enter it into an RAF contest for a new primary trainer and planned for a batch of ten Fairey Primer Trainers to be built at Hamble. The first incorporated many parts of G-6-1 and was flown from White Waltham as G-ALBL on 14 August 1948. It was powered by a DH Gipsy Major, later changed to a Cirrus Major. The second aircraft was powered by a Cirrus Major and was tested as G-6-5 (G-ALEW not carried) at Boscombe Down at the end of 1948 in competition with the DHC Chipmunk. The Chipmunk proved 'excellent', won the competition, and was ordered into production for the RAF. Although it was still promoted at the Farnborough Air Show in September 1950, no further Primers were completed. Part of the Hamble factory was kept busy with overhaul work on Fireflies. This included five Firefly Is, which were converted in 1954–55 into target tugs for the Indian Navy. The factory rebuilt 'hack' Swordfish G-AJVH in 1955 – this is still flying today as LS326 of the Royal Navy Historic Flight. So marked the end of aircraft work at Hamble, with Fairey Aviation purchased by Westland Aircraft in the spring of 1960.

The directors of Fairey were keen sailors and had turned their attentions to pleasure-boat building from 1946. The construction sheds passed to Fairey Marine Ltd for the production of sailing dinghies, some designed by Uffa Fox. Types included the Firefly, the Albecore and the Swordfish. Later, the company turned its attention to the building of GRP powerboats, with the first Spearfish appearing in 1969. Spearfish construction was then subcontracted to Fairey's aircraft site at Ringway. The Fairey Boat Park was managed by Peter Twiss, Fairey's test pilot in the 1950s. Fairey Marine ceased boat building by the end of 1973, but not before they built a replica Vickers Viking IV amphibian for the film *The Land that Time Forgot*. Boat construction continues at Hamble Point, now in the hands of many other companies. A century on, the deserted spit of land is now covered by parked yachts of all shapes and sizes.

A. V. ROE & CO. LTD ('AVRO')

A. V. Roe & Co. was one of Britain's pioneering aviation companies. Its founder Alliott Verdon Roe built his first Avro aircraft in 1907. With his brother, Humphrey Verdon Roe, he established A. V. Roe & Co. as aeronautical engineers in Manchester in January 1910 – trading under the now-familiar Avro name. Avro became a limited company in January 1913 and by the time of the First World War, its main factory was at Newton Heath, Manchester. Anticipating an increase in naval aircraft production for the war, coupled with a lack of capacity at Newton Heath, a site at Hamble was chosen for a second factory. This was built in 1916 adjacent to a new 100 acre grass airfield, which was bounded on the west by Southampton Water, having a frontage of one mile. In addition to the factory and design office, Avro intended to build a 'garden city' for its workers, who would be housed in 350 new houses. A. V. Roe said, 'I conceived the idea of establishing modern works and a garden city for employees on the south coast, where we could build aeroplanes or flying boats and our employees could breathe God's fresh air.' The harsh wartime economy meant that only twenty-four houses were completed – the remaining funds were needed for the construction of nearby Eastleigh Airfield and the Weston Rolling Mill. As from 1 January 1917, the new factory was planned to be run by A. V. Roe (Southampton) Ltd as a separate entity from the Manchester operations. Avro's design office moved to Hamble in February 1917, under a newly appointed chief designer, Roy Chadwick. It was shortly after this that Humphrey left the company to join the RFC.

The Manchester factory was at full capacity building Avro 504s for the RFC, with prototype testing being undertaken from Hamble. In order to use the

Avro's factory at Hamble was built in 1916 overlooking Southampton Water. Anticipated orders for naval aircraft did not materialise, so the site never reached its full potential. By the 1930s it had become surrounded by other buildings.

surplus capacity of Hamble, Avro 504Js and Ks were built from 1917. Hamble also supported the licensed production of 504s by Eastbourne Aviation and S. E. Saunders of Cowes. Avro had hoped to obtain orders for new RFC and RNAS fighters and bombers but, with the end of the war in sight, these were not forthcoming. This meant Manchester continued with 504 production, but there was less work for Hamble, which was absorbed back into the Manchester operations.

Hamble continued to be used by Avro for experimental testing of a large number of new types, but none were to enter production. The Avro 519 was a bomber intended for the RNAS and the RFC. The second RFC prototype 1615 arrived at Hamble in November 1916 in preparation for military trials in December. It was later joined by RNAS prototypes 8440 and 8441. They were only intended for evaluation, and little more is known of their fates. The Pike was a twin-engined multi-role RNAS aircraft and prototype N523 was moved by road to Hamble in the summer of 1916 and flown in November. A second Pike A316 was built at Manchester for trials by the RFC. Again, no orders were received and both aircraft ended their days as trials aircraft at Hamble in 1917–18. Developed from the Pike, the prototype 529 naval biplane fighter 3694

Avro anticipated that Hamble would become a major production centre, but it was mainly used for building and testing experimental prototypes. Two Avro Manchester bombers were built at Hamble in 1918, but the type did not enter production.

was built at Manchester, but was sent to Hamble for flight-testing in March 1917. The second prototype 3695 was sent to Hamble for completion, and made its first flight in November 1917. Both aircraft crashed while undertaking trials at Martlesham Heath. Following on from the Pike and 529, Avro developed the 533 Manchester bomber. The prototype F3492 was built in Manchester, but was transported by road to Hamble for its first flight in December. After military trials at Gosport and Martlesham Heath, the Manchester returned to Hamble in September 1919. The second Manchester F3493 was flown in the summer of 1919, and undertook trials at Martlesham Heath from October. Although performing well, the RAF no longer had a need for bombers such as the Manchester, and so no order was placed. The 530 fighter flew in July 1917 but lack of a suitable engine meant no orders were forthcoming. Early in 1918, Avro worked on the 531 Spider lightweight fighter, which was based on a 504 fuselage with new wings. The prototype flew in April and early tests showed promise. However, as the similar Sopwith Snipe had already been selected for the RAF, no production order was placed.

With the return to peace, the outlook was looking bleak for Avro and other aviation companies, with many existing orders being cancelled. Diversification was needed and the company decided to enter into car production at Manchester, with aircraft production being undertaken at Hamble. A number of cars were produced at Newton Heath, but in May 1920 the majority shareholding of Avro was purchased by Crossley Motors Ltd. Seeing the Avro car as a rival, Crossley stopped production and used Newton Heath to produce parts for its own designs.

Avro also turned its attention to civilian flying. For the Easter Holiday in 1919, three Avro 504s were pressed into use at Hamble to undertake £1 joy flights. Word spread of these activities and 350 passengers were flown on the first day alone. This success resulted in Avro Transport Co. being formed at Manchester equipped with a fleet of 504s for joy flights around the country. Various bases were set up, with the local one established at Southsea. The majority of these 504s still flew in military markings at the time, as a system of civil registrations was still being devised. A number of 504s were modified as 536s, which had a widened cockpit area to accommodate four passengers as well as the pilot. The prototype K-114 first flew from Hamble as a landplane in April 1919, but was equipped with floats in June. A further nine followed, but they only had short careers. Further 536s were built at Manchester, plus a batch of four at Croydon in 1926–27. Joyriding 504Ks continued until the end of 1935, but the 536s had disappeared by the end of 1930. Another update of the 504 was the 548, which was a re-engined three-seat version. Avro wanted to move on from rotary engines and used an air-cooled Renault for the 548. Displayed at the Olympia Aero Show in July 1920 as the Avro Tourist, the prototype G-EAPQ had already flown from Hamble at the end of 1919. A handful of 548s were built by Avro at Hamble and Manchester, but they were competing with large numbers of surplus RAF 504s. However, various other companies around the country converted 504s into 548s, some as late as 1932. A further update of the 504 was the 552, which was powered by a 180 hp Viper water-cooled engine originally produced for the SE5A fighter. The prototype G-EAPR flew in the spring of 1921 and was operated in various guises. In August it was flown with twin floats, and in this form was ordered by the Argentinean Navy. Production was underway by the end of the year, by which time G-EAPR was flying with a single float plus outriggers. This was in connection with an RCAF order for both landplane and floatplane versions. These aircraft were built by Canadian Vickers in Montreal. G-EAPR reverted to a landplane in 1922 and took part in a number of races, remaining in use at Hamble as a 'hack'.

Avro continued to develop the 504 line for a number of years. The Avro 552 was basically a 504K fitted with a Wolseley Viper engine. G-EAPR was fitted with floats in 1921 in connection with an order from the Argentine Ministry of Marine.

The success of 504s in civil use saw Hamble involved in overhauling and building new versions of the famous trainer. One was supplied to Spain in August 1919 for use by the king. Six were rebuilt for the Belgian Air Force and delivered in April 1921. Unfortunately, records do not show full details of other deliveries from Hamble. In 1924, a Mk II version of the 504K was produced at Hamble and although it flew in RAF markings, no serial was allocated. It remained a one-off. Going back to the original intention of Hamble producing naval aircraft, the 504L floatplane appeared at the end of 1918 and flew the following February. The underpowered prototype flew with military marking C4329, but the 504L three-seater was also aimed at the civil market. Six others followed and were employed in the summer of 1919 on joy flights along the south coast, with two further 504K conversions operated from Lake Windermere. Ten were delivered to the Japanese Navy with further aircraft built in Japan. The 504M Limousine was a one-off modification with an enclosed cabin for two passengers. Flown as K134 in June 1919, it later became G-EACX, but only survived until the following summer. In 1922, a number of 504Ks were converted at Hamble to take a radial engine, producing the 504N. A variety of engines could be used and testing continued over the next few years. This resulted in the RAF ordering two for trials in 1924, following which a production order for 200 was placed in March 1927 for a Lynx-powered version. This entered service as the RAF's standard primary trainer and remained in production until September 1933. Production was shared between Hamble and Manchester, although all the final ones were from Manchester. Again there were export orders, but records do not confirm which were supplied from Hamble. A number of civilian 504Ns were still flying on the outbreak of the Second World War – including a number of ex-RAF machines. Hamble used development aircraft G-EBKQ as the factory 'hack' from summer of 1925 and it was entered in a number of races. Fitted with floats in 1930, it was used by locally based Air Service Training, now known as the 504O. Due to its low-powered engine, it spent most of its time taxiing on Southampton Water rather than flying. Another one-off floatplane was the 504Q G-EBJD, which again had a widened fuselage to accommodate two side-by-side seats. Built in 1924 for the Oxford University Arctic Expedition, the pilot still only had an open cockpit in front of the cabin. Flown from Southampton Water in the spring, in July it was delivered to the expedition, who had it shipped to Spitzbergen. Avro's final development of the 504 was the 504R Gosport, with prototypes

Versions for the 504 continued to appear for a number of years. This 504Q was prepared in 1924 for the Oxford University Arctic Expedition. The explorers had a cabin but the pilot sat up front in an open cockpit – still the normal procedure for the time.

In 1923, Hamble produced the 504N, which had an improved undercarriage compared to the skid and wheels fitted to earlier marks. Large numbers were ordered to supplement the RAF's existing 504Ks, and they stayed in production at Manchester until 1933.

Last of the 504 line was the 504R, which also received the name Gosport. A number of prototypes, including G-EBNE, were built in 1926, resulting in orders from Argentina, Estonia and Peru, but not from the RAF, although it tested one in 1929.

Following the return to peace, Avro anticipated the need for a private sporting aircraft. The Avro Baby got off to an inauspicious start when the prototype crashed on its first take-off in April 1919. Undeterred, it was rebuilt as G-EACQ, leading to limited sales.

G-EBNE and G-EBNF built at Hamble in the spring of 1926. G-EBNE first flew in July and it was intended that the Gosport be a lighter version of the 504K. Other prototypes were built at Manchester and a variety of engines were tried in these aircraft. One was tested by the RAF at Martlesham Heath, but no order was placed. However, orders were received from Argentina, Estonia and Peru, with deliveries commencing June 1927.

Further peacetime activity included the design of a lightweight biplane for private owners – the 534 Baby. Due to be flown by its designer, Roy Chadwick, the prototype flew from Hamble on 30 April 1919 with another test pilot, but crashed almost immediately from a low level when its ignition switch was cut in error. A second aircraft, K-131, was already under construction, flying in May, and was used in a number of air races. A further seven aircraft followed over the next two years – all being slightly different. The Water Baby G-EAPS was equipped with floats and first flown in November 1919. Next was G-EAUG in July 1920, but this crashed after only four weeks' flying while en route to Martlesham Heath for trials. At the end of 1920, another appeared at Hamble with narrow-chord, Venetian blind-style 'wings' but it never flew. Chadwick was seriously injured while flying G-EACQ in January 1920 when he hit some trees and crashed into the garden of Everard Verdon Roe's house. (He was another of Alliott's brothers, also the vicar of Hamble). The wrecked Baby was rebuilt and flown by Avro's new test pilot, Bert Hinkler, who later shipped it to Australia. An Avro advertisement for the Baby proclaimed 'London to Turin in 9½ hours – 650 miles on 20 gallons of petrol'. This referred to a non-stop flight made by Hinkler. The other Babies all had varying careers, ending up in India, Australia and Russia. One was used in Newfoundland for spotting seals.

Many aircraft companies hastily prepared entries for the 1919 Schneider Trophy Race, which was held in Bournemouth. Avro produced the 539 – a small float-equipped biplane with a powerful Puma engine. Time was tight, as it flew on 29 August and had to be at Cowes for elimination trials on 3 September. In the event, G-EALG ended up as the race reserve machine. So it returned to Hamble and was converted into a landplane the following year. As such, it took part in the Hendon Aerial Derby in July, but force-landed with a broken fuel line. It returned to Hamble for further modifications in 1921, including fitting a 450 hp Napier Lion engine. Now registered G-EAXM, it flew on 13 July and was entered in the Hendon Aerial Derby three days later. But at the end of its landing run on 15 July, it overshot the runway at Hamble and was destroyed when it hit a bank.

In what now seems a backward step, the Avro 547 reverted to a triplane 'airliner' carrying four passengers in a fully enclosed cabin. The idea of a triplane was that of Alliott, not Chadwick. The wings and tail were those of an Avro 504K, married to a new fuselage and engine. G-EAQX was flown on 6 February 1920, followed by G-EAUJ in August. Attempts to sell the 547 to Instone Airlines in June 1920 failed, but in November G-EAQX was sold to the newly formed Qantas for £2,798. Shipped to Australia and flown from Mascot the following March, it did not prove suitable for airline services. It is reported that as a result of the 547s shortcomings Qantas refused to buy another Avro aircraft. G-EAUJ fared no better. It underwent trials at Martlesham Heath in August 1920, but performed badly against other entrants in the Small Commercial Airliner Competition. The 547 returned to Hamble at the end of October, but only flew a few more times. So Avro would rather forget the 547.

Returning to military aircraft, Avro was now having some success in obtaining orders. They designed the 549 Aldershot to an Air Ministry requirement for a single engine, biplane bomber/transport. Prototypes J6852 and J6853 were ordered by the Air Ministry in December 1920 and the first flew from Hamble in the spring of 1922 powered by 680 hp Rolls-Royce Condor engine. Later in the year J6852 was re-engined with an experimental 1,000 hp Napier Cub to try to improve performance. Becoming the Aldershot II, it flew again on 15 December. It was also referred to as the 'Avro-Napier Bomber – the most powerful single-engined Aeroplane in the World'. After various demonstrations, it was delivered to RAE Farnborough in 1923 for engine trials, and was promoted as the Avro Cub – which was its type of engine. By this time, fifteen Condor-powered aircraft had been ordered for the RAF as the Aldershot III, but these were built at Manchester. Powered by a 480 hp Napier Lion, the 555 Bison, a fleet reconnaissance biplane, first appeared in 1921, when prototypes N153–55 were built. All had differing layouts, with the final one flown in the spring of 1923, by which time an order had been placed for an initial batch of twelve. As with the Aldershot, these production aircraft were built at Manchester. N9594 was fitted with a central float to undertake trials as an amphibian at Felixstowe in 1924. Then followed forty-four Bison IIs, some of which were built at Hamble. The 557 Ava was the result of an Air Ministry requirement for a torpedo-carrying, coastal-defence aircraft. A large, twin-engined biplane powered by Rolls-Royce Condors, the prototype N171 flew from Hamble in 1924. However, the second, which was of metal construction, did not fly until April 1927, by which time the requirement had disappeared and there was no production order. The 561 Andover was an ambulance transport that combined the 549 Aldershot's wings and tail with a new, enlarged fuselage. As such, there was no prototype, and the RAF ordered twelve in January 1924 for use in the Middle East. However, these transport duties were taken over by Imperial Airways and so the order was reduced to three – J7261–63. All were flown in 1924 and delivered to the RAF at Halton for use as flying ambulances. Even at this date, the pilot and navigator were still housed in an open cockpit under the upper wing. A fourth aircraft was fitted with twelve seats for use by Imperial Airways and, registered G-EBKW, it flew from Hamble at the beginning of 1925. It was delivered to Imperial in the summer for proving flights on its continental routes, mainly to build up hours on its Condor engine. It was only used for a few months before passing to the RAF in January 1927 to join its sister aircraft.

Britain's aircraft manufacturers produced a variety of light aircraft designs in the 1920s, culminating in the famous DH Moth. Avro produced a number of designs. The single-seat 558 was an attempt to produce a very light biplane for the 1923 Lympne Light Aircraft Trials. Powered by motorcycle engines, two were built at Hamble in the summer for the event in October. Strangely, the first was never registered, only carrying the Avro name on its fuselage with competition number 5 on its rudder. The second appeared at the trials as G-EBHW. Avro also produced two monoplanes for the trial, but only the 560 was completed. As with

Four Avro Andovers were built in 1924 for RAF transport/ambulance duties. The final one was used by Imperial Airways for a while in 1925 before joining the RAF in 1927. It carried twelve passengers; the pilots sat in the open behind the engine.

The Avenger was a private venture fighter first flown from Hamble in June 1926. As such it flew as a civil aircraft. It failed to receive an RAF order and was retained by Avro for trials with different Napier Lion engines and varying wing shapes.

the 558, it only flew with Avro titles and competition number 6. The Lympne Trials demonstrated that there was still some way to go to develop a reliable light aircraft, so a further event took place the following year. For this, Avro produced the slightly larger twin-seat 562 Avis with a choice of two engines. The sole aircraft was entered in the trials as competitor 10 when fitted with a Cherub engine, and as competitor 11 with a Thrush engine. Engine problems meant the Avis did not complete the trials, but did win the final race, which was not part of the trial. Having been taken by road to Lympne, the race success gave pilot Bert Hinkler the confidence to fly the Avis back to Hamble. Now registered G-EBKP, the Avis undertook further engine trials in 1925, before appearing at the Lympne Trials again in August. By the following year's trials in September the Avis was flying with its Thrush engine. Again the trials confirmed that more reliable aircraft would be needed by private owners.

Avro found that the Hamble airfield site was becoming too restrictive and in 1926 purchased 200 acres of land to the north of its factory to be the new airfield.

The Buffalo was produced in 1926 as a private venture naval aircraft. It undertook military trials later in the year, but failed to win an order from the Navy. As with many prototypes of the time, it ended its days test-flying for the Air Ministry.

This meant all new production aircraft had to be taken across the adjacent road to reach the new Hamble (North) Airfield.

Two private-venture military aircraft emerged from Hamble in 1926. As neither had been ordered by the Air Ministry, they both flew with civil registrations. First was the 566 Avenger biplane fighter, which flew on 26 June as G-EBND. Powered by a 525 hp Napier Lion, the new fighter had streamlined looks. It was demonstrated at the RAF Hendon Display in July and undertook trials at Martlesham Heath in October, but did not attract an RAF order. Hoped-for overseas sales were also not forthcoming. So the Avenger was used by Avro in a number of races in 1927–28. In September 1928, it flew to Bucharest in an attempt to gain an order from the Romanian Air Force. None was received and the Avenger returned to Hamble to be pushed to one side. The second private venture was the 571 Buffalo multi-role naval biplane. Flown as G-EBNW in 1926, it undertook competitive trials at Martlesham Heath. These were won by the Blackburn Ripon, and so there was no need for the Buffalo. However, it was rebuilt and re-engined in 1927, flying again as the 572 Buffalo II. Again, there was no hope of any orders, and so the Buffalo was converted to a floatplane in the summer of 1928. Now with military markings, N239 was tested on Southampton Water before delivery to Felixstowe for experimental flying. Two

A view inside Avro's hangar in the summer of 1928. A variety of aircraft and autogyros can be seen, including the Buffalo II N-239 being prepared for MAEE Felixstowe, where it served as a trials floatplane.

other types were then built to Air Ministry requirements, but neither entered production. The 584 Avocet was a small, square-cut, all-metal biplane fighter powered by an AS Lynx, with prototypes N209 and N210 built at Hamble in 1927. N209 was completed as a landplane, flying in December 1927. N210 was fitted with floats and flown in April 1928, but had wheels fitted in June, prior to both Avocets undertaking trials at Martlesham Heath in February 1929. On its return to Hamble, N210 had its floats refitted and was used as a trainer by the RAF High Speed Flight at Calshot. The 604 Antelope was a single-engine, high-performance day bomber, but only prototype J9183 was built. It was flown from Hamble in November 1928, and competitive trials at Martlesham Heath resulted in orders being placed for the rival Hawker Hart. The Antelope was exhibited at the Olympia Aero Show in July 1929 to attract interest. Upon its return to Hamble, it was fitted with dual controls and delivered to RAE Farnborough for propeller trials. The Antelope was the last of a line of military aircraft from Avro at Hamble.

Two Avocets was built in 1927 for trials as naval fighters – one with wheels and one with floats. An ungainly-looking aircraft, the Avocet was not ordered by the Navy. N-210 was the aircraft used for landplane trials in 1928.

In March 1926, Avro let the newly formed Hampshire Aeroplane Club use their north airfield. It was in the expanding light aircraft market that Avro found success with the 581 Avian biplane. Similar in size to the Avis, prototype G-EBOV was built from a spare autogiro fuselage at Hamble and flown in the summer of 1926. Along with the Avis, it took part in the Lympne Trials in September and showed great promise. Unfortunately, it did not complete the trials due to a broken magneto, but it did win the subsequent air race. Returned to Hamble for modification and re-engining, it appeared in the following spring as the 581A Avian. As such, it was purchased by Avro's test pilot, Bert Hinkler, who raced it with great success. In February 1928, he flew G-EBOV 11,000 miles to Darwin, Australia, amid much publicity. Production aircraft appeared from early April 1927, with sufficient alterations made for it to become known as the 594 Avian. G-EBQL and G-EBQN were completed in time to take part in the Bournemouth Air Race in the middle of the month; both continued to participate in races in 1927–28. The next aircraft, G-EBRC, was successfully demonstrated at Copenhagen in September, but failed to make it back to Hamble. A faulty compass meant that it flew too far south and ran out of fuel south of Ventnor, Isle of Wight; the pilot was rescued by boat. G-EBVA was tested as a floatplane from Southampton Water in 1928. Large numbers of Avians were sold, both in the home market and overseas, and were fitted with a variety of engines. These included approximately forty to the United States. One of these was fitted with floats and, as NX6663, it was collected by its owner from Hamble in September 1928. It departed on a flight to Seattle, flying eastwards on 15 September, but was badly damaged on take-off from Corsica a week later. It finally made it to Seattle by sea. As well as at Hamble, Avro undertook production of the Avian at Manchester, where it developed the metal-tubed fuselage Avian IVM variant.

The Avian prototype first flew in the summer of 1926 and was successfully raced by test pilot Bert Hinkler. Avian production commenced at Hamble, but was switched to Manchester in 1929. Produced in various versions, it saw worldwide sales.

Changes took place within the Avro organisation in the spring of 1928. Crossley Motors, as majority shareholder, was in financial trouble and in April sold its shares to Sir John Siddeley, who was the major shareholder of Armstrong Siddeley and Armstrong Whitworth. Alliott also sold his shareholding to Sir John. With Avro now part of the Siddeley Group, it was decided to concentrate activities in Manchester, where a new factory and airfield were in use at Woodford. In October 1928, Alliott resigned from Avro and along with two other Avro directors took a controlling interest in the Cowes firm of S. E. Saunders. Avro's Hamble design and development staff moved north early in 1929, but Avian production continued for a while. Interestingly, the staff considered they worked for A. V. Roe – not Avro. Avro also assisted Cierva with its autogyro developments, but finally sold the Hamble factory to Air Service Training in April 1931. However the site was still used by Avro to test some of its Manchester products when fitted with floats. Tutor G-ABGH was tested from Southampton Water in 1931 and Avro 626 demonstrator G-ACFZ in the summer of 1933.

Similarly, the first 626 for the Estonian Air Force was tested in 1934, with one for Chile the following May.

In July 1935, Avro at Manchester became one of the founding members of the newly formed Hawker Siddeley Aircraft Co.

CIERVA AUTOGIRO CO. LTD

Juan de la Cierva commenced his many years of autogiro development in Madrid in 1920. This started with the C1 and had reached the C6, which employed the fuselage of an Avro 504K, by 1924. It retained the 504's engine for forward flying, but a rotor was fitted above the cockpit area. Cierva was invited to RAE Farnborough, where his C6 was demonstrated by his test pilot in October 1925. The Cierva Autogiro Co. was established in March 1926 with its offices at Hamble and headquarters in Aldwych. Although Cierva was involved, the driving force was the company chairman, Air Commodore James Weir, who also provided financial backing. He was also owner of the engineering firm G. & J. Weir, based in Glasgow, and set up his own autogiro and helicopter firm, Weir Helicopters, in 1933. Following the Farnborough trials, the Air Ministry order two similar C6C 'Gyroplanes', which were to be built by Avro at Hamble. J8068 was flown on 19 June 1926 and shown at RAF Hendon Display in July. Experimental flying continued over the following months, but J8068 crashed at Hamble on 7 February 1927, following the failure of its rotor blades. The second aircraft was completed as a C6D two-seater and flew without markings on 29 July 1926. The next day, de la Cierva flew as passenger – a novel experience as it was his first flight in an autogiro. In the event it was not delivered to the Air Ministry, but was registered as G-EBTW in the summer of 1927 and used at Hamble for further development flying. It was joined by a further aircraft, which was rebuilt from an Avro 552 and flown as G-EBTX on development work. In 1930 it was converted back to a 552 biplane. Although they had Cierva-type numbers, since the autogiros were built by Avro they also had Avro-type numbers. So G-EBTW, later modified as a Cierva C8R, was also an Avro 587.

In 1926, the Air Ministry ordered two further autogiros, which were to be based on Avro 504N fuselages. J8930 appeared as a Cierva C8L (Avro 575) and first flew in the spring of 1927, piloted by Bert Hinkler. Frustrated at not being able to fly his own product, Cierva obtained his Private Pilot Licence at Hamble in 1927 and followed this with autogiro instruction from Hinkler. Now able to fly his design, he delivered J8930 to RAE Farnborough in September 1927. The second C8L was completed to the order of Air Commodore Weir and flown as G-EBYY in May 1928. It took part in the King's Cup Race in July and in August

Juan de la Cierva experimented with autogiros in Spain in the early 1920s. For these he used the Avro 504 fuselage as the basis of his design. When he arrived at Hamble he continued to use 504 fuselages – as in this Cierva C8V of 1928.

undertook a 3,000 mile round-Britain tour, taking in Air Commodore Weir's Scottish Estate at Dalrymple. Returning south, it flew from Croydon to Le Bourget on 18 September 1928, becoming the first autogiro to cross the English Channel. Two other C8Ls were flown at the end of 1928 – one for the Italian Government and the other for the USA. The similar-looking C9 J8931 had a new, slimmer fuselage. Cierva next designed the C17 (Avro 612) as a lighter version based on an Avian fuselage and intended for private owners. Flown by Cierva in October 1928, the C17 G-AABP did not live up to expectations, and proved to be underpowered. After test-flying in 1929, the second was converted into the C12 Hydrogiro G-AAGJ and fitted with floats from an Avian. As such it was unsuccessfully tested by Cierva on Southampton Water in April 1930. In 1935, it was reconverted back into an Avian.

Then came the Cierva C19, which was a more substantial-looking two-seat machine, fitted with stub wings and powered by a 105 hp AS Genet engine. More importantly it was fitted with an automatic rotor starter. The C19s were built as

Cierva C8L, which was built for military trials at RAE Farnborough in 1927. First flown in July, it was delivered to Farnborough by Cierva at the end of September. As with all Avro-built Ciervas, J8930 bore the dual-designation Cierva C8L/Avro 575.

Avro 620s in the former Avro factory by Cierva workers. The first two appeared in the summer of 1929 as G-AAGK and G-AAGL and were used as demonstrators. Unfortunately G-AAGL only lasted a month, as it was badly damaged during an air display at Haldon in September. Various marks of the C19 were produced, but all had relatively short flying lives – the majority ending in accidents. This was at variance with Cierva's advertising of the time: 'Safety in Flight – Vertical Descent – No Stalling!' Mk III G-AAYO became K1696 and was prepared for trials at Farnborough in 1930. The final version was the Mk IV, which had an improved tail section and, more importantly, an improved rotor start-up system. Fifteen were produced in 1931–32, by which time Cierva had moved to Hanworth, Middlesex. Records seem to indicate they were flown from Hanworth, not Hamble. This marked the end of Cierva's association with Hamble.

AIR SERVICE TRAINING LTD

Air Service Training (AST) was established by Armstrong Whitworth Aircraft in January 1931 at Whitley in Oxfordshire as the Armstrong Whitworth Flying School. Lack of room at Whitley saw the school move to Hamble in the spring, taking over the former Avro factory and the north airfield. Its prime aim was to operate a reserve flying school, which was officially opened on 25 June 1931 and proclaimed as 'Britain's Air University'. An additional hangar was erected in the summer of 1932 at the southern end of the north airfield to house the training fleet. AST became part of Hawker Siddeley Aircraft in 1935. It operated a large number of Avro training types – 504, Tutor, Cadet – as well as Cierva Autogiros.

The Cierva C19, which flew in the summer of 1929, had a more substantial fuselage than earlier examples, plus stub wings. After a number of trials aircraft, the Mk III version entered production in 1930, with later examples completed at Hanworth.

Although not an aircraft production company, AST receives mention due to its involvement with the Ensign airliner. The Ensign, designed by Armstrong Whitworth, was a large aircraft with a span of 123 ft and powered by four 800 hp AS Tiger IX engines. Prototype G-ADSR was ordered in September 1934, followed by eleven production aircraft for Imperial Airways in May 1935. As Armstrong Whitworth had insufficient capacity at its Whitley factory to build the new airliner, the work was passed to AST. Construction commenced at the end of 1936 in the former Avro factory, and the fuselage of G-ADSR was completed in March 1937, although the aircraft did not fly until 24 January 1938. This was later than originally planned due to changes requested by Imperial. The Empire version of the Ensign carried twenty-seven passengers and the European version forty passengers. After flying from Hamble the airliners undertook their flight-testing at Coventry and they proved to be underpowered. Two further aircraft, G-AFZU and G-AFZV, were ordered as Ensign IIs with more powerful Wright Cyclone engines, but due to the outbreak of war they were not completed until the summer of 1941. AST also built the prototype AW41 Albemarle bombers P1360 and P1361 on behalf of Armstrong Whitworth in its own hangar in 1939–40, with P1360 first flying on 20 March. As opposed to the metal Ensigns, the bomber was an all-wood construction in order to conserve strategic materials. After completion in the former Avro factory, both Albemarles were flown to Bagington for flight-testing, but they proved underpowered in RAF service. At the end of the war, the remaining seven worn-out Ensigns were withdrawn from service and flown back to Hamble. They were offered for sale by AST but, as there were no bidders, they were scrapped in the spring of 1947.

AST was appointed a Civilian Repair Organisation (CRO) by the Ministry of Aircraft Production and undertook major repairs on at least 2,500 Spitfires and Seafires on the south site. In addition, large numbers of Spitfires were converted into Seafires for the Royal Navy. The first Spitfire BL676 arrived in January

Armstrong Whitworth, along with Air Service Training, was part of Hawker Siddeley Aviation. Lack of capacity at Coventry led to the Armstrong Whitworth Ensign being built at Hamble. G-ADSR, the first, is seen here during testing at Coventry in the spring of 1938.

1942 for basic conversion to a Seafire IA, which retained the fixed wings. It was followed by a further forty-seven. BL676 flew again in March, was renumbered MB328, and was delivered to the Navy in June 1942. Not all the CRO work was undertaken at Hamble; some was undertaken at other sites, including Exeter. Other aircraft passing through the CRO included Mitchells, Mustangs and Fortresses. As a result of all the Spitfire rebuilding, the airfield resembled a Spitfire graveyard at the end of the war.

Post-war, AST's Aircraft Division consisted of the main factory south of Hamble Lane (former Avro) and the training school north of Hamble Lane. In 1946 it described itself as 'Britain's foremost aircraft repair and service organisation' although other firms would probably challenge that. AST undertook the design work relating to the conversion a number of Lancasters and Lincolns as engine testbeds. This ranged from the 'simple' fitting of a turbo-prop in the bomber's nose to the installation of a turbo-jet under the bomb bay. Modified were Mamba Lancasters ND784 and SW432, the first in October 1947; Sapphire Lancaster VM733 in the winter of 1949; Derwent Lincoln SX971 in the summer of 1950 to test reheat; Lancaster RA805 with an underfuselage Dovern jet for Sweden in 1950–51. Another Avro type seen was the York. AST undertook modifications

AST converted surplus bombers into engine test beds, including Lancaster SW732 for use by Armstrong Siddeley Engines. On this aircraft, the Mamba is surrounded by a metal rig that sprayed water onto the engine during flight trials.

on BOAC and RAF aircraft from the spring of 1947 until the summer of 1949. During the period of the Berlin Airlift, AST deep-cleaned Transport Command aircraft to remove coal dust, flour, etc.

AST was also involved in two Gloster fighters, building parts for Meteors and 30 per cent of parts for the Javelin. In the autumn of 1951, Meteor F4 testbed RA491 was fitted with two French Atar jet engines on behalf of SNECMA, and Meteor WA820 was later converted to Sapphire engine power. In the spring of 1956, AST built the prototype Javelin T3 trainer WT841, which was delivered by road to Moreton Valence, where it flew on 20 August. In 1956 it converted Hunter XF310 with new nose radar and underwing pylons for Fireflash missile trials.

Promoted by Hawker Siddeley, a high-speed, towed target with a span of 25 ft was developed in 1953. The prototype AST C4 undertook trials from Boscombe Down in the spring and summer, but the target was not adopted by the military.

From the mid-1950s, as the College of Air Training, AST concentrated on pilot training. These operations moved north to Perth in April 1960 when Hawker Siddeley Aircraft sold out. The former Avro factory was absorbed into Folland's complex.

ARMSTRONG WHITWORTH AIRCRAFT

Armstrong Whitworth was the parent company of AST; both were part of Hawker Siddeley Aircraft. As such, its name would sometimes crop up in connection with Hamble. It was AST that built the Ensign airliners for Armstrong Whitworth.

AST was one company in the early 1950s that worked on a towed target for the RAF. Trials of the AST C4 were undertaken in 1953, but were not very successful. As a result, surplus Meteor fighters were used by the RAF as targets.

BRITISH MARINE AIRCRAFT LTD

British Marine Aircraft was formed in February 1936, having acquired the rights to construct the Sikorsky S-42A flying boat as the British Marine BM-1, under licence from Sikorsky. This was a four-engine, long-range aircraft carrying thirty-two passengers in comfort. Orders totalling £225,000 had, reportedly, already been placed when the company commenced business. The chairman was Air Marshal Sir John Higgins, who had previously been with Avro and AST. Premises adjacent to Southampton Water were acquired, about half a mile north of the Avro waterfront site. An erection shed capable of housing three S-42s was built, along with the necessary slipway, costing £120,000. At the AGM in December 1936 it was stated that 'five boats were being built to fulfil orders'. This was rather optimistic, as construction of the first BM-1, G-AEGZ, had only just started and did not progress very far. Sikorsky had decided to pull out of the flying-boat market and so were not keen to supply parts and plans to British

British Marine Aircraft commenced work on the first S-42/BM1 in 1936, but it was never completed. This is a Sikorsky S-42 of Pan American visiting Hythe. It has a smaller fuselage compared with the contemporary Short C-Class being built for Imperial Airways.

Marine. Additionally, the anticipated British and Empire market for the British-built S-42 did not materialise, as the new Short C-Class flying boat fulfilled the need. So the company gave up ideas of the BM-1, tried to obtain subcontract work, and considered amalgamation with another aviation company. Failure to do so resulted in British Marine going into liquidation in May 1937. At the time, its new factory was described as the 'finest in the country' and a possible link with a group formed by Henry Folland was being studied. This went ahead in December 1937, and the company was renamed Folland Aircraft.

FOLLAND AIRCRAFT CO.

Folland Aircraft was formed on 24 December 1937 to take over the assets and waterfront premises of British Marine Aircraft at Hamble. Its new managing and technical director was Henry Folland, who had been the chief designer of Gloster Aircraft, and brought other Gloster design staff with him. In order to keep the workforce busy, Folland initially undertook subcontract work for other aircraft manufacturers, mainly Spitfire tails for Supermarine at Woolston, but also Blenheim and Beaufort noses for Bristol. It also undertook maintenance work on Imperial Airways' fleet of C-Class flying boats, which were based on Southampton Water.

The arrival of Henry Folland saw a flurry of aircraft designs. These resulted in the company receiving its first contract in November 1938 for its Fo108, designed to Specification 43/37 for a testbed aircraft for large aero engines. This was a bulky aircraft with a pilot and two test observers; twelve were ordered. Having obtained the order, Folland was unable to build the aircraft at Hamble due to lack of space. So the first two 43/37s, P1774 and P1775, were completed by Oddie, Bradbury & Cull at Eastleigh and the rest were built at Staverton – where part of Folland's operations moved to in 1940 due to the wartime danger of being near the south coast. The flying qualities of the 43/37s were marginal, resulting in pilots referring to them as the 'Folland Frightful'. As well as at Staverton airfield, Folland also took over dispersed manufacturing garage sites in Cheltenham and, nearer to home, Southampton. In 1939, Hamble was undertaking subcontract work on Wellingtons and Spitfires.

Folland's first design to take to the air was the Fo108-engine test-bed aircraft in 1940. In the event, the twelve aircraft ordered were not built at the Hamble factory, but two were built at Eastleigh and ten at the company's Cheltenham works.

Folland was given the task of fitting floats to Spitfires. W3760 was worked on in 1940–41 and, as well as the large pair of floats, it was fitted with a redesigned tail unit. Initial trials were undertaken from Southampton Water.

A November 1939 Folland advertisement showing a modern, twin-engined, twin-finned, twelve-seat airliner, G-FOLL, claimed that the company had twenty-seven years of experience. This implied establishment in 1912, whereas Folland Aircraft had only been formed in 1937. The 1912 date was when Henry Folland designed his first aircraft prior to joining Gloster Aircraft. The claim was still being relied upon post-war – in September 1947, the company claimed thirty-five years as pioneers in aviation design. Early in 1940 Folland described itself as 'Designers and manufacturers of aircraft. Contractor to the Air Ministry. Extensive factory at Hamble most up to date in the country.'

Folland was involved in fitting floats to Spitfires on behalf of Supermarine. In May 1940, Spitfire I R6722 was received from Supermarines and fitted with the floats from a Blackburn Roc. The work was completed and R6722 was delivered to the RAF, but the contract was cancelled before flight trials could be undertaken. In August 1941, W3760 arrived to be fitted with Supermarine-designed floats, but delays meant that its first flight was not until October 1942.

MJ892 was a further Spitfire fitted with floats in the spring of 1944. Although it was successfully tested, the need for floatplane fighters disappeared as the war progressed and so further planned conversions were cancelled.

The former BMA slipway was used to gain access to Southampton Water. On one occasion the Spitfire was shot at by local AA gunners, so for safety flight-testing moved north to Beaumaris. Spitfire Vs EP751 and EP754 were both fitted with floats in August 1943 and delivered to the RAF for service trials in Egypt. Finally, MJ892 was fitted with floats in May 1944. In the summer of 1944 there was talk of a further eight conversions, but no order was placed. There was a proposal in February 1943 for producing floats for Seafires, but again they were never ordered.

In February 1941, Folland was awarded a contract to build a research torpedo reconnaissance bomber to Specification E28/40. Powered by a 2,400 hp Bristol Centaurus engine, the Fo116 design had variable incidence wings and was fitted with a fixed undercarriage. Construction work on DX160 was underway at Cheltenham when the Air Ministry cancelled the contract early in 1943. The Ministry were more interested in Folland proceeding with its Fo117A fighter design, which was intended to be a Tempest replacement. Powered by a

Folland's factory at Hamble, with wartime camouflage paintwork applied. The main section is the former British Marine factory with plenty of wartime additions. The slipway to Southampton Water is bottom left.

Centaurus engine, six prototypes were ordered in September 1943. Due to lack of room at Hamble, these were to be built by English Electric, but in the end the Fo117A was also cancelled. Subcontract work was now being carried out at Hamble on Brigands and Buckinghams for Bristol, Mosquitoes for de Havilland, Seafire wings for Cunliffe-Owen/Supermarine and Wellingtons and Warwicks for Vickers. Some of this work was undertaken at Folland's dispersal site in Southampton, which remained in use well into the 1950s.

Post-war aviation work was hard to come by for Follands. This resulted in a switch of some of the factory space to the production of electric trucks and domestic refrigerators in 1946–48. Then, in 1948, a contract was received from de Havilland, which took Folland heavily into wing construction. Initially, these were for Doves, then Vampire and Venom fighters and Chipmunk trainers. There were still a large number of Folland projects emerging from the design office, but none reached the construction stage. The Fiona of 1947 was a three-engined feederliner, similar in shape to the Percival Prince. However, it had a strange look as one of its Gipsy Major engines was in the nose, with the other two mounted under the wing, pusher fashion. There were other small airliner designs made at around the same time.

Management changes in October 1950 saw Teddy Petter appointed deputy managing director. He had been chief designer at English Electric, where he had designed the Canberra bomber and worked on early designs of the P1 fighter. Due to ill health, Folland stood down as managing director, and was replaced by Petter from 1 July 1951. Petter already had plans for a lightweight fighter, having brought these ideas with him. In July 1951 there was an Air Ministry requirement for a lightweight interceptor fighter; Petter submitted his design, but there appeared to be no interest. In February 1952 there was a fresh requirement for an interceptor fighter, which eventually led to the Avro 720 and SR53. So, early in 1952, Folland decided to proceed with his lightweight fighter without official backing, but a request for four AS Viper engines for use in the prototypes was turned down. A mock-up was built in the spring of 1953 and Folland confirmed in the autumn that two Fo140 Gnat prototypes were being built. The compact design was originally to be powered by a Bristol Saturn jet engine, but this had been cancelled in the autumn of 1952. A new engine was needed for the fighter that was under construction. To save time, a lower-powered Viper was installed in the first prototype aircraft, which now become the Fo139 Midge, although it was realised that the Viper would provide insufficient power for a production version. In August 1953 the Air Ministry said that the Gnat was 'unlikely to meet RAF specifications', but this did not deter Petter and his team. The Midge was rolled out on 31 July 1954 as G-39-1, but could not be flown from the grass runway at Hamble. Folland had established a flight-test base at Chilbolten, but for its first flight the Midge was taken by road to Boscombe Down on 11 August and flown later the same day. It moved to Chilbolten in the middle of the month for development flying. Alongside developing the Midge and Gnat fighters, Folland's 'bread and butter' work included building Vampire Trainer wings for de Havilland and Hunter tails for Hawker.

With the cancellation of the Saturn engine, Petter searched for a more powerful engine for the second prototype Fo140, and settled on the Bristol Orpheus by the end of 1953. The airframe of the second prototype had to be widened to take the new engine. It became the Fo141 Gnat and was still constructed as a private venture. Completed by the early summer of 1955, prototype G-39-2 was taken to Boscombe Down for its first flight on 18 July. Folland already had an eye to the future, as a notice by the factory door stated 'Folland Gnat Mark One'. The Air Ministry showed interest in the Gnat, with Folland also hopeful of meeting a 1954 NATO lightweight ground-attack fighter requirement. The Ministry of

Folland promoted the advantages of a lightweight fighter and produced the Midge demonstrator in 1954. It is seen here between Winchester and Stockbridge on the morning of 11 August 1954 en route from Hamble to Boscombe Down. Its first flight was later the same day.

Supply ordered six Gnats for evaluation in the spring of 1955 (Folland had hoped for twenty-four), and they were built at Hamble the following year. XK724 was the first of the trials aircraft, and it flew from Chilbolten on 16 May 1956. XK768/ G-39-3, the final one, flew in August 1957. Despite the limited Ministry order, Folland was not too despondent, as back in March 1955 the Indian Air Force had shown interest in the Gnat, and talked of production in India. This led to a £3 million contract in September 1956 for twenty-five to be built by Folland, with a further fifteen kits to be built by Hindustan Aircraft in Bangalore.

On behalf of the Ministry of Supply, Folland started work on the improvement of a Saab-designed lightweight ejector seat in 1952. In due course, trials were undertaken from Chilbolten using a Meteor T7, with the first live firing taking place in December 1955. The new seat was then used in production Gnats. The old BMA slipway was used by flying boats again in the early 1950s. Aquila Airways had collected together ten Hythe flying boats, of which three were made serviceable and flown on services from Southampton. Maintenance of the fleet was carried out on the slipway, but the hangar was now used full-time by Folland, so Aquila engineers had to work in the open.

While the Ministry of Supply was making its mind up about Gnats for the RAF, two export orders were obtained. In October 1956 the Finnish Air Force ordered twelve Gnats with a possible licence to produce further aircraft in Finland. Yugoslavia also purchased two in 1957 for evaluation, but no production order was forthcoming. With these orders, and hopefully an RAF one to follow, Folland set up additional facilities at Eastleigh to produce the Gnat fuselages.

The Midge over the Hampshire countryside on one of its test flights from Chilbolten in 1954. The Midge was only ever intended as a demonstrator aircraft prior to production of the higher powered and slightly larger Gnat.

Development batch Gnat F1 XK741 was the trials aircraft for underwing stores. Here it carries two bombs and two additional fuel tanks. Other trials included the firing of underwing rockets. The additional weight and drag reduced the fighter's range.

Pre-production Gnat Trainer XM693 on display at Farnborough in September 1960. Production aircraft had a more pointed nose fitted, which contained a landing light. The Gnat proved a leap forward for trainee pilots, compared to the Vampire Trainer.

Final assembly was at Hamble, with flights made from Chilbolten. The first Indian Gnat flew in August 1957, with deliveries to India made by C-119 Packet from January 1958. The Finnish Air Force received its first Gnat in July. Petter designed a thin-wing Gnat F2. The wing was built with the intention of fitting it on pre-production Gnat No. 6 in 1959. This did not happen, the Air Ministry having announced that there was 'no use for the Gnat Mk 2'. However, hopes for an RAF order were raised again in May 1958 when the Secretary of State for Air said that he was considering the Gnat as a Venom FB4 replacement. In August, Gnat XN122 competed against the Hunter and Jet Provost in trials held in Aden. Follands hopes were high, as the RAF did not have any interest in the Hunter at the time. In the event, it was the Hunter that won the trials and obtained orders for its FGA9 version.

At last the RAF showed real interest in the Gnat, but as an advanced trainer, not a fighter – a replacement for the Vampire Trainer, not the Venom. In any case, the Defence White Paper of April 1957 said there was no longer an RAF

The former British Marine building provided plenty of working space for Follands. Initially this was on subcontract work, but Gnat production commenced in 1956. This early 1960s view is of Gnat Trainers built for the RAF.

Following their RAF service, a number of Gnat Trainers continued flying in private hands – this one is based at Bournemouth. As well as the UK, a large number was exported to the USA. An example still guards the entrance to the Hamble factory.

need for fighters. Folland was already working on a two-seater and quickly responded to a July 1957 specification. This resulted in an initial order for fourteen Fo145 development aircraft in January 1958. With a lengthened forward fuselage, the first XM691 was completed by the summer of 1959 and flown from Chilbolten on 31 August. A follow-on order for thirty production Gnat T1s was placed in February 1960, followed by others, making a total of 105 Gnat T1s. The first for the RAF was delivered in June 1962, although instructors and pupils soon found the cockpit area a tight fit. However, its advanced performance over the Vampire made it well-suited for training front-line pilots. Mention must be made of the RAF's Aerobatic Team, the Red Arrows. Initially equipped with seven red-painted Gnats, the Arrows' first public demonstration was in May 1965. From that time onwards the team has amazed people worldwide with their performances – something that Teddy Petter had probably not imagined. XS111 was the final Gnat delivered to the RAF in May 1965, and was outshopped from Hamble in its Red Arrow colour scheme.

Through Folland, Hawker Siddeley Aviation decided to dabble with hovercraft in the early 1960s. This proof-of-concept craft was known as the Ground Effect Research Machine (GERM). Initial trials were carried out within the Hamble factory grounds.

Hawker Siddeley was responsible for building the huge opening nose doors for the five Airbus Beluga transports. They were built in the former Folland works in 1993 and shipped to France for fitting to the aircraft.

HAWKER SIDDELEY AVIATION

Changes in Britain's aircraft industry followed a Government directive in the spring of 1958. This saw Folland Aircraft become part of Hawker Siddeley Aviation in September 1959, at which time it sought more civil-orientated subcontract work. Petter resigned as director and designer; his place was taken by Maurice Brennan. Production of the Gnat T1 continued, but now they were test-flown from Dunsfold, not Chilbolten. The design office continued work on advanced Gnat projects, but none got beyond the drawing board. Continuing the practice of building wings for other companies within Hawker Siddeley, Hamble now produced Sea Vixen wings for the Christchurch site. Further new work included building HS748 wings for Woodford and Trident 1 wings for Hatfield in the early 1960s. In July 1963, the Hamble site became part of the Hawker-Blackburn Division of Hawker Siddeley. With the delivery of the final Gnat in 1965, the Hamble site undertook Harrier and Hawk subcontract work for Hawker Siddeley at Kingston, mainly fuselage sections. The company also started building wings in late 1964 for the HS P1154 fighter, but this was cancelled in February 1965.

In the summer of 1960, Hawker Siddeley decided to venture into hovercrafts, with work undertaken by Folland. Initial trials were undertaken by the simple Folland GERM (Ground Effect Research Machine) G39-15 in 1960, but it proved unsuccessful. It was planned that the GERM would be followed by a series of Hovertrucks, starting with the design of one with a 5 ton payload. However, in July 1962, Hawker Siddeley pulled out, saying that it was not the right time for hovercraft research and development. The design staff were transferred to Westlands at Cowes.

The Hawker Siddeley Group became part of the nationalised British Aerospace on 1 January 1978, with Hamble becoming part of the Weybridge Division in 1984 and then the Military Aircraft Division in 1986. In January 1989, the former Folland factory was renamed Aerostructures Hamble Ltd, still within British Aerospace. It continued work for Dunsfold and also a large number of other aircraft companies. It developed the manufacturing of cockpit canopies for Harriers and Hawks, and came to specialise in such mouldings. In 1991, British Aerospace announced that Aerostructures was no longer part of its core business, and in May 1992 the company was bought out by its management. Following various changes of ownership, the site continued to be actively involved in aerospace subcontract work for multinationals such as BAE Systems, Airbus and Boeing. It is currently part of GE Aviation and the site is symbolically guarded by a pole-mounted Gnat Trainer.

High Post

Situated alongside the main road between Amesbury and Salisbury, High Post airfield opened in the summer of 1931 for club flying, the main user being the Wiltshire School of Flying. Operations continued until the outbreak of the Second World War, when civilian flying was banned. The airfield closed in the spring of 1947.

VICKERS- SUPERMARINE

High Post was selected by Supermarine in the summer of 1940 as one of its many Spitfire dispersal production sites. It undertook the final assembly of Spitfires built in the various requisitioned small factories around the Salisbury area. New hangars were erected to the south side of the airfield and the High Post Hotel was taken over as offices. The large number of Spitfires being produced locally meant that Supermarine also had to use Chattis Hill for final assembly. Spitfire Vs (commencing W3175) were assembled from April 1941, followed by the first production version of the Griffon-powered Spitfire (EN221) – the XII. These appeared from October 1942 and were followed by large numbers of VIIIs from June 1943. The first production PRXIX RM626 was flown in April 1944, there being no prototype of this version. A prototype F21 'Victor' PP139 was ordered in June 1943 and was flown in August. Well over 300 Spitfires were assembled and flown from High Post.

In October 1941, a study commenced on fitting the Spitfire V with a hook and catapult gear for naval operations, and so it became the Seafire IB. A number of these conversions were carried out at Worthy Down. The first new Supermarine Seafire (originally ordered as Spitfire VCs) was IIC MA970, which flew from High Post in May 1942. Assembly of this fixed-wing version continued until April 1943, and many were ferried to AST at Hamble for fitting out, prior to delivery to the Navy.

Spitfire and Seafire assembly at High Post continued until the spring of 1944, when the airfield took over from Worthy Down as Supermarine's flight

The all-yellow Spitfire Trainer was first flown in August 1946 wearing 'B Condition' marking N32. It was soon repainted and was allocated civil registration G-AIDN in 1947. Supermarine had anticipated an RAF demand for such conversions.

development unit. Extra hangarage was provided adjacent to the High Post Hotel and the road to the south of the airfield was closed to enable the grass runways to be extended. A number of prototypes were built at Hursley Park and then brought to High Post for assembly and first flights. These included Griffon-powered Seafire XV prototypes PK240, PK243 and PK245, which were completed in January 1945. Flight-testing of Seafire XVIIIs was also undertaken. The Spitfire Trainer N32 arrived from Hursley Park in August 1946 for its first flight, and was soon registered as G-AIDN.

Supermarine designed the Spiteful as the successor to the Spitfire, with three prototypes ordered in February 1943. The first, NN660, was built at High Post. It was a Spitfire XIV fuselage fitted with a new laminar flow wing, powered by a Griffon and first flown on 30 June 1944. Unfortunately it was lost in a crash ten weeks later. The second prototype NN664 was built from new. It flew on 8 January 1945, and was followed by NN667. Their fuselages were based on the Spitfire F21. The theoretical speed increase offered by the laminar flow wing did not work out in practice. The initial production Spiteful FXIVs were assembled at High Post from the spring of 1945, with RB515 first flown in April. Main production was due to be undertaken at South Marston from 1946, but the RAF order had been drastically cut back in the spring of 1945. RB518 was modified at the end of 1945 as the sole FXVI, with a higher-powered Griffon, which enabled it to reach a maximum speed of 494 mph. This was the fastest British piston-powered fighter of the time, but its overall performance was little better than the Spitfire F22s then in production at South Marston.

Above: The prototype Spiteful NN660 was assembled at High Post in the spring of 1944. To save time it incorporated a new laminar flow wing married to the fuselage of a Spitfire. Regrettably, it crashed early in its flight-test programme.

Right: The initial Spiteful FXIVs were assembled and test-flown from High Post early in 1945. Production was to be undertaken at South Marston, but was cancelled. This view of RB515 clearly shows the laminar flow-wing shape.

The replacement for the Seafire was intended to be the Seafang. Spiteful RB520 was fitted with an arrester hook early in 1945, but it did not undertake service trials. It was followed by two new-build Seafang prototypes ordered in March 1945. VB893 was to be a F31, but VB895 was completed as an FR32 with a higher-powered Griffon and it was first flown in June 1946. Following the mass cancellation of Spitefuls in the spring of 1945, 150 of the order were switched to the Navy in May 1945 as Seafangs. Ten early production Seafang F31s, fitted with fixed wings, were erected at High Post in 1946 (VG471 was first flown January), although only nine were fully completed and were used for limited trials. Main production at South Marston would have been the FR32 with folding wing tips

Development of the Seafang was protracted. Envisaged for sometime by Supermarine, it was not until the spring of 1945 that Spiteful RB520 was fitted with an arrester hook and became a Seafang. However, no official trials were carried out with this aircraft.

The Seafang was intended to follow on from the Seafire. Prototype VB895 was tested in 1946 and although it was ordered into production, this was soon cancelled. The Navy already had Sea Furies on order and the prototype Attacker jet had flown.

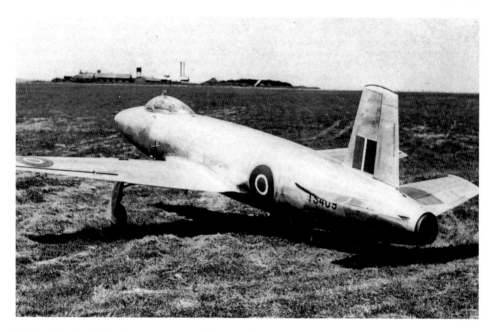

Built at Hursley Park, the prototype E10/44 Attacker was assembled at High Post prior to its first flight from Boscombe Down in July 1946. It returned to High Post's grass runway for further flight trials before moving to Chilbolten in 1947.

and contra-rotating propellers. Only the first production aircraft, VG481, was completed and flown from High Post, and the production order was cancelled at the end of 1946. Neither the Spiteful nor the Seafang entered full production, as propeller fighters were quickly becoming outdated due to advances with jet propulsion.

Arriving from Hursley Park, the three E10/44 jet fighter prototypes were completed at High Post in 1946–47. They were then taken the short distance to Boscombe Down for their maiden flights, with TS409 first flown on 27 July 1946. TS413 was completed to naval standards, with the E10/44 receiving the name Attacker in 1947. Some test-flying was undertaken by TS409 from High Post's grass runways prior to moving to Chilbolten in 1947.

The Wiltshire School of Flying reopened in April 1946, but was restricted by Supermarine as to the amount of flying it could undertake. Eventually, High Post airfield proved to be too close to the Aircraft & Armourment Experimental Establishment at Boscombe Down for further flight-testing. As a result, all flying ceased in spring of 1947, and Supermarine moved to Chilbolten.

Hungerford

There was no airfield at Hungerford, but small-scale aircraft production was undertaken in the late 1930s in the grounds of a local country house.

CHILTON AIRCRAFT

While at the de Havilland Technical School at Hatfield in 1936, two of the students – the Hon. Andrew Dalrymple and A. R. Ward – designed a single-seat, all-wood, ultra-light aircraft. Ward's parents owned Chilton Lodge in the village of Chilton Foliate, to the north-west of Newbury, and one of the outbuildings was taken over for the construction of the Chilton DW1 (DW = Dalrymple & Ward). Chilton Aircraft was formed in 1936 and the first aircraft was completed by the following spring. As there was no airfield, G-AESZ was taken to Witney for its maiden flight in April. Power was provided by a 32 hp Ford Ten car engine converted by Carden Aero Engines, which was taken over by Chilton in the summer of 1937. Two further DW1s, G-AFGH and G-AFGI, were completed in 1938 and flown from a private airstrip near Marlborough. These were followed in the summer of 1939 by G-AFSV, powered by a 44 hp train engine, which gave it a top speed of 126 mph. This was designated the DW1A. When used for air-racing, even the DW1s attained a respectable maximum speed of 112 mph. Sale price of the DW1 was £315 and it was £375 for the faster DW1A.

Work started on the improved DW2 in 1939, but the outbreak of war meant that it was not completed. During the war Chilton Aircraft undertook subcontracting work and in 1940 advertised its capacity for woodworking and small machined-metal assemblies.

In 1944, the company obtained drawings of the German DFS Olympia glider and set about anglifying them. The Olympia was a 15 m Standard glider and was offered for sale as the Chilton Olympia, with an initial batch of fifty planned. In November 1945, the company announced that work had commenced on the first and that six had been sold. Due to shortage of space at Chilton Lodge, arrangements were made with Elliotts of Newbury for them to build the

The four Chilton DW1s built have always proved popular for air racing, starting in the late 1930s and continuing in the present day. Here, G-AFSV is surrounded by a crowd of interested spectators.

At another meeting, DW1A G-AFSV shows ease of ground handling between races at Southend in 1947. Continued interest in the aircraft has resulted in the DW1 now being available for home construction.

As part of its Spitfire dispersal programme, Hungerford was one of the sites selected by Supermarine for production of major Spitfire components. This resulted in a new factory being built in the town in 1941.

wings. Unfortunately, Chilton's plans did not work out. Its managing director – Dalrymple – was killed in an air crash at Chilton Lodge on Christmas Day 1945. The company then found it was unable to produce the gliders quickly enough and so Elliotts took over all development and production. Only Olympia BGA434 was completed by Chilton, and this was transported to Theale in August 1946 for its first flight.

In 1948, Chilton Aircraft was still undertaking light engineering for the aircraft industry, but it was now mainly concerned with electrical components. The company still existed in 1951 but no aircraft work was being undertaken. Surprisingly, all four DW1s survive – two airworthy and two under restoration. To boost their numbers, plans are available that enable new DW1s to be completed as home-built aircraft.

VICKERS-SUPERMARINE

As part of Supermarine's dispersal programme, a new factory was built in Hungerford in 1941 for the production of major Spitfire components. These were then taken to assembly sites in the area, such as Chattis Hill.

Hurn (Bournemouth)

RAF Hurn was built to the north of Bournemouth for the RAF during the Second World War. It was active over the D-Day period and was later used by the USAAF. Hurn became a civil airport and BOAC base in the autumn of 1944, prior to services being able to operate from London Heathrow. Hurn continues to be a civil airport – Bournemouth Airport. However, it was always referred to by Vickers and BAC as their Hurn site.

VICKERS-ARMSTRONGS (AIRCRAFT) LTD

Vickers-Armstrongs' main factory was at Weybridge, where aircraft production had commenced in 1915. In May 1951, the company took over some of the former BOAC hangars at Hurn as their flight-test department. This involved the prototype Varsity trainer, Viscount airliner and Valiant bomber. The Varsity and Viscount were entering full production at Weybridge and were soon to be followed by the Valiant. The board of Vickers, headed by George Edwards, realised that there would not be enough space to produce all three types and considered ending Viscount production after fulfilling the initial BEA, Air France and Aer Lingus orders. Vickers then decided to expand the Hurn site, initially intending to produce the Valiant, but then settling on the Varsity.

The Varsity was a large, multi-role trainer for the RAF powered by two Bristol Hercules engines. Initially only Varsity wings and tails were built at Hurn, with fuselages coming by road from Weybridge. The first Hurn-assembled aircraft, WF386, flew in November 1951 and gradually, complete aircraft were built at Hurn. By the beginning of 1953, production was running at two per week, with the final example, WL692, flown in December 1953. Out of a total of 163 Varsities built, 146 were from the Hurn production line.

The original Viscount specification was for a thirty-two-seat airliner for BEA, powered by four Rolls-Royce Darts and, as such, the prototype flew on 16 July 1948. It was soon realised that greater capacity was required, leading to the lengthened forty-seven-seat Viscount 700, which entered BEA service in

Vickers-Armstrongs originally used Hurn in 1951 as a flight-test base, notably for the Varsity, Viscount and Valiant prototypes – the latter is seen here on a test flight in the autumn of 1951. The original plan was for the Valiant bomber to be built at Hurn.

The initial Varsity trainers were built at Weybridge, but the site was then needed for Valiant production. Construction at Hurn commenced in 1951 and WF386, the first Hurn-produced aircraft, is seen here on engine tests.

A multi-role trainer, the Varsity remained in RAF service until May 1976. Varsity WJ917 of No. 5 FTS at Oakington first flew from Hurn in January 1953. The final Hurn-built aircraft was handed over to the RAF in February 1954.

February 1953. Early in 1953, Vickers confirmed that Viscounts would follow Varsities at Hurn, with BEA's G-AMOO flying in December. At the time, Vickers announced that no further Viscounts would be built at Weybridge, so as to make way for 'super priority production' of the Valiant bomber. In the event, such was the success of the Viscount that it continued to be built at both sites, with an anticipated production of 100 annually from Hurn. The initial Viscount 700s suited European customers, but changes were needed to suit the worldwide market. The Hurn design office worked on major internal modifications, which included improved instrumentation and greater fuel capacity. This resulted in the Viscount 720, which enabled Vickers to break into the Australian and Canadian markets. It was these changes that ensured the future success of the Viscount. Then followed the Viscount 745, which was developed for Capital Airlines of the United States. The airline ordered sixty in 1954. In the winter of 1954/55, the Viscount assembly area was doubled, along with the workforce. To speed up final production, the wings were subcontracted to Saunders-Roe at Eastleigh.

The Viscount airliner helped to make Britain's aircraft industry a world leader in the early 1950s. Initial series 700 aircraft for BEA are seen here on the Hurn production line in 1954; they were soon to be followed by aircraft for Air France and Aer Lingus.

The first major development of the Viscount was the series 720 with additional fuel capacity and higher-powered Dart engines. Initially ordered by Trans Australia Airlines, the first aircraft is at the head of the production line in July 1954.

A later series 800 Viscount is seen here in February 1959 outside the Vickers hangars, which now clearly show their ownership. Ansett-ANA referred to their Series 800 aircraft as the Viscount II; this title was not used by Vickers.

The lengthened Viscount 800 was developed and produced at Weybridge, with fuselages built at Hurn from 1956 and delivered by road. All remaining series 700 orders were then completed at Hurn. An expanded drawing office was opened at Hurn in 1957, and it soon employed 350 staff. By the end of the 1950s, the Weybridge site was producing Vanguards and production of Viscounts at Hurn had slowed down.

On 1 July 1960, the British Aircraft Corporation officially came into being, with Vickers- Armstrongs being one of the major shareholders (40 per cent), along with English Electric Aviation, Bristol Aircraft and Hunting Aircraft. For the time being, the former names remained in use as subsidiaries of the new company. Limited Viscount production continued, and to provide additional work, overhauls were undertaken on RAF Valiants. The final Viscount order was received in December 1961 – six for Civil Aviation of China, which was a new market for Britain at the time. The final Viscount, G-ASDV, was rolled out early in January 1964 and delivered in April – the 438th and final production Viscount, of which Hurn had built 279. 31 December 1963 saw the name of Vickers-Armstrongs finally disappear – it was now British Aircraft Corporation (Operating) Ltd.

BRITISH AIRCRAFT CORPORATION (BAC)

The newly formed BAC inherited the design of the H107 short-haul airliner from Hunting Aircraft and from this was developed the BAC One-Eleven. This new airliner proved vital to BAC's future. In March 1961, BAC announced the launch of its 'bus stop jet', followed by an order for ten from British United in May. Typically fitted with seventy-nine seats, the One-Eleven was powered by two rear-mounted Rolls-Royce Speys. Design work on the initial One-Eleven 200 was

One-Eleven airliners followed the Viscount at Hurn from 1963, and remained in production until 1982. This December 1976 view shows series 500 aircraft destined for Tarom of Romania. The Rombac Deal of 1978 saw further aircraft built in Romania.

Completion of a One-Eleven fuselage in 1966. The front and mid fuselage sections were built at Hurn, the rear fuselage and tail at Filton, and the wings at Luton. This airframe emerged as series 400 for TACA of El Salvador.

The One-Eleven 400 had higher-powered Speys than the series 200. Channel Airways referred to its One-Elevens, produced in the summer of 1967, as 'Continental Golden Jets'. The production hangars now show BAC ownership.

undertaken at Weybridge and Hurn, with production split between Weybridge, Filton and Luton, and final assembly at Hurn. In October 1961, an order was received from Braniff Airways, providing BAC with a breakthrough into the North American market. In July 1963, American Airlines ordered fifteen (later to be doubled) of the more powerful One-Eleven 400, followed by the first flight of the prototype One-Eleven G-ASHG on 20 August. Tragically it crashed on 22 October during flight-testing, having entered a deep stall from which it could not recover. Undeterred, the first production aircraft G-ASJA flew in December 1963. From 1 January 1964, the original subsidiary companies all became part of BAC (Operating) Ltd. Up to then there was the strange situation where the initial One-Elevens were built by Vickers-Armstrongs on behalf of BAC. In the spring of 1964, the Hurn production site was expanded still further, and now employed 3,500 people. Of the initial orders for sixty, fifty were from the USA, but lack of further orders for BAC generally in 1965–66 led to financial difficulties within its commercial division. There was talk of the Hurn site having to close by the end of 1967, and perhaps even Weybridge as well. This situation was eased when BEA placed an order in January 1967. BAC had launched the lengthened One-Eleven 500 at the end of 1966, which resulted in BEA ordering eighteen, soon to be followed by British United and Caledonian. Development aircraft G-ASYD was modified as the prototype and first flew in June 1967. Further work carried out at Hurn included the construction of Jet Provost T5 and Strikemaster wings for BAC's Warton site and the resparring of Pembroke and Sea Prince wings.

At the end of 1969, BAC announced details of the Three-Eleven wide-bodied airliner, which was intended to be built in a new £4 million factory at Hurn, following on from the One-Eleven. It typically had 245 seats, and power was from two rear-mounted Rolls-Royce RB211s. BEA sought an initial fleet of twenty to be in service by 1974. Further interest was shown from airlines such as Britannia and Laker, so BAC sought Government financial aid to launch the Three-Eleven. Work on components for the prototype commenced at Weybridge in the summer

BAC had high hopes for the Three-Eleven, which was due to be built at Hurn from 1973. BEA indicated it wanted twenty and a number of other airlines placed provisional orders. Lack of start-up finance prevented the project going ahead.

BAC had great expectations for Concorde sales and arranged for sub-assemblies to be built at a number of its sites. In the mid-1970s, Hurn was responsible for the droop noses, which were delivered either to the Filton or Toulouse production lines.

To extend the appeal of the One-Eleven, a freighter version was developed in the 1970s, but few were sold. The Oman Air Force received three in 1975, one of those remained in service for thirty-five years – a record for a One-Eleven with just one operator.

Development flying was undertaken by G-ASYD. Built as a series 400, it was lengthened into a series 500 and then shortened to a series 475. Finally it was modified into a series 670 for the Japanese market. It carries both BAC and BAe titles.

of 1970. Then, in December, the Government announced that funds would not be available for the Three-Eleven. It had had to support Rolls-Royce, following the financial disaster over the development costs of its RB211 engine. BAC was unable to proceed by itself, and so the Three-Eleven was cancelled.

In January 1970, BAC announced a further development of the One-Eleven, the 475, which was intended for country routes. Trials aircraft G-ASYD was rebuilt as the prototype and first flew in August 1970. The new version did not prove as popular as hoped, with only twelve being produced. One-Eleven production almost ended at the end of 1972, but an order from the Sultan of Oman Air Force managed to keep production going. When these aircraft were delivered at the end of 1974, further limited orders kept production going for a further seven years. The One-Eleven 670 was announced early in 1977, and was intended to meet a Japanese short field requirement. G-ASYD was modified once more, and flew again in September 1977. Regrettably, no orders were forthcoming.

From 1 January 1978, BAC became part of the nationalised British Aerospace, having merged with the Hawker Siddeley Group.

BRITISH AEROSPACE (BAe)

At the time of British Aerospace's formation there was little One-Eleven work left at Hurn. However, after months of negotiation, a major agreement was signed in June 1978 between BAe and President Ceauçescu for the production of One-Elevens in Romania. This became known as the Rombac Deal. The initial aircraft were constructed at Hurn by Romanian engineers, with full production then switching to Bucharest. The contract covered twenty-five aircraft, although it was envisaged that at least eighty would eventually be required. Three fuselages were completed at Hurn and flown to Bucharest inside an Airbus Super Guppy. The first Rombac One-Eleven built at Hurn was Tarom's YR-BCO, which was delivered in March 1982. The first Bucharest aircraft flew in September 1982, but only nine were completed and flown as financial problems brought an end to the deal. Including Romanian production, 244 One-Elevens were built – 222 at Hurn. To provide additional work, ten partly completed Strikemasters arrived by road from Warton in the summer of 1979 for completion at Hurn; the first flew in August 1980. Only six were completed, and the other four returned to Warton. Hurn was also involved in the production of VC10 parts for Weybridge, Concorde noses for Filton, and A300 components for Airbus.

BAe had been hopeful of obtaining major work on the proposed Airbus A320 airliner. But its launch was delayed due to problems over funding, and the go-ahead was delayed until March 1984. As there was insufficient work for all BAe

With a drop-off in One-Eleven orders, BAe's Hurn site undertook the completion of ten Strikemasters in 1980–81 in order to keep the workforce occupied. Other work included the re-sparing of Sea Princes and the painting of Islanders.

The initial Strikemasters were completed without there being a customer for them. As a result, the first G-16-26 appeared in BAe house colours for its maiden flight in the spring of 1981. Later ones were completed for the Sudanese Air Force.

189

A view of BAe's Hurn site in 1983, shortly before closure. A One-Eleven is outside the production hangars – much expanded from BOAC days. The VC10 tanker was visiting for modifications. Because of a lack of aviation activity, many workers' cars are parked on the apron.

One-Elevens were built in Bucharest from 1982, but financial problems in Romania brought a premature end to production. YR-BRC is seen here at Farnborough in September 1984, unusually marked as a '1-11' rather than 'One-Eleven'.

sites around the country, in June 1983 it was announced that Hurn would close in the summer of 1984 'due to the depressed state of the civil aircraft market'. Following BAe's departure, the former hangars were taken over by various aviation companies, with one even used for storage of part of the EEC's grain mountain.

FLS AEROSPACE

FLS Industries A/S was a major Danish aviation company with a UK subsidiary, FLS Aerospace, whose Lovaux Division undertook aircraft maintenance at Hurn in the late 1980s. In July 1990 FLS purchased the production rights of the Optica Scout from Brooklands Aerospace at Old Sarum, followed in November 1991 by the SAH-1 from Orca Aircraft. In the summer of 1991, FLS established its Light Aircraft Division at Hurn to relaunch refined versions of both the Optica and SAH-1. Sales of fifty Opticas a year were anticipated, with a $3.6 million sale of twelve to an American distributor announced in December 1991. Brooklands built G-BOPN, now flown as the demonstrator FLS Optica. There were hopes of an RAF trainer order for the re-engined and renamed SAH-1, now the FLS Sprint. The basic

The original SAH-1 prototype G-SAHI appeared under the new FLS banner when it was launched as the Sprint in May 1992. Although FLS reported that a number of orders were in the pipeline, none of them materialised.

FLS set up its Light Aircraft Division in October 1991 with the intention of relaunching the SAH-1 Sprint basic trainer. Production of five new aircraft was undertaken in 1993, but there were no sales – civil or military.

Two versions of the Sprint were offered by FLS – the basic 115 hp version for club flying and the 160 hp version for military training. Hence the registration G-SCLX on this aircraft (*Sprint* + *CLX* = the Roman 160).

FLS relaunched the Optica observation aircraft using one of the Brooklands-built aircraft as the demonstrator. Although FLS commenced production of five aircraft in 1993, only two were completed and the project was put up for sale the following year.

aircraft was the Club Sprint, with the Sprint 160 trainer fitted with a more powerful 160 hp Lycoming engine. Production of both types commenced at the beginning of 1993 with an initial run of five of each aircraft. The first 'new' FLS Optica, G-BOPO, flew in April 1993, followed by Sprint G-FLSI in December. Unfortunately, the American Optica order did not proceed and this dampened further prospects. In May 1994, FLS decided to concentrate on its core overhaul business and put production rights of both aircraft up for sale. By this date only two Opticas and three Sprints had been completed. In April 1996, it was announced that the Optica rights had been sold. Production would be undertaken in the UK for a further twelve months and then pass to Gegasi Industries of Malaysia. The deal was never completed and there was no further interest in the Sprint, so in December 1997 the aircraft and jigs were moved to FLS's Stansted site for storage.

The next few years saw many new owners and proposals for the Optica and Sprint. By December 2004, their rights were with Aviation Group International, who intended to restart production for the US market. Major parts were to be built by Aerostar in Romania, with final assembly by Thrush Aircraft in Albany, USA. This did not happen and, by 2006, the Sprint was being marketed in the UK as the Redwing by British Light Aircraft, a subsidiary of Aviation Group International. The rights of the Optica and Sprint were then acquired by Aeroelvira in the spring of 2008 (see under Thruxton) – yet another twist in a protracted saga.

FR Aviation announced in July 1996 that had been appointed prime subcontractor to BAe on the Nimrod 2000 project. Design problems saw BAe take the project in-house, where it dragged on until it was finally cancelled in October 2010.

FR AVIATION LTD

Upon the closure of Tarrant Rushton airfield, Flight Refuelling moved its flying operations to Hurn. In the autumn of 1989, FR Aviation, in conjunction with British Aerospace, received a contract to modify eight (later increased to thirteen) RAF VC10s into dual-purpose tanker transports. A large new hangar was built to house the aircraft, with XV101 arriving in February 1991. Again in conjunction with BAe, in July 1996 FR Aviation became the prime subcontractor for the Nimrod 2000 conversion programme. FR Aviation was to strip down twenty-one Nimrod MR2s to leave just a gutted fuselage shell. BAe would build and supply new wings and tail surfaces, with the 'new' aircraft erected and test-flown from Hurn. Another large hangar was built in 1997 to house the Nimrods. Four gutted fuselages were awaiting their wings and tails at the beginning of 1999, when BAe ran into design problems and decided to take the Nimrod 2000 project back in-house, and transported the fuselages to Woodford. Here the programme dragged on, with the first 'new' Nimrod MRA4 flying in 2006. Cost overruns saw the RAF order reduced to nine, and then, after the first few were finally flying, the complete project was cancelled by the Government in October 2010 as part of defence cutbacks.

FR Aviation became involved in another protracted project in the summer of 2001. As part of the AirTanker consortium, it proposed the Airbus A330 airliner as a replacement tanker transport for the RAF's existing Tristars and VC10s. However, it was not until January 2004 that AirTanker was confirmed as the 'preferred bidder'. This status was upped in June 2007 to 'selection', prior to the contract finally being awarded in March 2008. Fourteen A330s were acquired by AirTanker on behalf of the RAF. The first two were modified by Airbus Military in Madrid in 2010, with ZZ332 finally arriving at Hurn in the autumn of 2011 as the first of twelve to be modified by what was now Cobham Aviation Services.

Hursley Park

There was no airfield at Hursley Park, situated between Romsey and Winchester, only the stately Hursley House – home of Sir George Cooper (chairman of Strong's Brewery) and his wife. Sir George died in 1940 and the house was requisitioned by Lord Beaverbrook as part of the Spitfire dispersal programme.

VICKERS-SUPERMARINE

Despite only being a country house, Hursley Park became famous as the headquarters of the Supermarine Works of Vickers-Armstrongs Ltd. Following the bombing of Woolston, Supermarine moved Joe Smith and his design staff to Hursley House in December 1940. In due course, a large design office building and a hangar were erected in the park for the Experimental Department to house mock-ups or prototypes of new Supermarine designs. The initial years saw the design team working on updated Spitfires and Seafires. After the initial Spitfire Is and IIs, the next major version was the 'stop-gap' V with a higher-powered 1,440 hp Merlin and increased armament. Its improved performance soon led to large numbers ordered; they were produced around the Southampton area's dispersed sites from June 1941. By early 1942, the RAF Spitfires were having problems countering the Luftwaffe's new Fw190s. Rolls-Royce test-flew an improved 1,660 hp Merlin 61 in the spring of 1942 and this was fitted into some Spitfire Vs. This proved successful and so was ordered into production in April 1942 as the Spitfire IX. The XVI was similar, but powered by a Packard-built 1,750 hp Merlin. The VII was pressurised for high-altitude operations. The VIII featured a number of design improvements, including a strengthened forward fuselage to absorb the increased power from the engine, plus a retractable tail wheel.

Supermarine had been working on the design of a Rolls-Royce Griffon-powered Spitfire and two prototypes were ordered in May 1941. DP845 and DP851 were built at Hursley Park that summer, with Mk IV DP845 flown from Worthy Down in November. It entered production as the Spitfire XII and was followed by the

The magnificent Hursley House is situated in Hursley Park and was requisitioned by the Air Ministry at the end of 1940. It was used by Supermarine as offices, and there was no need to change the building's historic exterior. Today it is within IBM's huge complex.

As soon as Supermarine arrived at Hursley Park, it erected a large hangar in the grounds. For over ten years prototypes of the various Supermarine designs from Spitfire to Scimitar were built in the experimental hangar.

Work in progress on Spitfire prototypes and development aircraft during the war. These would then be taken to either High Post or Worthy Down for flight-testing. The hangar was used in the 1950s for construction of Supermarine's various jet fighters.

XIV. Based on the earlier VIII, this was the first major Griffon-powered version to enter production. JF316 was converted from a VIII into the prototype XIV in the spring of 1943, and large numbers of this Griffon version were produced. To take full advantage of the Griffon's increased power (2,050 hp), Joe Smith redesigned and beefed-up the Spitfire's airframe in 1942, losing the classic elliptical shaped wings. As an interim measure, the 'Super Spitfire' FXVIII was produced, but delays meant it did not appear until November 1944. The final efforts of the design team led to a much-changed airframe. Due to these changes, it was intended that the name Victor would be used for production aircraft, which were ordered in August 1943. In the event, the change of name did not prove popular and so production aircraft appeared from South Marston as Spitfire F21s from March 1944. The design office developed the PRXI into the Griffon-powered, pressurised PRXIX, and a prototype was ordered in March 1944. More design work was undertaken on the proposed F23 Valiant with an interim laminar flow wing, as was originally proposed for the Victor. DP851 was rebuilt as the prototype XX, but its role was overtaken by the development of the Spiteful. The final Spitfires were the F22 and its F24 development. Both were similar to the F21, although they were fitted with a cut-down rear fuselage for improved pilot vision.

In November 1941, design work was undertaken on a hooked Spitfire for the Royal Navy, with the prototypes tested at Worthy Down. The first production aircraft were converted by AST at Hamble, and received the type name Seafire in January 1942. These initial Seafire IBs and ICs had fixed wings; they were basically hooked Spitfire VBs and VCs. A folding-wing version was developed by General Aircraft in the summer of 1942, and entered service as the Seafire III in the spring of 1944. Production was undertaken by Cunliffe-Owen and Westland Aircraft. The Griffon-powered Seafire XV was developed in 1943, and three prototypes were ordered in March 1943, with NS487 completed in December. Production aircraft were built by Cunliffe-Owen, but did not enter service until May 1945. Three Spitfire F21s were delivered from Castle Bromwich in 1944 for conversion into prototype Seafire F45s TM379, TM383 and TM389 by the addition of an arrestor hook. The first Griffon-powered, fixed-wing version was completed in October 1944 and forwarded to Cunliffe-Owen for flight-testing. The Seafire F46 was a hooked Spitfire F22 with contra-rotating propellers to cope with the Griffon's increased power. The final development of the Seafire was the F47, which had folding wings as well as contra-rotating propellers. Little design work was needed as it was similar to the F45 and F46. Production of these three versions was undertaken at South Marston. It is generally accepted that 20,351 Spitfires and 2,622 Seafires (including conversions) were built.

In 1942, Joe Smith's team worked on the Spiteful as the Spitfire's replacement and the Seafang as the Seafire's. Three prototype Spitefuls were ordered to Specification F1/43 in February 1943, but the Seafang prototypes had to wait until April 1945. The aim was to reach 500 mph, but neither entered full production due to the end of the war and the advances of jet fighters. Development work was undertaken at High Post.

Back in 1937, Supermarine had undertaken design work on a Merlin-powered dive bomber to meet naval requirement S24/37. Prototypes R1810 and R1815 were ordered, but work on developing the Spitfire meant there was a delay with the resulting Supermarine 322. The first prototype was not completed until the end of 1942 and was flown from Worthy Down in February 1943 – the type later receiving the unofficial name 'Dumbo'. No orders were placed due to the delays, the Navy having already selected the competing Fairey Barracuda. Following a June 1941 naval requirement, three prototype reconnaissance amphibians were ordered in April 1943, but continued work pressure meant that construction was delayed until after the war. Initially planned as a biplane to replace the Sea Otter, Supermarine considered that a monoplane aircraft would be more

In addition to fighters, the prototype Seagull amphibians were built at Hursley Park in 1946. They were then transported to the Itchen factory for test-flying from Southampton Water. PA143 was the first of the prototypes.

appropriate. Powered by a 1,815 hp Griffon, with contra-rotating propellers, the all-metal Supermarine 347 featured a variable incidence wing, which improved lift. Its speed range was 55–260 mph and for carrier operations the wings could be folded. The requirement was amended in November 1944 to cover a new air–sea rescue role as the Supermarine 381. Named Seagull in the spring of 1947, only prototypes PA143 and PA147 were fully completed, with Hursley Park responsible for building the fuselages plus final assembly. PA143 was taken to Itchen factory in June 1948, from where it flew the following month, but PA147 did not fly until September 1949. The Seagull did not enter production as, by the early 1950s, helicopters were becoming available to undertake air–sea rescue duties. In the spring of 1946, Spitfire XIII MT818 had a second cockpit added to become the prototype trainer version, and it undertook its first flight from High Post in August 1946. However, anticipated RAF orders were not received.

More importantly, Hursley Park was involved in the development of Supermarine's various jet fighters, commencing with a design to Specification

E10/44 in the summer of 1944, plus the construction of a mock-up. Joe Smith used the Spiteful wing married to a modified fuselage that retained a tail wheel. This layout was not favoured by the Ministry of Aircraft Production, but it hastened design work. Powered by a Rolls-Royce Nene, four 20 mm guns were specified for the fighter – as in the Spiteful. Prototypes TS409, TS413 and TS416 of the Supermarine 392 'jet fighter based on Spiteful' were ordered in September 1944 to be built at Hursley Park. In July 1945 the Royal Navy issued Specification E1/45 to cover its version of the Supermarine 392, which became the Supermarine 398. Six pre-production Supermarine 392s and eighteen Supermarine 398s were ordered in November 1945 as the 'Jet Seafang'. Such were the technical delays with the project in 1945–46 that the RAF lost interest and the Navy couldn't wait any longer, resulting in all the pre-production aircraft being cancelled. Work continued on the prototypes, with TS409 first flying in July 1946. The new fighter was named Attacker in April 1947, with TS413 first flying in May and TS419 not until December 1949. These two prototypes were completed to Supermarine 398 naval standards. The prototypes were taken to High Post for final assembly and then to Boscombe Down for their first

Three prototype Supermarine 398s were built in 1946–47 as a 'Jet Seafangs' before receiving the name Attacker in the spring of 1947. TS413 was the second of these prototypes, and was taken to Boscombe Down for its first flight in May 1947.

flights. The Navy finally placed an order for Sea Attackers in October 1948, with production undertaken at South Marston. As there was no longer an RAF version, the 'Sea' part of the name was dropped.

Then followed a swept-wing version of the Attacker, with Nene-powered prototypes VV106 and VV119 ordered in March 1947. A swept wing and tailplane were fitted to a modified Attacker fuselage that still retained its tail wheel. Again, they were built at Hursley Park, with VV106 completed as the Supermarine 510 and flown from Boscombe Down on 29 December 1948. VV119 was completed as the Supermarine 528, which had minor differences to VV106, and it was flown from Boscombe on 27 March 1950. The name Swift was adopted in September 1949 for the intended production version. Both prototypes were fitted with tail wheels, which was not practical for a jet fighter. So VV119 returned to Hursley Park in May 1950 to be rebuilt with a tricycle undercarriage, a lengthened nose and reheat. As the Supermarine 535, it returned to Boscombe in August for a 'new' first flight on 23 August. It was the first British aircraft to be fitted with reheat, which boosted its engine's performance on take-off. The 535's improved flying characteristics led to two further Avon-powered prototypes, WJ960 and WJ965, ordered in November 1950. This was immediately followed by an initial RAF Swift order for 100 production aircraft. This was due to the need to quickly re-arm the RAF upon the outbreak of the Korean War. *Flight* magazine of August 1951 likened the Hawker P1067 (still to be named Hunter) and Swift to post-war successors of the Hurricane and Spitfire. A Supermarine advertisement in the autumn of 1952 refered to the Swift as the 'First of the New' – referring to the famous wartime Spitfire film *The First of the Few*. WJ960 and WJ965 were

WJ960 was the first of two Supermarine 541s built at Hursley Park in 1951 and was flown from Boscombe Down. Along with WJ965, it represented a pre-production Swift fighter, with 100 ordered for the RAF in November 1950.

The first two production Swift F1s, WK194 and WK195, were built in the experimental hangar at Hursley Park in 1952–53. WK194 is seen here on an early test flight. From the third Swift in early 1953, production aircraft were built at South Marston.

built at Hursley Park as Supermarine 541s. WJ960 flew from Boscombe Down in August 1951, although WJ965 was delayed until July 1952. The first two production Swifts – WK194 and WK195 – were also built at Hursley Park, with further aircraft then following from South Marston from March 1953.

Supermarine design team developed a supersonic version of the Swift, with prototype Supermarine 545s XA181 and XA186 ordered in February 1952. Utilising modified Swift fuselages, the design underwent major changes in layout, engine and armourment. Completion was further delayed following the cancellation of RAF Swift fighter orders in March 1955. The second 545 had already been cancelled in October 1954, but work on XA181 continued until the summer of 1955, when it was 90 per cent complete. The 545 contract was cancelled in December 1955 – a 'rival' supersonic Hunter prototype having already been cancelled back in July 1953.

Supermarine also worked on advanced naval fighter designs from 1945; all were bulky, Avon-powered machines. First was the Supermarine 505 – a

The experimental Supermarine 529 was one of three large naval prototype fighters built in the early 1950s. VX136 is seen here undergoing deck-landing trials in the autumn of 1953. Development work led to the Supermarine 544, which entered production as the Scimitar.

single-seat, V-tail, undercarriageless, carrier-borne fighter – and a mock-up was soon completed. The idea of not having an undercarriage worked in theory, but planned full-scale trials kept being delayed. Supermarine decided to play safe and modified their design in 1946 into the twin-engined 508, which had a normal undercarriage. (Trials were eventually carried out at Farnborough and on HMS *Warrior* in 1948–49 with undercarriageless Sea Vampires. The idea worked on this 'lightweight' fighter, but probably would not have with Supermarine's 'heavyweight' strike fighter. So the company was correct in proceeding with the 508 design.) Prototypes VX133, VX136 and VX138 were ordered in August 1947, with a further mock-up constructed, which included four 20 mm guns. The programme proceeded slowly and VX133 was finally taken to Boscombe Down for its first flight on 31 August 1951. VX136 flew in August 1952 as the Supermarine 529, by which time the third prototype had been redesigned to have swept-back wings and a standard tail. Now designated the Supermarine 525, VX138 was taken to Boscombe Down for its first flight on 27 April 1954. Supermarine stated that although an experimental aircraft, the 525 was the fastest and most powerful aircraft designed for carrier operations. However, flight-testing revealed a number of problems, Supermarine having already

The third aircraft was completed as the Supermarine 525 with swept flying surfaces and a standard tail. VX138 is seen here at Farnborough in September 1954. Additional prototypes were built before production of the definitive Scimitar commenced.

realised that the 525 did not form the basis of a production aircraft. The Navy had issued Requirement N113D back in the summer of 1951, with prototypes WT854, WT859 and WW134 ordered early in 1951 as the Supermarine 544, again to be built at Hursley Park. Although similar in layout and size to the 525, the 544 was a major redesign of the earlier aircraft. Such was the anticipated need for the new fighter – to be named Scimitar – 100 aircraft were ordered in December 1952, with production undertaken at South Marston. The Scimitar had a very strong airframe, with plenty of power from its two Avon engines. Whereas the Supermarine 508 had 6,500 lb thrust Avons, the latest version used in the Scimitar had a 11,250 lb thrust. The prototype N113, WT854, was flown from Boscombe Down on 19 January 1956 – it still had yet to be named Scimitar. A two-seat, all-weather version of the Scimitar was developed by Supermarine, with the Supermarine 556 prototype XH451 ordered in September 1954. However, it had only reached the stage of a mock-up before the project was cancelled in July 1955, the Royal Navy having ordered a naval version of the DH110 instead. So the 544 prototypes proved to be the final aircraft to be built at Hursley Park. In the 1940s and '50s, it was the design teams from Supermarine and Hawker that systematically pioneered the development of jet fighters in Great Britain.

Reorganisation in December 1954 saw Hursley Park become part of the Supermarine Division of the newly formed Vickers-Armstrongs (Aircraft) Ltd. In April 1956, Supermarine announced that its drawing office would be transferred to South Marston, with some work moving to Weybridge. At the time of Supermarine's September 1958 decision to cease aircraft production, only a few design staff remained at Hursley. At the end of 1958, Hursley House passed into the hands of IBM UK, whose additional laboratory and office buildings now dwarf the original building.

Hythe

Situated on the western shore of Southampton Water, Hythe was selected by the Admiralty in 1915 to site a large building intended for the construction of seaplanes.

MAY HARDEN & MAY LTD

During the First World War, the Admiralty required seaplanes and flying boats, and devised a system of ordering major types from various manufacturers. To aid this, they funded the construction of an erecting shed at Hythe, which became known as the Admiralty Shed. This was run by the ship-building firm of May, Harden & May, who undertook the construction of hulls for various flying boats. First was the Porte Baby, which was to the design of Sqn Cdr John Porte. Despite its name, this was a large, three-engined flying boat with a wingspan of 124 ft. Records indicate that twenty-one were ordered (commencing with 9800), but that only twelve were fully completed in 1916. The hulls were transported from Hythe to Felixstowe for final completion. Next came the smaller Felixstowe F2A. Eighty hulls were completed in 1917–18 on behalf of the Aircraft Manufacturing Co. Again, the final ones were not completed, with a follow-up order for fifty Felixstowe F5s also cancelled in 1918. May Harden built AD Flying Boat hulls for Supermarine's Woolston factory in 1917–18, as well as the Phoenix P5s P86 and P87 and the hull of Fairey Atalanta N119 in 1919.

After the war there was no aviation work for May, Harden & May, so the shed fell into disuse for a number of years.

VICKERS-SUPERMARINE

In May 1927, Supermarine bought the Admiralty Shed and used it for final assembly and flight-testing of Southampton IIs and Seagulls – the hulls having been towed over from Woolston. The shed was also home to the Nanok, which

Supermarine took over the former Admiralty Sheds in 1927 to give themselves more production space. Southampton II S1249 awaits roll-out from the works in 1928. It carries the type's original colour scheme of a dark top and white lower hull.

Workers preparing a Southampton II for a test flight. Production of the Southampton totalled seventy-nine, with the earlier wooden-hulled ones having replacement metal hulls fitted from 1929 onwards. The boats are now in a silver colour scheme.

A nose view of the prototype metal-hulled Southampton II. The original Southampton Is were fitted with wooden hulls, but trials with N218 led to future Southamptons being metal-hulled. N218 is seen here in 1930 after it had been fitted with Bristol Jupiter radial engines.

had been built for the Danish Navy, but after flight trials in the summer, it was not accepted. So the Nanok was refitted with a luxury interior, and renamed the Solent. From the summer of 1928, G-AAAB was based at Hythe for the Hon. A. E. Guinness's flights between his local home and that in Galway, Eire. In November 1928, Supermarine amalgamated with Vickers, and production continued at both the Hythe and Woolston works, with the former's roof declaring itself the 'Vickers-Supermarine Works'. Supermarine designed a large reconnaissance flying boat for the RAF towards the end of 1927 and went ahead with a prototype. Delays in construction meant it no longer met the RAF's requirement, and so the flying boat was completed as a civil aircraft for the Hon. Guinness. The Air Yacht G-AASE was powered by three AS Jaguar engines and had a wingspan of 92 ft. The Air Yacht was first flown in February 1930, but due to delays in internal fitting-out it was not ready for delivery until the end of 1931. Trials earlier in the year showed the need for more powerful engines, and so AS Panthers were fitted. Although he had intended to replace his existing Solent

The Nanok was a three-engined version of the Southampton built for the Danish Navy. After trials in the spring of 1928, the Danes refused to accept delivery. So the Nanok was converted into a VIP aircraft and renamed Solent G-AAAB.

The private-venture Seagull V was built at Hythe in the spring of 1933 and was first flown on 21 June. After trials at Felixstowe, the Australian Navy ordered twenty-four in August 1934. From the Seagull V, Supermarine developed its famous Walrus.

with an Air Yacht, the Hon. Guinness now preferred landplanes, which he based at Eastleigh. The Air Yacht was not delivered, and was stored at Hythe until its resale in October 1932. In August 1931, Vickers Vildebeest VII floatplane G-ABGE was prepared for a sales tour of the Baltic, which took place the following month. The prototype Seagull V was built in 1933 for Australia, and first flew in June as N-1, with twenty-four production aircraft following in 1935–37. The Seagull V also undertook trials with the FAA, and was eventually ordered as the Walrus. Initially, production was undertaken at Supermarine's Woolston site, but in 1936–37, fuselages were towed across Southampton Water for completion at Hythe. As well as the Australian Seagulls, Hythe shared production of RAF Stranraers with Woolston, but by the end of the 1930s there was less work for Hythe. This was due to Supermarine's new Itchen factory opening in 1938 and taking on production of the Stranraer and Walrus.

Adjacent to Supermarine were the works of the British Power Boat Company, established in 1927 by former Supermarine director Hubert Scott-Paine. The

Although the sheds still carry the name 'Vickers-Supermarine Works', at the time of this photo they were in use by Imperial Airways. Their C-Class flying boats took up residence in the summer of 1936 and this July 1937 view includes a visiting Pan American Sikorsky S-42.

A present-day view of the former Vickers-Supermarine works at Hythe. They have seen many changes over the years, and are currently occupied by Griffon Hoverwork. One of Griffon's hovercrafts can be seen to the right.

works were almost completely destroyed by fire in August 1931, but were soon rebuilt. In 1936 the Supermarine Sheds were leased to Imperial Airways, who used them as a maintenance base for their new C-Class flying boats, which were entering service from Southampton.

GRIFFON HOVERWORK

The Admiralty Shed had many occupants after the departure of Supermarine. These included Imperial Airways, BOAC and the US Army. The site was purchased by SEEDA in October 2007 for redevelopment as a Marine Business Park, with the Admiralty Shed occupied by Griffon Hoverwork from May 2008. Griffon describes itself as the 'descendent of British Hovercraft Corporation' and holds the design authority for their former products. Griffon is successful in its own right, and sells a range of hovercraft worldwide.

Itchen

VICKERS-SUPERMARINE

Supermarine had become restricted by the amount of space available at its main Woolston site. With war looming, the company went ahead in 1938 with the building of a new factory a short distance upstream from Woolston. Orders for Walruses and Spitfires meant that much more production space was needed, and this was met by the new Itchen site. From early 1939 it became the main Walrus production facility, as well as completing the final Stranraers and, more importantly, assisting in Spitfire production. Walruses were flown from the River Itchen, with Spitfires taken to Eastleigh for erection and delivery. All this came to an end with the bombing of both the Woolston and Itchen sites by the Luftwaffe on 26 September 1940. No attempt was made to rebuild the gutted Itchen factory during the war, and the site was used for troop training.

VICKERS-ARMSTRONGS LTD

Following its destruction, the Woolston factory was never rebuilt. However, the Itchen site was rebuilt in 1947, as Vickers-Armstrongs Ltd's 'Aircraft Section – Supermarine Works'. It overhauled a number of Walruses for export, including eight for Argentina in 1947–50. The prototype Seagull PA143 arrived by road from Hursley Park in June 1948 and was first flown from the Itchen on 14 July. However, the second prototype PA147 did not fly until September 1949, after which it had deck-landing trials on HMS *Illustrious* in October. In 1949, Itchen assisted Vickers-Armstrongs by building the wings of the Viscount 700 prototype, which were then transported to Weybridge and attached to the fuselage, which had been built at South Marston.

Pre-war, Supermarine's flying boats were to the fore, but post-war it was to be jet fighters, Attackers, Swifts and Scimitars all completed at South Marston. The company was reorganised as Southern Area (Chilbolton, Eastleigh, Hursley Park and Itchen) and Northern Area (South Marston and Trowbridge). Early

The opening of Supermarine's Itchen factory in 1938 gave additional production space for Stranraers, Walruses and Spitfires. Seen here are a large number of Walrus Is destined for service with the Royal Navy.

A view inside Itchen in late 1938. Spitfires are nearing completion in the foreground, Walruses are behind, and in the distance are the final Stranraers. The Spitfires were taken to Eastleigh for assembly, while the Walruses and Stranraers were flown from the Itchen.

The Itchen works were situated just upstream from Supermarine's existing Woolston site. They were built on land between the Southampton–Portsmouth railway line and the River Itchen. From the start they carried Vickers-Armstrongs titles on the façade.

Prototype Seagull PA143 arrived from Hursley Park for its first flight in July 1948 and is seen here on the hardstanding outside the works. It did not enter production, as its Air Sea Rescue role was about to be taken over by Dragonfly helicopters.

production Swift fuselages were completed at Itchen, their wings were built at Eastleigh, and the parts were taken to South Marston for assembly. As in wartime, production still remained dispersed; i.e. Swift noses from a bus works in Hove and wings from Boulton Paul in Wolverhampton. Swift sections were still being produced at Itchen in the summer of 1955, followed by Scimitar sections. A new drawing office was brought into use in 1956. In the spring of 1958, the Government stated that Britain's aircraft industry must contract,

Itchen entered a new era in 1961 when it became involved in the development of hovercraft. Vickers-Armstrong's first machine was the VA-1, which is seen here proceeding up the slipway early in 1962. It was followed by the larger VA-2.

Following the experimental VA-2, Vickers' next hovercraft was the VA-3, which undertook trials from Itchen in 1962. The works prepared it for the world's first passenger hovercraft service – between Rhyl and Wallasey – in July.

resulting in Supermarine announcing in September that it would switch from aircraft production to general engineering. Delivery of the final Scimitar in 1961 marked the end of Supermarine's aircraft production and name. The Itchen site was then used for a new form of transport being developed by Vickers-Armstrongs.

The Supermarine Works' name and factory did not become part of British Aircraft Corporation when the latter was formed in June 1960. The former Itchen Division now became part of Vickers-Armstrongs (Engineering) Ltd, which was developing hovercrafts at South Marston. From 1961 these were brought to Itchen for testing on the Southampton Water. First was the experimental Vickers VA-1 G-15-252, which was followed by the slightly larger VA-2. Both undertook military trials with IHTU, with the VA-2 undergoing land-based assessment in Libya as XS856 in the spring of 1963. In the early summer of 1962, the twenty-four-seat VA-3 arrived and was prepared for passenger-carrying trials in connection with British United Airways between Rhyl and Wallasey. As G-15-253, it operated the first hovercraft commercial service in July 1962, but the trials were not as successful as had been hoped. Vickers realised that it was not sensible to build the hovercraft at South Marston and then transport them to Itchen so that they could operate at sea. So it was planned that the next project – the much larger VA-4 – would be assembled at Itchen towards the end of 1966. This was a massive craft that could carry 500 passengers or 140 passengers and twenty-eight cars.

In the mid-1960s, Britain's new hovercraft industry was mainly centred around the Solent and Southampton Water, but it did not expand as anticipated. So the main manufacturers amalgamated to form the British Hovercraft Corporation in March 1966. As part of the deal, all Vickers' South Marston hovercraft work was transferred to Itchen. Vickers' proposed VA-4 was very similar to the Saunders-Roe SRN4 design, which was the large hovercraft BHC chose to develop. So with little hovercraft work left, Vickers' Itchen site was closed in February 1968, with some of the staff moving to the BHC Headquarters at Cowes.

Newbury

There was no airfield at Newbury, but in 1940 the town became involved in Spitfire work following the dispersal programme introduced by Supermarine. The local firm of Elliotts also became involved in Spitfire work and later Hamilcar gliders.

VICKERS-SUPERMARINE

As part of Supermarine's Spitfire dispersal programme of the summer of 1940, the Ministry of Aircraft Production took over a number of garage company premises in Newbury. These produced fuselages, wings and sub-assemblies for the final erection sites at Chattis Hill, Henley and Aldermaston. Two new factories were built for Supermarine in 1941 and these works were still in use in the early 1950s.

ELLIOTTS OF NEWBURY

Elliotts of Newbury had been established in 1895 as joinery firm, and later became a furniture manufacturers. In 1940, the company's Albert Road premises were taken over by the Ministry of Aircraft Production on behalf of Supermarine for production of major Spitfire parts. These were then delivered to one of the final assembly sites. Due to its woodworking experience, Elliotts was also involved in subcontract work for Airspeed on Horsas and Oxfords – reportedly contributing 30 per cent of total Horsa components. Elliotts also supplied de Havilland with Mosquito parts and Walrus II hulls for Saro at Cowes. Following the woodworking experience with Horsas, Elliotts then built major Hamilcar sections under subcontract for General Aircraft and Harris Lebus.

Following the return to peace, Elliotts found that the Board of Trade would not allow it to resume furniture-building, due to the shortage of necessary materials. Wood was still regarded as a strategic material. However, for some reason, the

During the Second World War, Elliotts was heavily involved in producing major wooden sections for Hamilcar and Horsa assault gliders. Hamilcar parts were supplied to General Aircraft or Harris Lebus, who completed construction of the gliders.

company was able to continue building gliders. It was not until 1948 that the company returned to furniture-making.

Using the pre-war German DFS Meise design as a basis, Elliots developed the Olympia range of high-performance gliders, marketed under the EoN title – Elliotts of Newbury. It was a single-seat, wood-and-fabric design of standard 15 m span for club use. Initially, the Olympia was to have been built by Chilton Aircraft at nearby Hungerford, but it only completed BGA434 in 1945. Elliotts' prototype, BGA501, flew in January 1947 from White Waltham and, with an initial sale price of £425, soon proved popular with competition pilots. By April 1947, orders for twenty-five had been received. Under the chairmanship of Horace Buckingham, Elliotts' directors anticipated a high demand by private owners for gliders, as opposed to powered aircraft. As a result, production of 100 AP5 Olympias commenced, the majority being test-flown from nearby Welford airfield. Olympias VV400 and VV401 were supplied to ETPS at Cranfield in the summer of 1947, and the glider was exported to Australia, Denmark, India, Malaya and USA. As well as civilian gliding clubs, Olympias were also widely used by RAFGSA. Hoping to boost sales, Elliotts fielded its range at the Radlett SBAC Show of 1947 and at Farnborough in 1948.

Elliotts also built the Newbury AP4 Eon in conjunction with its associate company, Aviation & Engineering Projects. A three-seat, single-engine monoplane suitable for glider towing, its wooden construction was based on Elliotts' glider-building experience. Prototype G-AKBC was built in 1947 and flown on 8 August from Welford. A more powerful four-seater was proposed as the production version, with a sale price of £1,750. Although a further prototype was intended, the Eon did not proceed, as there was insufficient demand at the time from the UK private market. G-AKBC was then used for aerial delivery of new Olympias

Elliotts commenced production of the Olympia high-performance glider early in 1947. Anticipating high demand, the company optimistically started a production batch of 100. Seen here in the summer of 1949 is G-ALJZ – an Olympia 1.

Elliotts entered the world of powered aircraft in 1947 with the Newbury Eon. Prototype G-AKBC was a three-seater, although the production version would have had four seats. A depressed UK market at the time brought an end to the Eon.

to their purchasers. This included three Olympias for the Royal Danish Air Force in the spring of 1950. During the delivery of the final one, the Eon crashed at Lympne during a pilotless take-off in April 1950.

As well as Olympias, from 1947 Elliotts also built large numbers of AP7 Primary Eon and AP8 Baby Eon gliders. The Primary was the wartime German SG-38 basic glider updated by Elliotts; BGA577 first flew in February 1948. As well as the civilian market, ten were supplied to the RAF in 1951 for *ab initio* training as the Eton TX1. Primaries were also exported, and the customers included India and Pakistan. Production totalled ninety, but not all were sold. Later, Slingsby Sailplanes also produced a version of the SG-38, which was known as the T38 Grasshopper in RAF service. The Baby was a version of the pre-war German Grunau Baby 2B glider. It first flew in February 1948, and fifty were built. (Pre-war, a few Grunau Babies had been built in England by Slingsby.) The majority of these various gliders had been built in anticipation of orders that were not received. So, in the 1950s, there was a large store of completed Olympias and Babies at the Albert Road Works awaiting sale. At the time, Elliotts still undertook subcontract work for other aviation companies.

From 1947, Elliotts produced a range of private-owner gliders and sailplanes. The Baby Eon was based on the German Grunau Baby of the 1930s and G-ALRH, an early production aircraft, is seen here still active at Lasham in August 1986.

Olympia 460 prototype G-APWL in flight over Hampshire. Designed to take part in the World Gliding Championships, it first flew from Lasham in 1960 but did not enter production, since it was superseded by the Olympia 463.

Elliotts continued with glider construction, eventually producing a further fifty Olympias in the mid-1950s. Olympia 2 G-ALNF was rebuilt in 1954 as the improved Olympia 4 – later known as the Olympia 401. 1957 saw the improved 17 m AP6 Olympia 403, but only the prototype G-APEW was built. It was followed in the spring of 1958 by the 15 m Olympia 415 G-APLS and the 19 m high-performance 419 G-APLD. In 1960, Elliotts was still completing Olympia 2Bs at a price of £850 and producing a batch of ten 419s at a price of £2,150.

From 1959, Elliotts designed and produced a number of high-performance Standard Class machines for use in the annual World Gliding Championships. The first new design was the AP10 Olympia 460, with prototypes G-APWL and G-ARFU tested at Lasham in 1960. A production batch of fifty was planned, but in the event none were built. The 460 design was improved on in 1962 by the 463 – a standard 15 m glider, with a fibreglass nose and fabric-covered fuselage. It was first flown in April 1963, and forty-eight were built at an initial price of £1,000, along with two similar 465s especially for the 1965 Gliding Championships.

Mr Buckingham died in the summer of 1965, at which time a staff of twenty were employed on the glider-building side of the company. The remaining Elliotts directors decided to concentrate on furniture-making and so the rights to the Olympia 463 and product support were sold to Slingsbys in the spring of 1966. No further production was undertaken.

Old Sarum

Old Sarum, to the north of Salisbury, was originally a First World War RFC airfield. It still retains its original hangars and has never had a hard runway added. The military moved out in the mid-1970s, giving way to the expansion of light aviation.

EDGLEY AIRCRAFT LTD

In the 1970s, John Edgley developed his idea of an observation aircraft fitted with a unique bubble cockpit that gave the all-round vision of a helicopter, but at only a quarter of its operating costs. The prototype Edgley EA7 Optica G-BGMW was built at Islington and was first flown from Cranfield on 14 December 1979. It was a three-seater powered by a 160 hp Lycoming-ducted fan engine situated between the tail booms. Having proved the idea, John Edgley formed Edgley Aircraft Ltd to undertake Optica production. The company took over Old Sarum in May 1982, and set up production in one of the original hangars. Twenty-five Opticas had been ordered by an Australian distributor in July 1981 and there were plans to build seventy aircraft a year. Powered by a 260 hp Avco Lycoming engine, the first production aircraft G-BLFC flew on 22 August 1984 and became the demonstrator aircraft. It had a sale price of £140,000, and orders stood at eighty by the following year. However, production continued at a slow rate due to financial difficulties, and the company was forced into receivership in October 1985. At the time, only two Opticas had been delivered.

OPTICA INDUSTRIES LTD

Optica Industries was formed with new management in December 1985 to continue producing the retitled OA7 Optica. In the spring, funding of £2 million was being sought from the US, with anticipated sales of a refined aircraft reaching forty-eight a year. The first new delivery was G-FORK in June 1986.

With the airfield to the left, prototype Optica G-BGMW flies over the newly acquired Edgley hangars in May 1982. Production was underway by 1984. The hangars to the left of G-BGMW's cockpit are those destroyed in the arson attack of January 1987.

Limited work continued until the night of 16 January 1987, when the hangar and production line was destroyed by an unknown arsonist. Eight Opticas and many jigs were destroyed, and Optica Industries said it would start up production again. In the end, lack of finance resulted in the project being taken over by Brooklands Aerospace.

BROOKLANDS AEROSPACE GROUP plc

Brooklands Aerospace was formed in February 1987 and the first 'new' Brooklands Aerospace OA-7 Optica Scout appeared at the end of the year. Its sale price was still £140,000, with one sold to Hampshire Police in November 1987. A Scoutmaster electronic surveillance version was announced in September, but not developed, although G-BMPF was displayed at Farnborough in September 1988 as the Brooklands Scoutmaster. Six Opticas were sold to a Kansas distributor in July 1989 (price now $225,000), with the first delivered in November. Another was ordered by a Japanese distributor. It was Brooklands' intention that parts be built by UTVA in Pancevo, Yugoslavia, to reduce costs.

The prototype Trago Mills SAH1 arrived in September 1989, with Brooklands announcing it would also produce the trainer from the following summer, now

Left: A close-up of the 'bug-eyed' cockpit section of on Optica in the production hangar during Brooklands Aerospace ownership. Regrettably, Brooklands' various plans for Optica production came to nothing, and a receiver was appointed in the spring of 1990.

Below: Brooklands' Optica G-BMPF was acquired by the Hampshire Police at the end of 1987. Although there was interest in the Optica, Brooklands was unable to find a production site or finance. Hampshire Police continued aerial surveillance using an Islander.

marketed as the Brooklands Venture. Originally the SAH1 was to have been produced by Orca Aircraft, but they went out of business in August 1989. The aircraft's designer, Sydney Holloway, agreed that Brooklands could produce his design as the SHB1 (Sydney Holloway Brooklands). However, Orca said that it owned the rights and blocked production from going ahead at Old Sarum.

In April 1989, Croplease Ltd acquired the rights to the Fieldmaster crop-sprayer/water-bomber from NDN Aircraft of Cardiff. Croplease arranged for Brooklands to re-engine Fieldmaster G-NACL with a more powerful PT6A turboprop. It became the Firemaster 65, and was flight-tested in France in the summer of 1989. Through Brooklands contacts in Yugoslavia, a further five

In 1989, Brooklands re-engined an NDN Fieldmaster on behalf of Croplease with a more powerful PT6 engine. Now known as the Firemaster 65, it undertook fire-fighting trials in Southern France in the summer of 1989.

aircraft were to be built by UTVA and assembled by Croplease at Sandown, NDN's former home. The civil war in Yugoslavia at the time brought an end to the proposal. Croplease was unable to proceed with any production plans for the Fieldmaster, and so it sold the rights in 1994.

Brooklands said they had orders for the Optica Scout, but lack of cash prevented production of either the Optica or Venture. These production problems saw Brooklands Aerospace enter receivership in March 1990, and it was acquired by FLS Aerospace in the summer.

FLS AEROSTRUCTURES

FLS Industries A/S was a major Danish company that undertook aircraft overhauls, with FLS Aerospace (Lovaux) being one of its UK subsidiary companies. In July 1990, the company formed an Aerostuctures Division in the former Brooklands hangars at Old Sarum to relaunch the Optica. At the Farnborough Air Show in September, G-BOPN was displayed under the Lovaux banner, but later appeared with FLS titles. For a couple of years, FLS also produced aircraft components and structures for the aviation industry. FLS also intended to produce the SAH-1, but further, limited production of both types was undertaken at the Hurn (Bournemouth) site, where the production jigs were taken in the summer of 1992. FLS then closed its Old Sarum factory.

Portsmouth

The City of Portsmouth decided to develop a municipal airport in the late 1920s. To the north of the city, it was officially opened on 2 July 1932. There were three grass runways, and a terminal and hangars on the southern side. Airspeed arrived at the airport in the spring of 1933. The airfield closed in December 1973, and the redeveloped site is now known as Anchorage Park.

AIRSPEED LTD

When the Portsmouth Corporation proceeded with the construction of the airport, it was its intention to attract aircraft manufacturers as well as airlines. A large hangar was made available at a generous rental, and this was brought to the attention of Airspeed Ltd. The company had been formed in York in March 1931 under the directorship of Hessell Tiltman and Neville Shute Norway, who commenced work in a converted bus garage. They were soon joined by Sir Alan Cobham, who was looking for a rugged 'airliner' to undertake joy flights at his Flying Circus displays. Tiltman came up with the design of the AS4 Ferry a three-engined, ten-seat biplane, and Sir Alan ordered two in June 1931. Two of the engines were mounted on the lower wing, with the third on the upper wing. The Ferry was capable of short take-offs and landings, and was able to operate from smallish fields. Room in the garage proved rather tight in 1932, given the two Ferry aircraft under construction; this was eased when the first was flown in April 1932. In August, the directors confirmed to the Portsmouth Corporation that they wanted to move to Portsmouth, and so construction of the hangar on the south-east side of the airfield commenced in December. It was completed the following spring, with Airspeed moving south in March 1933. As well as tools and equipment, the almost-complete second Ferry also arrived by road. G-ABSJ was soon finished off. It flew in May and was delivered to Cobham's Flying Circus the following month. Two further Ferries were produced in 1933 for Midland and Scottish Air Ferries.

The Ferry was an ungainly-looking aircraft, but Tiltman had already designed a better-looking successor – the AS5 Courier. Construction of the prototype had

When Airspeed moved to Portsmouth in 1933, it brought the first Ferry, which had flown at York the previous spring. A 'basic' airliner, three more were built by Airspeed at Portsmouth, with two used by Sir Alan Cobham's Flying Circus.

commenced at York, but G-ABXN was moved to Portsmouth for its first flight on 11 April 1933. The Courier was a single-engine, low-wing five/six-seater and was the first British airliner fitted with a 'retractor undercarriage'. For this novel idea, much ground testing was undertaken to prove that retraction would be satisfactory. Despite Airspeed having been in business for only a short time, there was much interest in the Courier. The first production aircraft, G-ACJL, was delivered in September and the type entered airline service in May 1934. In September, G-ABXN was flown by Sir Alan Cobham on a non-stop demonstration flight to India by means of air-to-air refuelling. After take-off, the Courier was refuelled over the Solent before heading to Malta for a second refuelling link-up. Then Sir Alan found the throttle was not responding and had to make an emergency landing at Hal Far, ending the record attempt. In October 1934, G-ACJL took part in the England-to-Australia Air Race, and came third in the handicap section. Although this was good publicity for Airspeed, the company still had problems selling some of its stock of Couriers. So three were leased at favourable rates to the locally based Portsmouth, Southsea and IoW Aviation – a move that aided both firms. The final two Couriers were G-ADAX and G-ADAY, which were delivered to PS & IoW in April 1935. However, the final delivery was one of the earlier produced aircraft, which was not delivered to North Eastern Airways until February 1937. K4047 was used for research purposes by RAE Farnborough, who found it so easy to land that it was returned to Airspeed so that flaps could be added to make its wings less 'clean'.

The move to Portsmouth and production of the Courier put a financial strain on Airspeed by the summer of 1933. Ways of obtaining further capital were sought. This resulted in the Swan Hunter Group becoming a major shareholder

Courier G-ACLF nears completion at Portsmouth in the summer of 1933. This was the first of the Colonial version powered by an AS Cheetah engine. At the time there was insufficient demand for a full-scale production line.

The Courier was the first production airliner fitted with a retractable undercarriage. It could also be fitted with a variety of engines. Lynx-powered K4047 was supplied to RAE Farnborough in the autumn of 1935 for research purposes.

in July 1934; the reorganised company became Airspeed (1934) Ltd. This guaranteed continued production of the Courier and its follow-up, the Envoy.

Clearly based on the Courier, the AS6 Envoy, promoted as 'the Modern British Aircraft', was supposed to be powered by two Wolseley engines and to carry six to eight passengers in a comfortable cabin. The go-ahead was given in November 1933 for an initial production batch of six, the first of which, G-ACMT, flew on 26 June 1934. Although a civil machine, it still undertook trials at Martlesham Heath. G-ACMU appeared in August as the Viceroy, which was a one-off machine modified to take part in the England-to-Australia Air Race. The cabin had no windows. It was fitted with additional fuel tanks to supply the supercharged AS Cheetah engines. The attempt in October failed when the Viceroy had to retire after only getting as far as Athens. A Wolseley-engined version was being tested by Airspeed as V21 in the summer of 1935 and was joined by a Lynx-engined version V23. The Envoy entered airline service with North Eastern Airways in April 1935 and overseas sales included Czechoslovakia, France, South Africa and Japan – where it was built under licence by Mitsubishi. Three were delivered to the South African Air Force in the summer of 1936. These were fitted with an upper gun turret and underwing bomb racks, and were later modified for aerial survey work. An Airspeed advertisement of the time claimed, 'Conversion from luxury airliner to fast medium bomber in eight hours.' G-ACVI was delivered to Lord Nuffield named 'Miss Wolseley'. Airspeed had close connections with Lord Nuffield of Wolseley Motors and it was intended that Wolseley's engines would be used for the Envoy. Luckily, early ones had been fitted with other engines as, in September 1936, Wolseley suddenly pulled out of the aero engine business. So late-production Envoys flew either with Armstrong Siddeley Lynx or Cheetah engines. It was soon seen by Airspeed as an advantage for the airliner to be powered by a variety of engines, thereby offering choices to customers. Airspeed had been asked if it would undertake production of the Wolseley engines, but Swan Hunter, as majority shareholder, did not want to expand into the aero engine business. The Envoy II of 1935 introduced underwing flaps to reduce the aircraft's landing speed. The Envoy III was announced in January 1937, with Airspeed promising a four-week timescale for delivery. A major coup for Airspeed was in March, when a VIP Envoy III was ordered by the King's Flight. It was delivered as G-AEXX in June. G-AFJD and G-AFJE were handed over to the RAF in the summer of 1938 as N9107 and N9108, and were then shipped to Delhi for use as VIP transports. The majority of Envoys had been delivered by the end of 1937, but some airframes remained unsold. So, in January 1939, the RAF agreed to take the final five Envoy IIIs for delivery in the spring and summer.

In January 1935, Airspeed increased its share capital in connection with a forthcoming agreement with Fokker of Holland relating to the Douglas DC-2

Following on from the Courier was the twin-engined Envoy; the likeness is obvious. It first flew in June 1934. Sales were obtained worldwide, including this VIP version in the spring of 1937 for use by the King's Flight.

airliner. Fokker was Douglas's European agent, assembling aircraft shipped across from America, and the agreement was for Airspeed to build DC-2s and market them in the UK and the British Empire. Under the agreement, Anthony Fokker became a technical adviser for Airspeed. Airspeed allocated designation AS23 to the DC-2, with registration G-ADHO allocated in May 1935. There was a possible order for twelve from British Continental Airways in 1936, but at the AGM in December it was announced that Airspeed was no longer going ahead with plans for a large airliner based on Fokker and Douglas ideas. So no further work was undertaken on the AS23.

Staying with airliners, Airspeed designed the twin-engined, high-wing AS14 Ambassador airliner in 1936. A mock-up was completed at Portsmouth, but the aircraft was never built. An extension to the factory had been completed during the year, and was initially used to undertake subcontract work. The downside was that it was situated at the southern end of one of the runways, which had to be taken out of use. Despite having only been producing aircraft at Portsmouth for four years, Airspeed felt confident enough to submit a design to meet an Air

The Envoys supplied to the South African Air Force were unusual as they were armed. The upper gun turret can be seen. The aircraft was also fitted with underwing bomb racks. 253 is seen here on arrival in South Africa in the summer of 1936.

Ministry 1936 requirement for a twin-engined trainer. This resulted in the AS10, an all-wood aircraft based on the Envoy with a well-laid-out cockpit and ample cabin space. The initial plan was to use the Wolseley engine, but in the event, the AS10 was powered by the Armstrong Siddeley Cheetah X, which served it well. The Air Ministry were rather concerned about placing an order with a relatively new company, but in October 1936 placed an order for 136. In January 1937, the AS10 received the name Oxford, with the first aircraft, L4534, flying on 19 June. It was on show at the Hendon Display at the end of the month and the first RAF aircraft were handed over in November. In the summer of 1938, five were delivered to the Royal New Zealand Air Force and many more followed. Flying training schools equipped with Oxfords were established in a number of Commonwealth countries. Deliveries to the RCAF commenced in the spring of 1939, to the South African Air Force in the autumn of 1940, and to the RAAF at the end of 1940. The initial Oxford Is were general-purpose trainers, but the Oxford II was fitted out as a pilot, navigator and radio trainer. The Oxford III was a one-off, powered by Cheetah XV engines, and the IV was not built. The Oxford V was flown in 1941 powered by P&W Wasp Junior engines. 191 were built at Portsmouth and, as they had American engines, they were all shipped to flying schools in Canada. In July 1940, two ambulance versions were ordered by the Ministry of Aircraft Production and delivered to the RAF, but there was no follow-up order. Further large orders were placed for the Oxford, but there was no way that Airspeed could produce them all at Portsmouth. So, in June 1938, it was arranged that 200 would be built by de Havilland; the total would later exceed 1,500. Around the same time, an order was placed with Percival Aircraft for an initial 100 (for some reason cut back to twenty-five). Percival's final total was 1,350. Finally, Standard Motors were brought into Oxford production early in 1940, initially for 300 – later 750. Production at Portsmouth peaked early in 1942, with seventy-five a month produced.

Developed from the Envoy, the Oxford came along at the right time to meet the RAF's training requirements. Since it was of all-wood construction, it could be produced quickly by unskilled workers. It remained in production at Portsmouth from June 1937 until July 1945.

The Airspeed directors naturally felt pleased with the success of the Oxford. Having broken into the military market, they submitted designs for five other Air Ministry specifications. Unfortunately, all proved to be a let-down, no doubt to the frustration of the Airspeed directors and design team. First was the AS27 special defence aircraft, with prototypes K8846 and K8847, capable of slow-flying and powered by Wolseley engines, ordered in 1936. But the AS27 project was soon cancelled, following a change in Air Ministry requirements.

Second was the AS30 Queen Wasp, designed to a 1935 specification for a radio-controlled pilotless target aircraft. At the time, DH Queen Bees were being used by the RAF in this role, but the Air Ministry wanted a more reliable aircraft. Despite its anticipated limited flying life, Airspeed came up with a tubby biplane aircraft powered by an AS Cheetah with a cabin that could easily accommodate four. It looked more like an executive aircraft of the time, such as the Beech 17. Two prototypes were ordered in May 1936, and K8887 flew on 11 June 1937, appearing at the Hendon Show later in the month. K8888 followed

Early production Oxfords in service with No. 3 FTS at South Cerney in the summer of 1938. Initially the aircraft were painted yellow overall, then with top surface camouflage from 1939, then with overall camouflage from 1940.

on 19 October and was sent to Lee-on-Solent in June 1939 for the fitting of floats for further trials. It first flew as such on 4 July 1939. Flight trials on land and at sea showed problems at low speed, but otherwise the Queen Wasp fitted the requirements. An initial production batch of sixty-five was ordered, but delays meant that P5441 did not fly until 29 March 1940. By then the requirement had disappeared and the order was cancelled. The first five aircraft were delivered to the RAF's Pilotless Aircraft Unit for trials in 1942, with the rest scrapped.

The third new design was to an October 1937 Admiralty requirement for a carried-based aircraft for shadowing enemy shipping at night. For this it would need to fly silently at slow speeds, have a long endurance and be able to fit on a carrier. The design emerged as a rather ridiculous-looking aircraft, the AS39 Fleet Shadower (sometimes referred to as the Night Shadower). It had high-mounted folding wings, triple fins, a high-mounted cockpit, four 130 hp engines and a prominent fixed undercarriage. Two prototypes were ordered in 1938, but delays with design and construction meant that N1323 did not appear

The Queen Wasp was an impressive-looking aircraft, considering its intended fate was to be shot down. The first prototype is seen here at Portsmouth in the summer of 1937, along with Chief Test Pilot George Errington.

The second Queen Wasp was fitted with floats in the summer of 1939 and undertook trials from Lee-on-Solent. The first production aircraft were just appearing from Portsmouth when the requirement was cancelled – the RAF continuing to use Queen Bees.

The Admiralty's 1937 requirement for a 'fleet shadower' led to the ungainly AS39. Delays over considering the real need for such an aircraft meant that the prototype did not fly until the autumn of 1940. Only limited flight trials were undertaken.

A close-up of AS39 Fleet Shadower N1323 at Portsmouth in 1940. Having been faced with a demanding specification, the Airspeed designers came up with an aircraft that flew, only to have the project cancelled a few months later.

The Cambridge trainer was another unsuccessful design from Airspeed. It had been felt that there would not be enough advance trainers for the RAF in the early days of the war, but a sufficient number were ultimately available.

until August 1940. Its first flight was on 17 October and demonstrated that the strange design was underpowered and had extremely poor flying characteristics. The second prototype was not completed and the Fleet Shadower project was cancelled in February 1941. The Airspeed team was not too disappointed, as it had been faced with an impossible design requirement. Chief test pilot George Errington was also thankful, as he had doubts about the aircraft's airworthiness. A competing design was the General Aircraft GAL38, but, again, this did not progress beyond a prototype.

The fourth design appeared to have more promise. In July 1939, the Air Ministry requested an advanced trainer to supplement the Masters and Harvards that were entering service with the RAF. Two prototypes of the AS45 Cambridge were ordered from Airspeed. The design bore some resemblance to the Harvard, but was notable for its very small fin and rudder area. Prototype T2449 was flown on 19 February 1941, with T2453 following in August. By this time it was realised that sufficient numbers of Masters and Harvards were available and there was no need for the Cambridge. After unimpressive flight tests, the two prototypes were passed to the RAE Farnborough in July 1942.

The final design was the AS49 single-seat fighter trainer to Specification T24/40. By now Airspeed's design team had moved to Hatfield, as Portsmouth was considered in the front line of possible German attacks. The AS49 was an all-wood design powered by a 295 hp Gipsy Six engine and, following completion of a mock-up at Hatfield, prototype BS750 was ordered in 1940. This was soon followed by an order for fifty, but the project had to be abandoned following a bombing attack on Hatfield in October 1940 that destroyed the mock-up and plans. One can imagine the despair of Airspeed's design staff following all their efforts.

Airspeed had become involved with de Havilland in the summer of 1938, when it was arranged that Oxford production would to be undertaken at Hatfield. This led to de Havilland taking financial control over the company in June 1940, when it bought out Swan Hunters shareholding. De Havilland brought in its own board members, with Alan Butler as chairman. As already mentioned, the project design staff had moved to Hatfield. Other wartime changes brought about swift expansion for Airspeed. The Ministry of Aircraft Production had built a shadow aircraft production factory at Christchurch in 1939–40 and asked Airspeed if the company would run it. Having agreed, Airspeed undertook additional Oxford production at Christchurch.

When bombed out of Hatfield, the design staff moved into Salisbury Hall at London Colney, along with the de Havilland designers. In January 1941, work started on Airspeed's next project – a troop-carrying assault glider to Air Ministry Specification X26/40. The result was the AS57 Horsa, with prototypes DG597

Airspeed's Portsmouth factory was situated on the south-east side of the airfield, adjacent to Langstone Harbour. Gradual expansion of the site has resulted in an apparent clutter of small buildings being added to the original factory.

Airspeed directors and RAF VIPs gather in front of Oxford I RR382 at Portsmouth on 14 July 1945. This was a ceremony to mark the handover to the RAF of the last of 4,411 Oxfords produced at Portsmouth during the previous eight years.

and DG600 completed by the summer. Designed to be split into sections for ease of construction and movement, they were both taken to Fairey's Great West Aerodrome, and DG597 took to the air on 12 September 1941 behind a Whitley tug. Further pre-production prototypes were completed at Christchurch and Portsmouth in readiness for trials, but there was no spare capacity at Portsmouth for full-scale production. One of the aims behind the Horsa was that, as it was made out of wood and designed in small sections, it could be made by outside contractors who were used to dealing with wood. So it was that the vast majority were to be built by the London-based furniture manufacturers Harris Lebus. An initial order for 300 was placed in 1941 and the glider sections were then taken to an RAF Maintenance Unit for assembly and flight-testing. A further 100 were then ordered from the Austin Motor Company, who had spare production capacity. However, Horsas were also built by Airspeed at its Christchurch site, where production commenced in 1942. In April 1941, the Ministry of Aircraft Production asked that the Horsa design be adapted as a bomb-carrying glider

Post-war, many surplus RAF Oxfords were converted for other operators. G-AITB was one of a number used by AST at Hamble from 1947 for pilot training. It survived these duties and today is preserved with its original RAF marking, 'MP425'.

with a typical load of four 2,000 lb bombs. This resulted in the AS52, which had a bomb bay under the centre fuselage. Prototypes DK346 and DK349 were ordered and an order of 200 was anticipated, but in the end the Ministry did not proceed with its plans.

In January 1944, the company's name was changed from Airspeed (1934) Ltd back to the original Airspeed Ltd, with reference being made in publicity material to its affiliation with de Havilland. Airspeed was involved with RAF Dakotas, receiving FZ564 in February 1944 as its trials installation aircraft. However, work on Dakotas was undertaken at other locations, presumably RAF Maintenance Units. Portsmouth continued with full-scale Oxford production throughout the war. Luckily, the factory did not suffer enemy bombing as the rest of the city did. Portsmouth's final Oxford, RR382, was handed over to the RAF on 14 July 1945, just prior to the end of the Second World War. The handover ceremony was attended by the seventh production aircraft originally delivered in January 1938. Between November 1937 and July 1945, Portsmouth had built

4,411 Oxfords – an average of 588 a year, or forty-nine a month, figures more likely with fighter production. Post-war, many surplus RAF Oxfords were sold to overseas air forces. Some were direct from RAF stocks, with others overhauled by Airspeed. These included nine for Turkey in 1947 and fifteen for Burma in 1949–50. De Havilland arranged for Airspeed to build Mosquitoes, with an initial order placed for 300 FBVIs. RS637 flew from Portsmouth in March 1945 and the first half-dozen of the order were completed at Portsmouth. The rest were built at Christchurch, as had been de Havilland's original intention.

Well before the end of the Second World War (some reports say as early as 1940), Airspeed was thinking of further uses for the Oxford. Little work was needed to turn it into a post-war feeder airliner. The AS65 Consul – 'junior member of the Airspeed family' – was aimed at charter airlines as well as private owners and business executives. Minor changes saw additional cabin windows, a luggage compartment in the nose, and a partition between the five-seat cabin and pilots. With large numbers of often-unused Oxfords at RAF Maintenance Units, Airspeed was able to buy them back at rock-bottom prices. As such they were able to offer a fully equipped Consul for only £5,500, plus radio equipment. Portsmouth undertook the first conversion at the beginning of 1946, and it flew as G-AGVY in March. Sales were brisk, with orders received from all over the

Airspeed quickly developed the Consul in 1945 by converting many surplus Oxfords that the RAF no longer needed. As a feeder airliner, it carried five passengers, with others used as VIP transports. The basic version was offered for sale at £5,500.

An aggressive variant of the Consul was produced for the Burmese Air Force in 1949. UB345 was one of a number fitted with underwing rocket rails and is seen here at Portsmouth prior to delivery in the spring of 1950.

A number of Consul variants were offered by Airspeed. Fitted with an enlarged door, the ambulance version could carry two patients on stretchers. Limited sales included three to the Turkish Air Force in 1947.

Almost-complete Comet I fuselages were built at Portsmouth for incorporation into the Hatfield assembly line. In the mid-1950s, de Havilland also undertook work on Vampire, Venom, Sea Venom and Sea Vixen wings.

world – Congo, Indochina, Jordan, Spain, Sweden. 150 were converted within eighteen months, but conversions slowed up in the final months. A number were retained by Airspeed for communications duties and a fleet of five was delivered to the Ministry of Civil Aviation for airfield calibration duties. Three were delivered to the Turkish Air Force in 1946–47 for ambulance duties, ten to Argentina, and five to Israel, but those supplied to the Burmese Air Force early in 1949 were different. They were fitted with under-fuselage gun pods and underwing rocket projectiles. UB339 was tested at Boscombe Down with live firings of its eight underwing rockets in October 1949. Consul orders dried up by the end of 1948, at which time there were a number of unconverted Oxfords left lying around at Portsmouth and Christchurch. What may not have been realised at the time of the last Consul's handover was that it was the final complete aircraft to be delivered and flown away from the Airspeed factory.

After the Oxford and Horsa, the name of Airspeed will always be associated with the elegant Ambassador airliner. The wartime Brabazon Committee, set up to study the future of British civil airliners, recommended a DC-3 replacement. This

The Airspeed name disappeared from Portsmouth in 1951 when the company was absorbed into de Havilland Aircraft. At the time it was building major sections of the Comet I fuselages for Hatfield. Here, a nose is ready for departure.

was defined in their 1943 Type II specification and Airspeed was invited to submit a design, aided by de Havilland. The design team had moved from Salisbury Hall to Cobham, Surrey, in 1943 and design work commenced under Arthur Hagg. The AS57 started out as a forty-seat, high-wing, twin-engine airliner, but Hagg felt that the specification was short-sighted and that greater capacity would be needed. So the AS57, now named Ambassador, emerged with forty-eight seats. Prototype 'Transcontinental Air Liners' G-AGUA and G-AGUB were ordered by the Ministry of Aircraft Production in September 1945, by which time the design team had moved to Christchurch. Due to the restricted size of the grass airfield at Portsmouth, Airspeed decided to undertake development and production at Christchurch, although Portsmouth did build a fuselage for static test purposes. Major parts of production aircraft, such as flying surfaces, were also completed at Portsmouth and taken by road to Christchurch. G-AGUA visited Portsmouth on 17 June 1948 so that the local workers could see the results of their labours.

Portsmouth remained the Headquarters of Airspeed, with the business and design team based at Christchurch. The ties with de Havilland meant that there was plenty of work for the Airspeed factory, even before the Consuls were finished. De Havilland were building large numbers of Vampire fighters and its Venom replacement. So Airspeed was brought in to produce major assemblies for these fighters. In addition they were involved with the Comet airliner, producing a number of complete fuselages for the Hatfield production line.

In May 1948, de Havilland bought the outstanding Airspeed shares and so became the sole owner. This resulted in boardroom changes again, although the company still continued as Airspeed 'in association with de Havilland Enterprise' for another three years. In June 1951, the Portsmouth and Christchurch factories officially became the Airspeed Division of de Havilland Aircraft, and the de Havilland name appeared outside the factories.

PORTSMOUTH AVIATION LTD

When Portsmouth Airport opened, airline services were provided by the grandly titled Portsmouth, Southsea & Isle of Wight Aviation. Services ceased on the outbreak of the Second World War, and the company became a Civilian Repair Organisation involved in aircraft overhauls and repairs. Much of this work was undertaken on behalf of Airspeed in handling Oxfords, and it was also done in premises they had at Christchurch airfield.

In February 1943, the company was reorganised and renamed Portsmouth Aviation Ltd. Some airline services were operated post-war, but the company also moved into aircraft construction. In January 1946, it revealed details of the Aerocar series of four multi-purpose light twin aircraft, a mock-up having already been built. Designed by Major Luxmoore, these were of a high-wing, twin-boom layout, with a pod cabin area. The Minor would house four passengers, and the Major six – both having a retractable undercarriage. The Senior and Junior versions would have more simplified equipment and be fitted with a fixed undercarriage. An advertisement of June 1946 showed a likeness of Minor G-AGNJ. Work on two prototypes – a Minor and a Major – commenced in 1947. However, work on the Minor was halted and overtaken by the Major, which was seen to have greater sales prospects. In December 1946, there was talk of Portsmouth taking over space at Shorts Rochester factory for production of the Aerocar, but nothing came of this. The wood-and-metal prototype G-AGTG, powered by two Cirrus Majors, flew on 18 June 1947. Portsmouth Aviation announced there was much interest in the design, which, in its production version, would be all-metal. As well as Portsmouth, a new factory was to be built in Port of Sikka, India, and in September it was reported that there were 288 orders worth £2 million. The Indian plans faltered at the last moment, when the

Portsmouth Aviation had grand plans for a range of light twin aircraft, with the passengers housed in a central pod fuselage. Only the prototype of the Aerocar Major flew in the summer of 1947, with production plans thwarted by lack of capital.

country gained independence, and, combined with lack of capital, the Aerocar did not progress beyond the prototype stage. It appears to have continued flying until 1950.

Portsmouth Aviation continues in the aerospace business, providing aviation support equipment and vehicles. This work is undertaken from their original site, despite the airfield having closed at the end of 1973. Currently the company provides defence equipment to all three UK armed services.

DE HAVILLAND AIRCRAFT CO.

When the Airspeed name disappeared in June 1951 following its absorption into de Havilland, the site consisted of the main factory – No. 1 plant – and the smaller No. 2 plant. The Portsmouth factory continued to supply major assemblies for Hatfield, including Vampire and Comet 1 fuselages, with Vampire

The Airspeed factory had been built large enough to enable major Trident 1 fuselage sections to be produced for Hatfield in the late 1960s. This is the final one in 1968, marked, 'In loving memory. RIP Pompey.' Its completion heralded the closure of the factory.

and Venom wings from the No. 2 plant. In 1956 it produced fuselage assemblies for the Comet 4. There was plenty to keep the workforce busy, although there was no longer any flying activity. In 1960, de Havilland Aircraft became part of Hawker Siddeley, and the factory proclaimed itself 'Hawker Siddeley Aviation – De Havilland Division'. National cutbacks in aircraft production meant less work for the Portsmouth factory. At the time they were producing Sea Vixen wings for Christchurch, followed by Trident 1 forward-fuselage sections for Hatfield. The site was put up for sale, but there were no takers. So Hawker Siddeley closed the site in the summer of 1968, marking the end of aircraft production at Portsmouth. Eventually, the site was sold off and cleared for redevelopment as an industrial park.

Salisbury

There was no airfield at Salisbury, only the RAF airfield at nearby Old Sarum. However, the city was to play an important part in Spitfire production during the Second World War.

VICKERS-SUPERMARINE

Salisbury was one of the locations chosen by Supermarine in the summer of 1940 as part of its dispersed Spitfire production network. The garage premises of Anna Valley Motors, Wessex Garage and Wilts & Dorset Bus Company were requisitioned by the Ministry of Aircraft Production in 1940. Additional new premises were built at Castle Road to the north of the town, near Old Sarum Castle. Fuselages from Wessex Garage and Castle Road, wings from Wilts & Dorset, and tail units from Anna Valley were taken to either High Post or Chattis Hill for assembly and flight-testing.

Initially, Spitfire Vs were produced, with the first delivered to High Post in the spring of 1941. Other marks produced within Salisbury were VIII, XII and XIV. These were followed by various marks of Seafire. From the spring of 1944, the Spitfire and Seafire components were delivered to Chattis Hill, as High Post had a new role as Supermarine's flight development unit. Spitfire production within the city at Salisbury ran down with the return to peace, although the Castle Road premises remained in use for a while longer. The wings of the Seagull amphibian prototypes were built there in 1947 and taken to Hursley Park for joining to the fuselages.

Garages around Salisbury were typical of the dispersed sites set up by Supermarine for Spitfire and Seafire production. This view of work underway on fuselage assemblies is probably at the newly built Castle Road premises.

The Wilts & Dorset Bus Garage in the centre of Salisbury was another of the sites taken over by Supermarine towards the end of 1940. Fuselage and wing construction can be seen in this view; the completed sections are ready for transportation to High Post or Chattis Hill.

The larger premises at Castle Road enabled Supermarine to set up full-scale production lines, initially of Spitfire Vs, prior to the major sections being taken to Chattis Hill for assembly and flight-testing.

Sandown

Known locally as Lea Airport, the airfield opened at Easter 1935 as 'Isle of Wight Airport', with airline services operated from London and Southampton. It replaced the earlier Apse airfield at nearby Shanklin. The airfield was closed during the Second World War, reopening afterwards for private flying and limited airline services. It almost closed in October 2010 for redevelopment, but hangs on as an unlicensed airfield.

NDN AIRCRAFT LTD

The company initials referred to Nigel Desmond Norman, one of the founding directors of Britten-Norman at Bembridge. He established NDN Aircraft in 1976 to develop the NDN1 Firecracker high-performance trainer. The company's initial HQ was at Goodwood, where prototype G-NDNI, powered by a piston engine, flew on 26 May 1977. It appeared at the Paris Show the following month before undertaking development flying. NDN moved to Sandown in the summer of 1981 and occupied two purpose-built hangars on the south side of the airfield. Eventually, a P&W PT6A turbine version was built, with G-SFTR flying on 17 December 1981. NDN was hopeful of obtaining an RAF order for a new trainer to replace the Jet Provost. Work started on an initial production batch of five in 1982, but only G-SFTS and G-SFTT were completed. NDN realised that it would have insufficient capacity at Sandown to build these aircraft, and so entered into an agreement with Hunting at East Midlands in 1983 whereby they would build the RAF aircraft. Firecracker Aircraft (UK) Ltd was formed in anticipation of large-scale production, but the contract was awarded to the Short Tucano. The three Firecrackers were delivered to Specialist Flying Training at Carlisle in 1984, and eventually ended up in the USA, along with the prototype.

As well as the Firecracker, NDN also developed the NDN6 Fieldmaster, which was a large, crop-spraying aircraft also powered by a PT6A turboprop. Backed by the National Research & Development Corporation, a mock-up was built at Goodwood in the summer of 1980 and annual sales of thirty to forty aircraft

The prototype Firecracker was built at Goodwood in 1977 as a high-performance military trainer. The next stage of its development was as a possible COIN aircraft, with G-NDNI displayed as such at the 1980 Farnborough Show.

Re-engined with a PT6 turboprop, the Firecracker suited the RAF's need for a Jet Provost replacement. A batch of five was commenced at Sandown in 1981, with G-SFTR being the demonstrator seen here in the summer of 1984.

The Fieldmaster was a dual-role crop-sprayer/water-bomber, with the prototype flying from Sandown in December 1981. It was large machine with limited production undertaken by Norman Aircraft on its move to Cardiff in 1985.

The design of the Fieldmaster saw the pilot seated to the rear of the main tank, which was situated behind the PT6 engine. It is seen here on trials over the Solent with the water pick-up apparatus lowered, in readiness for the refilling of the tanks.

Norman Aircraft took over the Britten-Norman Nymph and rebuilt it as the Norman Freelance at Sandown. Still a four-seater, it was now intended for factory production – the company still anticipating a need for the design.

were anticipated. The prototype was built in 1981 and flown from Sandown as G-NRDC on 17 December. The project moved to Cardiff in the summer of 1985, where, under the reorganised Norman Aeroplane Co., it was redesignated the NAC6 Fieldmaster. Production aircraft G-NACL–CP were built there in 1986–87, but the company went into receivership in July 1988.

NDN also became involved in the Freelance light aircraft. While with Britten-Norman, Desmond Norman was involved in the Nymph, which did not progress beyond the prototype stage. NDN acquired the stored airframe, modified it, and installed a 180 hp engine. Fitted with folding wings, it was intended for storage within a normal garage. Reregistered G-NACI, the NAC1 Freelance first flew from Sandown on 29 September 1984. When the firm moved to Cardiff, a production batch was started, but only G-NACA was completed; it was flown in 1987. Five fuselages were built but never assembled as completed aircraft.

A small production batch of Freelances was undertaken at Cardiff when Norman Aircraft moved there. However, only G-NACA was completed and flown in 1987. Major assemblies of a further five then spent the next few years 'touring' the UK looking for a buyer.

SHERIFF AEROSPACE

Following his departure from Britten-Norman, John Britten formed Britten Aviation Technical Services in 1976 and set about the design of a light twin training aircraft. Named the Sheriff, details were announced in the spring of 1977, but John Britten died unexpectedly in July 1977. The project was continued by his brother Robin, who formed Sheriff Aerospace. In February 1980, it was announced that the prototype SA1 Sheriff would be built by Aircraft Designs Ltd at nearby Bembridge Fort. With four seats, it was aimed at company operators and the training market, with anticipated annual sales of 100 at a price of only £32,500. This was the tourer version, which was powered by two 160 hp Lycoming engines. The proposed trainer version had less power and only two seats. It was not intended that production would be undertaken by Sheriff Aerospace, but by a larger organisation. In view of the Romanian connections with the Islander, discussions were held for possible production by CNIAR in Romania. Construction of the prototype was protracted due to financing problems, and G-FRJB was 90 per cent complete when the receivers were appointed in January 1984. Although the first flight was only a couple of months away, funding had run out at a vital moment and the Sheriff project was cancelled. After a period of storage, the incomplete prototype was donated to the East Midlands Aeropark in 1986.

The ARV Super 2 was a compact two-seater planned for factory or home construction. The prototype was flown from Sandown in March 1985 and G-STWO was the demonstrator aircraft. Problems with the engine led to delays and loss of orders.

The cockpit of the Super 2 allowed easy access to the cockpit, but was rather cramped for two reasonably sized people. G-BNGY was one of a small number of aircraft operated by the Southern Aero Club at Shoreham in the late 1980s.

ARV AVIATION

The brainchild of Richard Noble, the ARV-1 Super 2 twin-seat light aircraft was designed for both factory and home construction. ARV Aviation was formed in December 1983, and took over a hangar on the north side of Sandown Airfield for the development of the Super 2. ARV stood for 'Air Recreational Vehicle' – a description then coming into vogue in the United States. Prototype G-OARV flew on 11 March 1985, followed by G-STWO, which showed excellent flying characteristics and ease of handling. At the time, it was estimated that annual sales could reach 200 at a competitive price of £26,000. Initial aircraft were powered by a Hewland AE75 two-stroke engine, but problems with the engine led to a slowdown in Super 2 production. Major problems with the propeller shaft were found at the end of 1987, and they took time and money to resolve. Lack of finance led to cash-flow problems, with a receiver appointed in June 1988, at which time just over thirty Super 2s had flown. Due to the engine problems, a private owner re-engined his aircraft in 1991 with a Rotax 912, and other owners followed suit.

ISLAND AIRCRAFT LTD

Island Aircraft was formed by a former ARV management team in the summer of 1988 to take over Super 2 production, initially at Sandown. The anticipated sale price was still £26,000. Later, at the Farnborough Air Show, it was announced that production would continue in Scotland and Aviation (Scotland) Ltd was formed in 1990 for this purpose. As with ARV, the Super 2 would be available factory-built or in kit form – the latter version being known as the Highlander. Progress was slow and in 1993 it was announced that Scottish-built kits would be shipped to Sweden for assembly by ASL Aero, who would market the Super 2 as the Opus 280. Later, full production would be undertaken by ASL, and Opus SE-KYP, powered by a Rotax 912, was completed by the autumn of 1994. In fact, it was a reworked and re-engined Super 2. Work stopped for some time due to certification problems, but commenced again in the spring of 1995. This was short-lived as, in September, ASL Aero went into receivership.

In 1995 it was announced that the Highlander kit version would now be produced by Highlander Aircraft in Minnesota, USA, with N280KT flying in February 1996. Also in America, Opus Aircraft was launched in Storeville, North Carolina, to continue production of the Rotax-powered ARV/Opus under the name of Opus Super 2. Two original ARV-built aircraft were imported as demonstrators N630A and N870A and FAA certification was obtained in

February 2008. However, no new aircraft appear to have been sold by either Highlander or Opus. Back in the UK, a number of ARVs continue to fly with either Hewland or Rotax engines.

CLARK-NORMAN AIRCRAFT

Desmond Norman returned to the Isle of Wight in 1995 to join with Alan Clark in the development of the Triloader freighter. A cross between a Trislander and Short 360, with a wingspan of 80 ft, this utility freighter was to be powered by three 600 hp PT6 turboprops. As well as large side doors, the nose was hinged for ease of freight-loading. Announced in August 1995, the prototype was to be designed and built at Sandown, with first flight anticipated in August 1997. Series production would be undertaken elsewhere, probably Belgium, but the project did not proceed due to lack of finance.

Another project of Desmond Norman in 2002 was the Weekender ultra-light two-seat biplane. Intended for home construction, it featured folding wings to enable the aircraft to be stowed in a lightweight container for ease of transport.

South Marston

A greenfield site to the north-east of Swindon was selected by the Ministry of Aircraft Production for a 'shadow factory'. Built in 1940 for use by Phillips & Powis, it was also used by Shorts Brothers and Vickers-Supermarine. Two hard runways were provided for production test-flying.

PHILLIPS & POWIS AIRCRAFT LTD

In the 1930s, the company produced the wide range of Miles aircraft at its Woodley factory, near Reading. Upon the receipt of large-scale wartime orders, there was lack of capacity at Woodley. So Phillips & Powis made use of the new South Marston factory for production of the Miles Master advanced trainer. The planned size of the factory was reduced and further sites were added nearby – thereby reducing any possible damage from enemy attack. Many of the workers were recruited from Swindon's railway works.

The first production Master flew from Woodley in March 1939 and the first from South Marston in the following spring. At times, production levels of Master IIs and IIIs reached eighty aircraft a month, with the final one delivered to the RAF in the spring of 1943. A total of over 900 were produced at South Marston. Early wartime advertisements of Phillips & Powis described themselves as based 'somewhere in England'. Reorganisation within the company in 1943 saw it become Miles Aircraft, named after the directors and now based at Reading.

With the anticipated run-down of Master production, overhaul work on Spitfire Vs commenced in the summer of 1942. From the following spring, thirty were converted into Seafire IBs, commencing with PA100. The factory passed to Vickers-Supermarine in the spring of 1943.

Large numbers of Miles Master were ordered by the RAF and Phillips & Powis was unable to cope at its Woodley site. The Ministry of Aircraft Production sanctioned the building of a new factory at South Marston. W8656 was a Master III delivered in 1942.

The all-wood construction of the Master meant that assembly could be undertaken by workers from outside the aircraft industry. Phillips & Powis took on staff from the Great Western Railway works, where the company had built wooden coaches or wagons.

As well as the Master, South Marston was used for the production of Short Stirling bombers from the beginning of 1942. This was to make up for the loss of production facilities at Rochester at a time when the RAF was desperate for heavy bombers.

SHORT BROTHERS (R&B) LTD

Shorts was well known for the production of flying boats and had received wartime orders for its Stirling bomber. Following the bombing of the Stirling production line at the Rochester factory in August 1940, the Ministry of Aircraft Production decided that production would be switched to South Marston. These were to be Wright Cyclone-powered Stirling IIs, as opposed to the initial Bristol Hercules-powered Stirling Is. Two prototype Stirling IIs were built at Rochester in 1941, but this version did not enter production. It was the Stirling III that was eventually built at South Marston – powered by the Hercules. Production was spread around the various factory sites – fuselages built at Blunsdon and Sevenhampton, with the flying surfaces at the Great Western railway works in Swindon. Final assembly was carried out at the new FS2 site at South Marston.

The first South Marston Stirling was delivered early in 1942, with deliveries eventually reaching sixteen a month. This total had slowed by the beginning of 1943, when it was anticipated that Stirling production would be succeeded by Avro Lancaster bombers. In the event the factory was turned over to fighter production.

The South Marston site passed to Supermarine in 1943 for production of the later Spitfire variants. This was to provide additional capacity to Castle Bromwich. F21s appeared from the beginning of 1944, followed by F22s (seen here) from March 1945.

VICKERS-SUPERMARINE

Despite the number of factories that were producing Spitfires in 1942, the Air Ministry saw the need for still more. So when a new version was designed by Supermarine it was decided to set up production at a new Spitfire site – South Marston. With the ending of Master and Stirling production, the two factory areas were taken over by Vickers-Supermarine in April 1943 as a satellite of its Castle Bromwich site. This was for production of an updated Griffon-powered Spitfire – the Victor. Orders were placed in June 1943 for 1,500 Victor F21 high-altitude fighters to be built at South Marston and Castle Bromwich. Due to opposition, the Victor name was dropped in November 1943, and the fighter was known as the Spitfire F21. Although a major redesign of the original aircraft, it still looked a Spitfire. The first production F21, LA187, was completed in January 1944 and taken to High Post for its first flight. 120 production aircraft were built at South Marston, and they were followed by the F22. Similar to the F21, this

The later Spitfires were too late for wartime service. As a result, production of F22s and F24s in 1946 was at a slower pace. Note the need for a female workforce. By this date, the factory had been purchased by Vickers-Armstrongs from the MAP.

version had a cut-down rear fuselage for better pilot vision. The first, PK312, was completed in March 1945 and flown from High Post. Production at Castle Bromwich continued until the site closed in December 1945, then switched to South Marston. Vast numbers of Spitfires were cancelled at the end of the war, including F21s and F22s. Production of the two versions at South Marston totalled 287.

The prototype Spitfire F21, PP139, was rebuilt with a new high-speed wing as the F23 high-altitude fighter and flown in the summer of 1944. It was supposed to enter production as the Valiant F23. As with the Victor, although there was a new name, the mark number followed on in the Spitfire sequence. In view of other Spitfire improvements, the Valiant was not proceeded with. It is interesting to speculate what – had both the Victor and Valiant entered service in 1946 – the RAF would have named its V-bomber force a few years later.

As well as Spitfires, South Marston was also involved with Seafires later in the war – initially the fixed-wing F45, the naval equivalent of Spitfire F21. The

As the Spitfire evolved, so did the Seafire. The ultimate versions were the F46 (fixed wing) and F47 (folding wing), both with Griffon's contra-rotating propeller. Pilots found it difficult to see over the large nose.

aircraft were built at Castle Bromwich, but were transported to South Marston for final assembly and flight-testing. The original order was greatly reduced, with only fifty completed, commencing with LA428 in January 1945. The F45 was regarded as only an interim version, to be followed by the F46. In the event, only twenty-four were completed, commencing with LA541, which was flown in June 1945. The F46 still had fixed wings, but was fitted with contra-rotating propellers to counter the power of the Griffon engine. This improved take-offs and landings for the pilot.

VICKERS-ARMSTRONGS LTD

In October 1945, Vickers-Armstrongs purchased the South Marston site from the Ministry of Aircraft Production for £500,000, and it became the company's 'Aircraft Section – Supermarine Works'. There was still plenty of Spitfire and

The final mark of Spitfire was the F24; VN479 was a late production aircraft. Its shape may have undergone many changes since the Mk I of 1938, but to everybody it is still a Spitfire, despite the MAP trying to impose the name Victor in 1943.

Seafire work to occupy the 450,000 sq. ft works and hangars. They continued to be refered to under their Supermarine name.

The final mark of Spitfire was the F24, which was similar to the F22. In fact, the final twenty-four F22s were completed as F24s, followed by new production aircraft from VN301. The aircraft were built at Vickers Trowbridge site, but were delivered to South Marston for final assembly. The first converted F24, PK678, flew in February 1946; the final one, VN496, in February 1948. Again, large numbers were cancelled.

Following on from the Spitfire was the Spiteful; initial aircraft were built at High Post in 1945. At the time, there were 800 on order, but this total was gradually reduced. The Spiteful F14 had only just entered production at South Marston in the spring of 1946 when the order was cancelled – the RAF was now re-equipping with Meteor and Vampire jet fighters. Commencing with RB522, only sixteen were completed, to be flown from High Post and South Marston.

The ultimate version of the Seafire was the F47, which appeared in 1946. Its price was quoted as £8,900 – the same as the first Spitfire Is from Woolston. As had always been intended with the later Seafires, these were fitted with folding wings and contra-rotating propellers. PS944 first flew in April 1946 and the last of ninety, VR972, flew in January 1949. Production of these final aircraft was not a swift process. The later aircraft were produced as FR47s. This final version of the Seafires was too late for the Second World War, but saw action during the Malaysian Emergency of 1949 and the early days of the Korean War in 1950.

In the same way that the Spiteful was intended to replace the Spitfire, so the

Seafang was to replace the Seafire. Vickers was informed by the Ministry of Aircraft Production that 150 of the cancelled Spitefuls could be completed as Seafangs. The first ten would be pre-production F31s, followed by production-standard F32s. Again, these orders were cancelled in favour of the development of jet fighters and, out of the 150, only Seafangs VG471–79 were flown from High Post from January 1946. They were only used for limited experimental flying.

Post-war, refurbishment of surplus aircraft was also undertaken at South Marston. Twelve Seafire IIIs were converted back to Spitfire VCs for the Irish Air Corps in 1946–47, with the first delivered in January 1947. Sweden was supplied with fifty Spitfire PR19s in 1948–49 as Cold War tensions built up with Russia, and Egypt received twenty F22s in 1950. In conjunction with the Eastleigh factory, twenty Spitfires were converted into trainer versions. Walruses and Sea Otters were also refurbished, including five Sea Otters for the Dutch Navy in the winter of 1949/50. In 1949, South Marston built the fuselage of Viscount prototype G-AMAV on behalf of Vickers' Weybridge site, where it was mated with the wings that had been built at Itchen.

The Supermarine E10/44 jet fighter entered production for the Royal Navy as the Attacker. An original order for eighteen 'Naval E10/44 Fighters' was

The first jet fighter to enter RN service was the Attacker, developed from the Supermarine E10/44 prototypes. Seen here in the summer of 1950, this is one of the early F1s; it was followed into service in 1952 by the improved FB2 version.

The Attacker's wing layout was based on that of the Spiteful. In 1950, a de-navalised version was ordered by the Pakistan Air Force. Three of the aircraft are seen here during a flypast over Karachi shortly after delivery in 1952.

placed in November 1945, but was cancelled three months later in favour of Sea Vampire F20s. A fresh order for sixty Attackers was placed in November 1948, as the Royal Navy had no suitable jet fighter in prospect. These were fitted with four 20 mm guns and powered by a Rolls-Royce Nene. The first production F1 aircraft, WA469, flew from South Marston in April 1950 and was followed by the fighter-bomber FB2 version in April 1952. A total of 148 Attackers were built for the Royal Navy. The Pakistan Air Force placed an order for thirty-six of a de-navalized version in 1950, and the first flew in July 1950. The final Pakistan Attacker was delivered in March 1953; the final Royal Navy one in March 1954.

Vickers' plan was that by the early 1950s all aircraft production would be undertaken at South Marston, with the other sites closed. But this changed with the outbreak of the Korean War. The Swift fighter followed the Attacker, with orders for 100 (commencing with WK194) having been placed by the RAF in November 1950 as a back-up for the Hunter. The outbreak of the Korean War saw the need for more RAF fighters, with both the Swift and Hunter ordered into 'super priority production' in 1952. The first Swift to be built at South Marston was WK196 – the third production F1 aircraft. To increase numbers, 140 were ordered from Short Bros of Belfast in April 1951. The Swift was introduced into RAF service in February 1954 while modifications were still being introduced on the production line. Hence twenty F1s were followed by sixteen 'improved' F2s with four 30 mm cannons, then twenty-five 'better' F3s. These were to be followed by the main production version – the F4. But only the first few had been completed when the RAF withdrew the Swift from service in March 1955 due to handling problems and cancelled the orders with Supermarine and

Shorts. Supermarine also discovered that the F4's reheat did not work at high level – not very satisfactory for a high-performance fighter. This seemingly left Supermarine with a line of unwanted Swift fighters. However, it had also been selected as a low-level reconnaissance aircraft with cameras in an extended nose; F1 WK200 flew as prototype FR5 in June 1953. So most of the partly finished F4s were completed as FR5s in 1955, and they were followed by new-build aircraft. They proved most useful for the RAF in their new low-level role. The Swift PR6 was intended for high-level operations, but was cancelled before the prototype flew. This was due to the fact that while in RAF service, the fighter version had been shown wanting at high level. The final Swifts were a batch of F7s for guided missile development trials. Originally, seventy-five F7s had been ordered, but most were cancelled in March 1956, leaving only the trials aircraft. Two pre-production aircraft were followed by the first of twelve production aircraft in August 1956. The final Swift built at South Marston was F7 XF124, which departed in July 1957.

Supermarine had worked on designs for a twin-engined naval strike aircraft in the late 1940s and early 1950s, resulting in a number of experimental prototypes. From the Supermarine 525 was developed the Supermarine 544, which became

Attacker FB2 WK338 on display at the Farnborough Air Show in September 1952. Due to its relatively low power, provision could be made for the fighter to be fitted with rocket take-off equipment, as seen here, for safer operations from carriers.

Despite the failings of the Swift as an interceptor fighter, Supermarine developed a low-level reconnaissance version for the RAF. WK275 is one of the FR5s delivered to the RAF from 1956 onwards. The aircraft proved successful in its low-level role.

Another version of the Swift to see service was the F7. Twelve aircraft were built for development trials of the Fairey Fireflash guided missile. As can be seen, one was carried under each wing, with trials undertaken at RAF Valley in 1957.

After a number of designs for a twin-engined naval fighter, Supermarine evolved the Scimitar. Although ordered in December 1952, the first production aircraft did not fly until January 1957. Development flying was mainly undertaken from Wisley.

The Scimitar fighters for the Royal Navy were the final aircraft built at South Marston, with the last flying in 1960. It was the last 'gunned' fighter used by the Navy, as Sea Vixens delivered around the same time were equipped with missiles from the start.

the Scimitar, built to naval requirement N113D. 100 were ordered for the Royal Navy in December 1952, and, although three prototypes were built at Hursley Park, production aircraft were built at South Marston. The fighter had been officially named Scimitar by the time the first production aircraft XD212 flew in January 1957. In the event, the order was reduced to seventy-six, with the first aircraft delivered to the Navy in August 1957. The final Scimitar was delivered in January 1961 and it proved a capable aircraft in naval service. It was the final aircraft type to be produced at South Marston.

In 1956, Vickers moved its main drawing office to South Marston, with staff gradually moving up from Hursley Park prior to its closure. Following a review of Britain's aircraft industry, Vickers announced in September 1958 that, after

Vickers entered the world of hovercraft in 1960. The VA1 was a research vehicle that was tested at South Marston in the autumn of 1961. Although only able to hover, it carried aircraft-style 'B Condition' registration G-15-252.

the Scimitar, all aircraft work would be transferred from South Marston to Weybridge, leaving a reduced staff of 1,700. The final design being worked on was the Type 571, a twin-engined tactical bomber that was the forerunner to the TSR2, which was fully developed by BAC at Weybridge. In the future, South Marston would house an apprentice training school and be involved in the design and building of nuclear reactors. One of the first tasks of the apprentices was to build a Bensen B-8 gyrocopter. Upon the formation of British Aircraft Corporation in June 1960, the South Marston site did not join the new conglomerate. It became Vickers-Armstrongs (South Marston) Ltd, and announced that it was also to be involved in the diverse fields of hovercraft development and nuclear engineering.

Vickers-Armstrong (Engineers) Ltd Hovercraft Division was established at South Marston in July 1960, with the first project being the VA-1 research hovercraft G-15-252. It was 'flown' in October 1961 to confirm the theory and was soon followed by the larger VA-2, which was considered suitable for overseas

To provide more practical experience, the larger VA2 followed in 1962. Early testing was carried out around South Marston airfield before the move to Itchen, where waterborne trials were undertaken on Southampton Water.

As the next stage of its hovercraft development, Vickers produced the VA3 in 1962. Again, after initial hovers at South Marston, it was taken to Itchen for sea trials. As can be seen, large, vertical vanes were required in order to maintain directional control.

In 1985, the South Marston site was purchased by Honda UK for car production. This successful operation has seen the addition of many new buildings. However, as this recent view shows, the main runway is still visible.

demonstrations. More practical was the twenty-four-seat VA-3 G-15-253, which was completed in April 1962. Capable of sixty knots, it was powered by four 360 hp turbo-prop engines and, after initial trials on the airfield, was taken to the Itchen works for further sea trials on the Solent. Vickers set its sights on the much larger VA-4, which would carry 200 passengers or 30 tons of freight and was estimated could be ready by 1966. In March 1966, most of the hovercraft work being undertaken in Great Britain was supervised by the British Hovercraft Corporation. As a result, Vickers' hovercraft development work was transferred to the Itchen works, leaving Vickers Engineers at South Marston to carry on the historic name.

On 24 June 1967, the Vickers Group chose South Marston to host its centenary show flying display, with aircraft ranging from Gunbus to Scimitar. Vickers Engineers were still at the site at the time, and moved out in 1983.

In 1985, the former factory and airfield was taken over by Honda UK Manufacturing for car production. A large new factory was built on the western side of the airfield, leaving little trace of its aviation past. Part of the runway now forms a high-speed test track.

Tarrant Rushton

The airfield was built for the RAF in 1943 and handed over in May. During the Second World War it was used by airborne forces. The RAF moved out in the summer of 1946 and Flight Refuelling arrived the following summer. The airfield closed in the summer of 1980.

FLIGHT REFUELLING LTD

Flight Refuelling had always envisaged in-flight refuelling as a necessity for long-distance airline operations. Limited trials had been carried out in 1939–40 with BOAC C-Class flying boats. Further trials were undertaken with BSAA to Bermuda in the summer of 1947 and with BOAC to Montreal in the spring of 1948. During the period of these trials, Flight Refuelling's design office came up with its own proposals for flight-refuelable airliners. In the summer of 1948, for example, there were proposals for four-engined, long-range airliners. It is not certain if there was contact with other major aircraft companies, as there was no capacity or expertise to build them at Tarrant Rushton. There was a rapid change of direction for Flight Refuelling in the spring of 1949, when the USAF showed serious interest in flight refuelling. From then on, the company became involved in military refuelling contracts. However, it was some time before the RAF showed serious interest. Two Canberras were modified at Tarrant in 1955 to act as trials tankers, and they replaced an outdated Lincoln. Their bomb bays were rebuilt to accommodate a refuelling pod.

In the early 1950s, Flight Refuelling undertook subcontract work on behalf of Armstrong Whitworth to build rear fuselages for Sea Hawk fighters in production at Coventry. Construction was undertaken in wartime Nissen huts. This was followed in the mid-1950s by major overhaul work on RAF Meteors. As Gloster Aircraft was heavily involved with the Javelin, Flight Refuelling was given the task of rebuilding and overhauling second-hand Meteors for many overseas air forces.

Flight Refuelling became involved in an Air Ministry requirement for target drone aircraft. Initially, the plan was to use surplus Lincoln bombers, with

Flight refuelling trials for military jet aircraft revealed the need for a jet tanker. As a result, two Canberras were converted in 1953 to house refuelling drum units in their bomb bays. Later, as can be seen here, they were modified to carry a refuelling pod.

Flight Refuelling entered the world of aircraft production in the early 1950s. The company undertook the building of Sea Hawk rear fuselages for Armstrong Whitworth at Coventry. No major assembly buildings were used – just existing Nissen huts.

the first conversion RF395 flown in the spring of 1956. The Air Ministry then cancelled the project, turning its attention to a smaller aircraft. Initial trials had been carried out at RAE Farnborough with a Meteor in 1954. Flight Refuelling then received the contract to develop the system fully and convert surplus Meteor F4s for drone work as Meteor U15s. The first conversion RA421 flew in March 1955 and was followed by ninety-two further conversions. They were followed

Having overhauled many Meteors in the early 1950s, Flight Refuelling then undertook the conversion of Meteors into target drones. Initially Meteor F4s were converted into U15s, followed by F8s converted into U16s (later D16s), as seen here.

from September 1958 by over a hundred Meteor F8s, which were converted into U16 drones. Conversion work continued until the end of 1963, by which time the Meteors had been redesignated D16s.

In the 1970s, Flight Refuelling developed its Universal Drone Pack. This was installed in an existing aircraft's cockpit to quickly convert it into drone or pilotless configuration. Development work was undertaken on four surplus Sea Vixens in 1977–78, and the result was known as the Sea Vixen D3. The Air Ministry indicated that at least a further twenty-four would be required. In the end, the project was cancelled, as the Sea Vixen proved unsuitable in its new role. Tarrant Rushton closed in the summer of 1980, by which time Flight Refuelling had moved its equipment production facilities and UAV work to its site at Wimborne.

In the late 1970s, Flight Refuelling designed and built an Advanced Subsonic Aerial Target for Army-training purposes; it was later named Falconet. It had a pod-like fuselage with a Microturbo TRS18 turbojet mounted under the fuselage to give the target a maximum speed of 400 kt. It was first flown in February 1982 from a test site at Larkhill. Later versions had a more powerful TJA24 engine. In service the Falconet was launched from a circular 'runway' and recovered

In the late 1970s, the Army had a requirement for a sub-sonic target drone. Flight Refuelling produced the Falconet, which flew early in 1982 and was ordered into production for the Army. A prototype Falconet is seen here on its special launch trolley.

In the 1980s, Flight Refuelling designed the Phoenix UAV. This was a reconnaissance vehicle for the Army, and was launched from a special rig on the back of a lorry. Production was undertaken by BAe prior to final assembly by Flight Refuelling.

by parachute. Following twelve pre-production Falconets, an initial order for twenty-five was placed in 1984. Eventually more than 300 were built. A ship-launched version was first flown in February 1985, with the capability of a zero-length, rocket-assisted take-off.

The Phoenix reconnaissance UAV was developed in the late 1980s in conjunction with GEC Avionics. A contract was placed in 1985 for production on behalf of the Army, but the project suffered a number of development delays. With a span of 18 ft and a twin-boom tail unit, the Phoenix was powered by a 25 hp piston engine. As major subcontractor, Flight Refuelling, designed the Phoenix and its mobile launch system, but production was under the control of BAe Avionics at Rochester, with final assembly by Flight Refuelling at Wimborne.

Flight Refuelling expanded its activities into many countries in the 1990s. This led to a rebranding of all associated companies under the Cobham Group name in 2008.

Thruxton

The airfield was built for use by the RAF in the Second World War, and was also used by USAAF. Civil flying training commenced in 1947, one operator being the Wiltshire School of Flying. In the mid-1950s, a number of former RAF Tiger Moths were reconditioned here. Thruxton is now a thriving general aviation airfield.

JACKAROO AIRCRAFT LTD

With its experience of Tiger Moths, the Wiltshire School of Flying designed a modified version in 1956. The airframe was rebuilt to allow for a four-seat cabin area and retain the original wings and tail units. Alternatively, the enlarged cabin area could house a 60 gallon tank to feed underwing crop-spraying units. Jackaroo Aircraft was formed to undertake the conversion work. The first two conversions, G-AOEX and G-AOEY, received their Certificate of Approval in July 1957; G-AOEX entered service with the school and G-AOEY became the crop-sprayer demonstrator. In the summer of 1960, 'new' Jackaroos were advertised at £1,400 – or £800 for conversion of an existing Tiger Moth. The crop-spraying version would cost £1,827 10s. During the next two years, a total of eighteen Jackaroos were converted at Thruxton, plus, later, one at Croydon.

A number of the Jackaroos that survived into the 1980s were converted back to Tiger Moths by their owners. Tiger Moths were more historic and valuable than Jackaroos.

The follow-up to the Jackaroo was the Paragon four-seat ultra-light. This was announced early in 1959, with the intention of two prototypes being completed by the spring of 1960. The main version was a four-seater powered by a 175 hp engine. Later, a two-seater would be built, powered by a 125 hp engine. If sufficient orders were received, the Paragons' anticipated sale price was £2,500. An agricultural version with an 80 gallon tank was also proposed. In 1961, Paragon Aircraft was formed to continue development, a mock-up having been built. This differed from the original plans as it was fitted with a nose-

The Jackaroo was basically a Tiger Moth fitted with a four-seat cabin. It was devised by the Wiltshire School of Flying in the mid-1950s, and Jackaroo Aircraft was formed by the school to undertake the modifications at Thruxton. A crop-spraying version was also available.

A close-up of a Jackaroo fuselage shows the new cabin arrangement and wider fuselage. In later years, many Jackaroos were converted back into Tiger Moths due to their greater historical and financial value.

wheel undercarriage. However, the box-like design looked very basic – it was no match for the Cessnas that were available from America. The Paragon failed to attract orders (although it was still being mentioned in summer 1964), and the prototypes were never built.

As a follow-on to the Jackaroo, the Paragon was designed in 1959 with two prototypes reportedly under construction. However, only this mock up – which shows a rather basic design compared to contemporary American thinking – was completed.

In 2008, John Edgley re-acquired the rights to his Optica design and formed Aeroelvira with the intention of starting production again. The Optica was now offered as a multisensory surveillance platform, but lack of funding once again saw the project stall.

AEROELVIRA LTD

In the summer of 2008, John Edgley re-acquired the rights to his Edgley Optica design. He formed a new company, with some former Edgley personnel as directors. Its office was in Tisbury, west of Salisbury. Aeroelvira also acquired the rights to the FLS Sprint 160 and the Edgley EA9 Optimist high-performance glider. Hangarage was taken at Thruxton, where Optica G-BOPO was flying again in June 2008 under the Aeroelvira name as a multisensor surveillance aircraft. Lack of interest at home led to Aeroelvira seeking an overseas manufacturer for future production.

Trowbridge

There was no airfield at Trowbridge, but the town played an important part in Spitfire production during the Second World War. Flight-testing was undertaken from nearby RAF Keevil.

VICKERS-SUPERMARINE

Trowbridge was one of the locations chosen by Supermarine in the summer of 1940 as part of its dispersed Spitfire production network. A number of garages within the town were requisitioned by the Ministry of Aircraft Production in the summer of 1940, with production jigs soon arriving from Woolston. The garages soon proved insufficient for Supermarine's needs and so three additional premises were built for the production of Spitfire assemblies. The main site at Trowbridge was the Bolton Glove Factory, and in 1941–42 additional factory premises were built at Bradley Road for the completion of fuselages and wings. The various components were taken to the RAF airfield at Keevil, to the east of the town, where Supermarine had a hangar for assembly and flight-testing. Post-war the Keevil site continued to overhaul a large number of Spitfires.

Initial production was of Spitfire Vs, followed by IXs and XIIs. FRXIVs and FRXVIIIs were produced from early 1945, followed by F24s in the spring of 1946 (commencing with VN301). Trowbridge and Keevil were responsible for producing over 600 Spitfires. By 1947, many of Trowbridge's F24s were taken to South Marston for completion. The requisitioned premises were disposed of, but Supermarine still retained a factory in Trowbridge, producing Swift and Scimitar parts for South Marston. This was closed in the summer of 1958. Present-day 'memorials' to Trowbridge's wartime effort are the Spitfire and Merlin retail parks.

As with many dispersed Spitfire sites, Trowbridge soon ran out of sufficient production space. This resulted in a new factory at Bradley Road (seen here) being brought into use in 1943. After Spitfire production ended, Supermarine retained the factory until the mid-1950s.

A busy 1943 scene inside the Bradley Road factory with Spitfire components being produced. This view is typical of many of the dispersed sites around Wessex. Much of the work was undertaken by women, since the men were away fighting.

This view of a Trowbridge-built FR XVIII emphasises the powerful combination of the Griffon engine and a five-bladed propeller. This version remained in RAF service post-war, with many serving in the Far East.

Trowbridge-built FR XVIIIs continued in service with the RAF for a number of years. This one has lost its camouflage paint scheme and serves with 226 OCU at Stradishall. To the rear of the cockpit is the window hatch for the camera.

The Spitfire components built at Trowbridge were transported to nearby RAF Keevil. Here, Supermarine had its own large hangar for the final assembly and flight-testing of locally built aircraft, such as the FR XVIIIs in 1945, seen here.

Weston

Weston is close to the eastern shore of Southampton Water. There was no airfield, but the village, now 'lost' within the eastern suburbs of Southampton, was the site of aircraft production for a short while.

SIMMONDS AIRCRAFT LTD

Following the success of the Spartan biplane built by Oliver Simmonds at Woolston, Simmonds Aircraft was formed in September 1928 and premises were acquired at Weston for production of the aircraft. This factory had served from 1917 as the Royal Navy's Rolling Mill for the production of brass shell cases. Simmonds Aircraft and the Spartan were officially launched on 31 December 1928. The first production Cirrus-Spartan, G-AAFP, appeared shortly after and was taken by road to Hamble, where it was flown in March. It was offered at a price of £620, and orders were soon received, including twelve for National Flying Services for training at Hanworth. An April 1929 advertisement showed a Spartan in RAF markings, but none were ordered by the RAF. However, the Spartan was exported to Commonwealth countries including Australia, Canada, India and New Zealand. A few Spartans were completed as 'taxiplanes' with enlarged front cockpits to carry two passengers; they were priced at £735. Early aircraft were powered by the Cirrus engine; later ones were fitted with a 100 hp DH Gipsy or 100 hp ADC Hermes. Production continued at Weston until 1930, by which time forty-nine Spartans had been completed.

Reorganisation took place on 1 April 1930, with investment in Simmonds by Whitehall Securities, who became a 50 per cent shareholder. The company was then renamed Spartan Aircraft.

SPARTAN AIRCRAFT LTD

Under the Spartan Aircraft name, Spartan production continued for a while, but was superseded by the slightly larger Arrow. Powered by a DH Gipsy II engine, the prototype G-AAWY first flew from Hamble in May 1930. Sale price of this version was £710, but a Cirrus III-powered version was only £650. One other Arrow was completed at Weston before a move was made to the Isle of Wight. Whitehall Securities bought out Oliver Simmond's 50 per cent shareholding in Spartan and, as they already had connections with Saro, future Spartan aircraft were produced at East Cowes. The move to the Isle of Wight was completed by February 1931.

Simmonds Aircraft set up production in the former Naval Rolling Mill at Weston. Seen here outside the factory is the first production Spartan G-AAFP at around the time of its official launch in December 1928. Production continued at Weston until the summer of 1930.

The prototype Simmonds Spartan G-EBYU was built in the spring of 1928. Production aircraft soon followed from Weston, and fifty Spartans were built there before the company moved to Cowes.

Woolston

Situated on the eastern bank of the River Itchen at Southampton, Woolston was another of the boatyards in Wessex that turned its hand to aviation in the early 1900s.

PEMBERTON-BILLING LTD

Noel Pemberton Billing was a businessman with a strong interest in early aviation. He obtained his Aviator's Certificate in 1912 and later that year purchased a boatyard on the banks of the River Itchen, just upstream from the Woolston Floating Bridge. The yard produced yachts and fast launches, but Pemberton Billing had other ideas. He was to use the yard for the development of flying boats, and commenced work on the small PB1 in the autumn of 1913. The yard was extended in the winter of 1913/14 with additional workshops and a covered floating dock. The unflown PB1 was displayed at the Olympia Aero Show in March 1914 and, although exhibited on the Pemberton Billing stand, it carried the name Supermarine PB1. The Supermarine name was coined by Pemberton Billing to indicate that he was building supermarine craft designed for the navigation of the seas, as opposed to submarines. The name was also used as the telegram address for Pemberton-Billing Ltd, which was established in June 1914, the company adopting a hyphen to its name. The PB1 failed to take off from the Itchen in April 1914, its 50 hp Gnome providing insufficient power. A major rebuild was undertaken in May, during which the engine was remounted to drive two pusher propellers, but this layout still proved unsuccessful. The next design on which construction started was the PB7 Supermarine Flying Lifeboat. This was a biplane flying boat whose wings and tail could be discarded if it made an emergency landing, with a marine engine enabling the hull to reach land. An order for two was anticipated from Germany, but this disappeared upon the outbreak of the First World War in August 1914. Pemberton-Billing completed the hulls as launches. The company then decided to switch to land planes. Built to a Government order, the first Pemberton-Billing design to fly was the

PB9 scout fighter 1267, which flew from a local field in August. Publicity of the day stated that the Gnome-powered PB9 had been designed and built within a week, and it became known as the 'Seven Day Bus'. However, it failed to win orders from the RFC. Next to appear was the PB11 single-engined box-kite-style biplane 1374, which was powered by the same Gnome. It was followed by the small PB23E pusher scout biplane, with the pilot accommodated in a pod fuselage, which also housed the Le Rhône engine. The prototype 8487 was taken to Hendon for its first flight in September 1915. Twenty PB25 production versions, commencing with 9001, followed for the Admiralty, but a shortage of engines meant only a few flew. Records seem to indicate that the majority were scrapped without ever being assembled. The PB23E was followed by the large PB29E quadruplane fighter, which was intended for high-level operations by the Navy against Zeppelins. It was thought that the lift of the four wings would enable the fighter to reach a significant height, but the prototype was unsuccessful, crashing after only a few flights. Ironically, considering its intended target, it was powered by two Austro-Daimler engines. The PB31E NightHawk, a quadruplane with a span of 60 ft, was an improvement, and two were ordered by the Admiralty. Unusually for the time, the crew were housed in an enclosed cockpit and the aircraft was fitted with a powerful searchlight in its nose plus a 1½ pounder gun to bring the Zeppelin down. However, only NightHawk 1388 was completed; it was delivered to Eastchurch for its first flight.

As with many south coast aviation firms, Pemberton-Billing soon received an Admiralty production order, in this case for twelve Short S38 training flying boats, 1580–91, in 1915. Again, records indicate that these were either not completed or else not delivered. Changes were coming, as Pemberton Billing himself decided to follow a career in politics, and he departed Woolston in 1916. The company was now under the control of its works manager – Hubert Scott-Paine – who was appointed managing director in September 1916. Shortly afterwards, the firm was renamed Supermarine.

SUPERMARINE AVIATION WORKS LTD

The Supermarine Aviations Works Ltd was established in November 1916 and the 'new' company promoted itself as 'Designers and Constructors of Aircraft, also of speed boats and racing craft'. The Admiralty were happy to place contracts with Supermarine, the first being for 105 Norman Thompson NT2B trainer flying boats in 1917. While the first batch of thirty was being completed, the Navy order was cancelled and only about eighteen were delivered. A similar fate befell thirty Short 184s also on order, with only twelve delivered to the Navy and then probably

Pemberton Billing's first design was the PB1 flying boat. It is seen here at the 1914 Olympia Show in its original form with a tractor engine and propeller. As such, it was unable to take off from the Itchen and was modified with pusher propellers. It still refused to take off.

Pemberton Billing designed the PB7 as a combined launch/seaplane. In the event of an engine failure over the sea, the wings and tail would be discarded, leaving the cockpit to proceed as a launch. The aircraft was not completed and the idea was never put to the test.

not used. Three of the aircraft appear to have ended up being delivered to Estonia, but whether by Supermarine or the Admiralty is not certain. During the war, the Admiralty's Air Department designed its own flying boats, with Supermarine entrusted with the building of prototypes 1412 and 1413 of the AD Flying Boat. Powered by a 200 hp Hispano engine, the first flew in 1917. Batches totalling a further eighty were ordered but only a few had been completed by early 1918. The ADs proved both seaworthy and airworthy and influenced Supermarine's post-war fortunes. The majority on order were cancelled, with only a few delivered to the Admiralty, leaving a number on Supermarine's hands. Another design built by Supermarine was the AD Navyplane, which had the looks of a two-seater PB23E fitted with floats. Two prototypes were ordered, but only 9095 was completed and flown. The second was cancelled, as was a small production batch.

Another Pemberton-Billing design was the PB 31E of 1917, which was intended to attack raiding Zeppelins. A quadruplane, it was intended to undertake slow-speed, night-time patrols. The 'sun' on the nose is a searchlight, behind which is the crew's compartment.

Supermarine designed the N1B Baby in response to a requirement for a single-seat naval scout flying boat. Blackburn came up with a similar design and three prototypes were ordered from each manufacturer. The prototype Baby N59 flew in the spring of 1918, but a change of requirement meant that the second was delivered for spares use only, and the third was cancelled. Such were the problems for all aircraft manufacturers towards the end of the First World War.

With a return to peace, Supermarine was left with a number of ADs on its hands, and looked for other uses for them. As built, they had two open-air seats in the nose, but were easily modified to take three or four passengers. They were then known as the Channel. In addition to Supermarine's own aircraft, further ADs were acquired from the Admiralty, with ten registered as civil aircraft in spring 1919. Supermarine formed its own airline to operate the Channels. From July, services were flown from Woolston and Southampton's Royal Pier to Bournemouth and Cowes (fare £2 2s), then across the Channel to Le Havre from the end of August. Supermarine advertised these as the 'First Flying Boat Passenger Services in the World'. Channels were also used for 'airline' services in Norway, Bermuda, Trinidad and New Zealand. Military versions were supplied to Chile and Japan.

Supermarine built the two-seat Commercial Amphibian G-EAVE in the summer of 1920 to an Air Ministry requirement for a civilian seaplane. The competition

In conjunction with Admiralty designers, Supermarine produced the AD Navyplane in 1915. Intended as a reconnaissance bomber, the AD 1 was beset by engine problems, resulting in only prototype 9095 flying in the summer of 1916.

The Sea King of 1920 was intended as a single-seat seaplane fighter. This is the Sea King II of 1921, which had twice the power of the original aircraft. Modified as the Sea Lion II, it won the 1922 Schneider Trophy Contest at Naples.

in September was won by the rival Vickers Viking, and the Amphibian crashed in October. The Amphibian was followed by the Sea Eagle, which was based on the Commercial but with a new wing. The Sea Eagle housed six passengers and it first flew in June 1923. G-EBFK gained the company publicity when it was entered into the King's Cup Race in July. By this time, Supermarine had reorganised its airline services under the name British Marine Air Navigation Co., with the title 'Marine Airport' used for the Woolston terminal. Services using

A Supermarine Channel underway. The Channel was developed from the wartime AD Flying Boat, and a number were built in 1919–20. As can be seen, the pilot and passengers sat in an open cockpit in front of the lower wing.

The Channel was used by Supermarine's own airline in 1919 for services to Bournemouth, Cowes and across the English Channel to Le Havre. The type proved successful, with sales made to Japan, New Zealand, Norway and the West Indies.

The Sea Lion was a racing seaplane entered in the 1919 Schneider Races held at Bournemouth. Its Napier Lion engine gave a top speed of 145 mph, but G-EALP disgraced itself by crash-landing at the end of the race. However, it was the forerunner of other racing seaplanes.

three Sea Eagles to the Channel Islands commenced in September 1923, and from April 1924 they passed to the newly formed Imperial Airways. So ended Supermarine's entry into airline operations. The Spanish Navy ordered twelve of a developed bomber version of the Sea Eagle II powered by a Rolls-Royce Eagle and known as the Scarab. M-NSAA, the first, flew in May 1924, but the type saw little service in Spain. While being flown by a Spanish test pilot, one of the Scarabs crashed into the side of a liner in Southampton Water.

Supermarine built the Sea Lion, which was based on the unsuccessful Baby fighter, as a single-seat, single-engine racing flying boat to take part in the 1919 Schneider Trophy race, which was held at Bournemouth in September. In place of the Baby's 200 hp engine, G-EALP was fitted with a 450 hp Napier Lion, giving it a top speed of 145 mph. The race proved a fiasco, with G-EALP crash-landing at the end of the race. However, it did introduce Supermarine to the world of racing aircraft. Sea Lion II G-EBAH was built for the 1922 Schneider Race, held in Naples in August. Piloted by Henri Biard, the Sea Lion II won the race at an average speed of 145 mph, at one stage almost reaching 200 mph, which enabled Supermarine to promote it as the 'World's Fastest Flying Boat'. For the 1923 race at Cowes, Supermarine hastily prepared G-EBAH as the Sea Lion III with a

525 hp Lion engine and reduced wingspan. However, Biard was beaten by the US team, which had Government backing. The Sea Lion was handed over to the Air Ministry as N170 in December 1923 for trials as a fighting scout. Development of the Sea Lion racers was funded by Supermarine, whereas the overseas entries for the Schneider Race were all Government-funded.

Supermarine continued military development with the Sea King pusher flying boat fighter, which flew in the spring of 1920, but only two prototypes were built. Then followed the larger Seal, which was a fleet-spotter. N146 flew in May 1921, but only flew a short time in its original form. Lack of work in 1922 led to Supermarine considering reducing its workforce, but the Air Ministry considered Supermarine to be a valuable aviation asset and placed an order for eighteen of a developed Seal known as the Seagull. Seal N146 was rebuilt as the prototype, followed by two Lion-powered development Seagull IIs before delivery of production aircraft commenced in 1923. As a fleet-spotter, the Seagull was able to operate from aircraft carriers or be catapulted from capital ships. However, the Navy showed little interest, although six Seagull IIIs were supplied to Australia from February 1926, with one remaining in service until 1933.

An important event within Supermarine Aviation was the appointment of a young Reginald Mitchell as chief designer in 1919. His early work included the Sea Eagle and Sea Lion. At the same time, Henri Biard was taken on as Supermarine's test pilot; it was a post he held for the next few years. James Bird was also taken on as a pilot in 1920 and later joined the management team. Having guided the company for seven years, Hubert Scott-Paine sold his shareholding in 1923. Bird took over as managing director. Having shown his early ability, Mitchell became technical director of Supermarine in 1927.

The Sparrow was a two-seat, ultra-light biplane built in the summer of 1924 for the Light Aeroplane Competition later in the year. It was taken to Hamble for its first flight on 11 September and flown to Lympne for the competition at the end of the month. It did not perform well as it kept suffering engine failure. Although allocated the registration G-EBJP, this was not carried. Mitchell completely rebuilt it as a high-wing, parasol monoplane. As the Sparrow II, it was entered in the 1926 Light Aeroplane Competition, but fared no better than before. So it was pushed into a corner of the hangar at Hythe and forgotten about.

Supermarine's first twin-engine flying boat was the Scylla, with prototype N174 built to an Air Ministry order. It was delivered by road to Felixstowe early in 1924, but appears not to have flown. In December 1923, the Air Ministry ordered another reconnaissance flying boat – the Swan. Powered by two 450 hp Napier Lions, prototype N175 was flown on 25 March 1924 and later completed successful trials at Felixstowe. However, no order was placed, so the Swan returned

The Swan was built as a reconnaissance flying boat, but failed to win any orders. N-175, the prototype, was later used by Imperial Airways as an airliner. Further development of the design led to the Southampton, which was ordered in large numbers by the RAF.

to Woolston to be converted to carry ten passengers in comfort. Civilianised as G-EBJY, it flew again in June 1926, and was later used by Imperial Airways on its Channel Island services. The Air Ministry requested an RAF version of the Swan, which led to Mitchell designing the Southampton. Using his experience, the twin Napier Lion-powered reconnaissance flying boat was built to a high standard – which was appreciated by the RAF over the next few years. In fact, the first six Southamptons were ordered in August 1924 without the need for a further prototype, with N9896 first flying in March 1925. Following the existing boat design, these Southamptons were built with wooden hulls. However, the Air Ministry was already thinking of metal hulls and ordered an additional Southampton with a metal hull. N218 was built in 1925 as the prototype Southampton II, but in the meantime further wooden-hulled Southampton Is had been ordered. Trials with the Mk II showed the advantage of the metal hull and so all subsequent Southamptons were completed to this standard, with some of the earlier ones being converted. The initial Southampton Is entered service with the RAF in September 1925 and remained in service until 1936 – a long service life in those days. The RAF obtained publicity with the delivery of six Southamptons to its Far East Flight in Singapore. The aircraft left Plymouth

In RAF service the Southampton flying boats often undertook 'flag-flying' cruises, including to the Mediterranean and the Far East. Sometime the cruises were nearer to home, such as Bournemouth in the summer of 1926.

in October 1927, but on arrival in Singapore immediately departed on a tour of Australia. They finally returned to Singapore in December 1928 after covering 23,000 miles – an unprecedented feat for those times. Production totalling seventy-nine aircraft continued over a number of years and included eight for Argentina in 1929–30 and six for Turkey as late as 1934. Two were supplied to Australia and a single example to Japan. Interest was shown by Denmark, who wanted a three-engined flying boat capable of launching two torpedoes. The design was modified and Denmark ordered one in June 1926. Known as the Nanok, it was built and flown from Hythe.

The failure of the Sea Lion III in the 1923 Schneider Race was due to it being an outdated design outclassed by the new Curtiss racing floatplanes. Initially, Mitchell considered a further small flying boat powered by a 600 hp Rolls-Royce engine. Delays, mainly with engine development, led to the idea being abandoned in 1924. Mitchell then concentrated on a racing floatplane, with his new revolutionary Supermarine S4 given the go-ahead in March 1925 and completed at Woolston in August. The streamlined monoplane was nearly all wood, with the S4 powered by a 700 hp Napier Lion that should have given it a top speed of over 225 mph. After work commenced, the Air Ministry placed an official order for two S4s – N196 and N197. The S4 was first flown by Biard on 25 August and the lack of vision for the pilot was immediately obvious. However, this did not prevent Biard from breaking the seaplane speed record by attaining 227 mph in September. The S4 was shipped to Baltimore in October for the Schneider Race, which was marred by bad weather. Three days before the event, while being flown by Biard, the S4 crashed due to wing flutter. The race was won by the Americans at a speed of 234 mph. This setback did not deter Supermarine, although the second S4 was not built. The Air Ministry agreed to fund further development of high-speed flight in order to take on the Americans. In March 1926, it ordered three further racing floatplanes from both Gloster and Supermarine for the 1927 race. Mitchell's new design emerged as the S5, which was slightly smaller than the S4 and had a duralumin fuselage and floats, with wooden wings. Power was from a 900 hp Napier Lion, which promised an increased top speed of 320 mph. The S5s N219–21 were built at Woolston in the spring of 1927, with N219 delivered to Felixstowe for its first flight in June. All three were shipped to Venice for the race at the end of September, which was won by N220 at a speed of 282 mph, with N221 second. The 1929 race was held at Spithead on the Solent. Four new racers were ordered by the Air Ministry in May 1929 – two from Gloster and two from Supermarine. Mitchell's new S6s, N247 and N248, were slightly larger than the S5 and powered by a new Rolls-Royce R engine of 1,900 hp. Such power was only available for the short period of time. The race was held in September, with N247 the winner at 329 mph. A few days later it claimed the air speed record at 358 mph. The next Schneider Race was due to be held in 1931, but the Air Ministry said it would not be supporting it due to increasing costs. Supermarine, Mitchell and the British press soon picked up on the point that Britain would be able to retain the Schneider Trophy if the team won a third time. But the Air Ministry still said 'no', leaving it to millionairess Lady Houston to fund the building of racers for the 1931 event. The new aircraft were S6Bs S1595 and S1596, with the earlier N247/48 brought up to similar standard as the S6As. Float design was improved and Rolls-Royce produced an R engine giving 2,350 hp. S1595 first flew at the end of July 1931, and the race was held at Calshot on 13 September. Technical problems for the other teams meant that only Britain was able to fly on the day, with S1595 completing the course at 340 mph. Later in the day, S1596 raised the air speed record to 379 mph and on 29 September it broke the 400 mph barrier by setting a record of 407 mph. So, Supermarine triumphed with Mitchell's design, which meant that the Schneider Trophy was now retained by Britain. The Air Ministry finally gave up further high-speed flight development. At the present time, N248, is displayed at Solent Sky and race winner S1595 is at the Science Museum.

A quantum leap in design saw Mitchell produce the Supermarine S4 for the 1925 Schneider Race. Its sleek monoplane design drew much attention, but regrettably it crashed in October while preparing for the race.

Supermarine S5 N219 prepares for another test flight in 1927. Mitchell had learned a lot from his S4 design and improvements were incorporated in the new racing seaplane. Its companion, S220, won the Schneider Trophy Race at Venice in September 1927.

Supermarine S6B N1595 nears completion at Woolston early in the summer of 1931. The tight fit of the new Rolls-Royce R engine can clearly be seen. The S6B was the ultimate development of Supermarine's racing seaplanes.

S6B S1595 won the 1931 Schneider Trophy Contest with a speed of 340 mph. Later, S1596 took the world record with a speed of 407 mph. The winning of the Schneider Race meant that Britain retained the Schneider Trophy.

VICKERS-SUPERMARINE

A lack of capital within the company saw Bird sell out to Vickers (Aviation) Ltd in November 1928, although he remained on the board. The company retained its existing Supermarine name for future designs, now being Supermarine Works of Vickers (Aviation) Ltd. An alternative title, Supermarine Aviation Works (Vickers) Ltd, was in use in 1934.

In the summer of 1928, Supermarine fitted floats to Vickers' Vivid G-EBPY for brief waterborne trials. This was followed by the Vildebeest VII G-ABGE in October 1931. Supermarine was also entrusted by Vickers with the construction of its Viastra ten-seat, twin-engined airliners. The first fuselage arrived from its Crayford site and was completed by September 1930. As a landplane, G-AAUB was shipped to Hamble for its first flight on 1 October. Four more Viastras were built at Woolston – the final one early in 1933. This was a VIP version for the Prince of Wales and was flown from Hamble in April 1933.

Seeking an updated Southampton, the Air Ministry ordered the one-off Southampton X N252 in June 1928. Larger than the existing Southampton and powered by three Bristol Jupiters, it was flown in the spring of 1930. The X had a completely new metal fuselage married to wings built by Vickers at Weybridge. Due to its poor performance, a variety of engines were fitted during trials at Felixstowe, which showed that the design was too large. Future Supermarine designs reverted to the company's favoured twin-engine layout. Mention was made at the end of 1929 of a civil version of the Southampton X, known as the Sea Hawk II. Powered by three AS Panther engines, it was intended to carry ten passengers in service with Imperial Airways. But the Sea Hawk was never built. The success of the existing Southamptons in RAF service eventually led to design improvements to Specification R20/31. Southampton S1648 returned to Woolston for a major rebuild and re-engining with Rolls-Royce Kestrels, which gave greater range, and it flew again as the Southampton IV in July 1932. The following summer, twelve were ordered for the RAF under the new name of Scapa, with the first flying in July 1934. They entered service in 1935, at which time the final original Southamptons were still being produced at Woolston. A contemporary Supermarine advertisement showed a picture captioned 'Southampton IV' and then a few months later the same advertisement appeared captioned 'Scapa'.

The RAF issued requirement R24/31 for a larger patrol flying boat, so, instead of seeking further orders for the Scapa, Supermarine concentrated on a new design. This emerged as the Stranraer – a larger aircraft than the Scapa, powered by two 920 hp Bristol Pegasus radial engines, carrying a crew of six and having greater endurance. Prototype K3973 flew in July 1934 and was delivered to

An experimental metal-hulled version of the Southampton was flown in the spring of 1930. However, the aircraft proved too large for the RAF, who ordered the smaller Scapa instead. So the Southampton X was used for engine-development trials.

To replace the Scapa, Supermarine developed the larger Stranraer in 1934. Prototype K3937 flew in July and was followed by production aircraft built at Woolston, Hythe and Itchen. It was the final biplane flying boat to serve with the RAF.

Supermarine built seventeen Stranraers for the RAF, with the final one delivered in April 1939. Forty further aircraft were built by Canadian Vickers in Montreal to serve with the RCAF, one of whose machines is seen here.

Felixstowe for trials in October. These resulted in an order for seventeen, with K7287 delivered to the RAF in April 1937 and the last, from the Itchen site, in April 1939. This was the final biplane flying boat in RAF service – it was withdrawn in October 1942. A further forty were built by Canadian Vickers at Montreal as patrol aircraft for the RCAF; the first was delivered in November 1937. These Canadian aircraft long outlived their RAF counterparts, with the last one soldiering on until February 1946. Many of the Canadian aircraft were then employed a civil aircraft – some as twenty-seat airliners.

So the Stranraer ended the line of Supermarine large flying boats for the RAF. However, there were two further civil types dating from 1929. The first was the 92 ft span, three-engined Air Yacht built to the order of the Hon. A. E. Guinness in 1929. Reginald Mitchell had already been working on designs for a large reconnaissance flying boat and these were used for the new Air Yacht. It was fitted with a luxury interior, including provision for ten beds. Built at Hythe, it first flew in February 1930 as G-AASE, but undertook little flying before being sent to Felixstowe in May 1931 for further trials. After all this, it was rejected by the Hon. Guinness, who purchased a much smaller Saro Cloud instead. The Air

A view of the Woolston works in the early 1930s. Much development has taken place, with the old wooden shipyard sheds replaced by modern buildings. The Woolston Floating Bridge can be seen at the bottom right.

Yacht was eventually purchased by an American millionairess in the autumn of 1932, still as a luxury aircraft. While flying near Capri in January 1933, it stalled and was badly damaged in the ensuing forced landing. It was declared a write-off. The second large flying boat designed by Mitchell was the Type 179, later refered to as the Giant. Originally intended to meet a military requirement of November 1928, it was modified to meet a new Air Ministry request for a luxury forty-seat civil flying boat. A prototype was ordered in April 1930, with the design showing the influence that the huge Dornier Do-X had on Mitchell. The Supermarine 179 had a span of 185 ft and was initially to be powered by six 900 hp Rolls-Royce H engines mounted above the wing. Due to a number of design changes, construction work did not begin until the spring of 1931. Work proceeded on the hull while further design changes were made to the wing, tail and engines, but in January 1932 the contract was cancelled by the Government as an economy measure. Had the 179 entered service with Imperial Airways as planned, one wonders what effect it might have had on the Empire Class flying boats ordered from Shorts.

Building on the knowledge he had acquired while designing the Schneider racers, Mitchell responded in February 1932 to Air Ministry Specification F7/30 for a 195 mph fighter – a tame speed compared to the racers. Development was protracted, with the Type 224 emerging as an all-metal, gull-wing, open-cockpit, liquid-cooled-engine fighter. It was not until the summer of 1932 that Supermarine was given the go-ahead to build prototype K2890, which first flew from Eastleigh on 19 February 1934. Its performance was below expectations and there were problems with the steam-cooling system of the 600 hp Rolls-Royce Goshawk engine. After flight-testing, Supermarine and the Air Ministry agreed that this was not the aircraft they were looking for. Mitchell felt he had been restricted by the official specifications – he favoured working with a free hand. Interestingly, due to the time taken by the Air Ministry in ordering the prototype, the original specification was met by the Gloster Gladiator – a biplane.

The lack of performance from the Type 224 led Mitchell to persuade Supermarine that a fresh design was needed. Work started in November 1934, utilising the new Rolls-Royce PV12 engine based on experience with the Schneider racers. Supermarine took the bold step of proceeding with a private-venture aircraft, and built a mock-up in the spring of 1935. By then, the Air Ministry had ordered a prototype to new Specification F37/34, which included the requirement for eight .303 machine guns. (Interestingly, the preceding Specification F36/34 resulted in the Hawker Hurricane.) Officially ordered in December 1934, the new fighter was built at Woolston in the winter of 1935/36, and first flew as K5054 from Eastleigh on 5 March. It soon showed its promise, resulting in an initial RAF order for 310 of the now-named Spitfire being placed in June. Rolls-Royce's engine, now named Merlin, produced 1,030 hp. Supermarine realised that it would be hard-pressed to produce the Spitfires at the Woolston site and so it was arranged that production would be spread between a number of aircraft firms. Supermarine would build the fuselages, General Aircraft the wings and Folland Aircraft the tails. Smaller parts would be supplied by other local companies. The various sections would be brought together on the final production line at Eastleigh. At the same time as Supermarine were developing the Spitfire, its parent company – Vickers-Armstrongs – was developing its own fighter to Specification F5/34. This emerged as the Venom, which first flew in June 1936. But it was a tubby, angular aircraft powered by a radial engine – the designers obviously unaware of the sleek design that Mitchell had produced. It remained a prototype only. Early in 1938, Supermarine proclaimed the Spitfire the 'Fastest military aeroplane in the world'. The first production Spitfire, K9787, was completed and flown in May 1938, with the first for the RAF delivered for trials at the end of July. At the time nobody realised how the combination of Spitfire and Merlin was to influence future events.

Two more successful military amphibians appeared from Supermarines in the 1930s. First was the Walrus, which originally started out as the Seagull V to meet an Australian requirement. Having been pleased with their original Seagull IIIs, the Australians asked Supermarine in 1932 to come up with a replacement. So, starting off as a private venture, the metal-hulled prototype Seagull V was built at Hythe in 1933, and flew as N-1 in June. At the end of the month it surprised guests at the Hendon Show by undertaking a loop. Despite the reports not

The Spitfire prototype, initially refered to as the F37/34 fighter, was hand-built in the winter of 1935/36. It was then taken to Eastleigh for its first flight on 5 March, and showed great promise. In June, 310 were ordered for the RAF.

being too favourable, the Australians ordered twenty-four Seagull Vs in August 1934, with the first delivered in September 1935. Although the flying boat was called the Seagull V, it bore no resemblance to the earlier Seagulls other then the general shape. Meanwhile, the prototype was tested as K4797 by the FAA in 1934, although British interest was lukewarm. These trials resulted in an initial order in May 1935 for twelve, with the contract specifying a change of name to Walrus. The first British aircraft flew in March 1936, followed by an order for a further eight. By now it was realised that the Walrus could be a very useful aircraft and a further 168 were ordered in July. As with the Seagull, it could be catapulted from capital ships, to undertake reconnaissance sorties for the fleet, as well as operating from carriers or land bases. Later in its life, it played a valuable air–sea rescue role.

It was the Walrus orders, plus those for Spitfires, which led to Supermarine building a further large factory known as Itchen, just upstream from Woolston. From early 1939, this took over as the main Walrus production facility. Overseas

Early production Walrus K8552 in the spring of 1937. Originally the Air Ministry showed little interest, but its hand was forced when the Australians ordered the similar Seagull V. In later years, the Walrus proved invaluable in its air–sea rescue role.

air force orders included Argentina (two), Eire (three) and Turkey (six). Even before the Walrus entered service, Supermarine had designed its replacement – the Type 309, later named the Sea Otter. Larger than the Walrus and powered by an 800 hp Bristol Perseus, prototypes K8854 and K8855 were ordered in April 1936 and built at Woolston. Production commitments of Spitfires and Walruses delayed the first flight of K8854 from Eastleigh until 29 September 1938. As Supermarine had insufficient capacity, a production order for 190 Sea Otters was placed with Blackburn Aircraft in 1940. But Blackburn also suffered lack of capacity and so the order was cancelled. Production finally got underway at the end of 1942 with the aircraft built by Saro at Cowes – and now powered by a 965 hp Bristol Mercury engine.

In addition to the design work on the Spitfire fighter, Mitchell also developed the Supermarine 316 bomber to Specification B12/36. In July 1936, two prototypes were ordered, along with two of the competing design from Shorts, which emerged as the Stirling. Supermarine's design was a four-engined

The two Sea Otter prototypes were built at Woolston in 1938. Insufficient production capacity, combined with the bombing of Woolston and Itchen works, resulted in production being undertaken by Saunders-Roe at Cowes from 1942.

bomber, fitted with twin fins and carrying its bomb load in its wing. Progress was slow, especially with changes in Air Ministry requirements issued in 1937 and 1938. A mock-up was built at Woolston, the type was amended to the 317, and construction commenced on the prototype aircraft L6889/90 late in 1938. By the outbreak of war, only the fuselages had been completed, as the layout of the wings was still being finalised. Following Mitchell's untimely death from cancer in June 1937 at the age of forty-two, Joe Smith was promoted from chief draughtsman to chief designer. As such, he ably developed the Spitfire over the next ten years. In October 1938, the company's name was amended to 'Vickers Armstrongs Ltd – Supermarine Division'.

With war looming, the RAF placed a second order for 200 Spitfires in September 1938. By this time, work had started on a number of Air Ministry-funded 'shadow' aircraft factories around the country. One at Castle Bromwich was to be run by Lord Nuffield's car organisation to build Spitfires – the first order in April 1939 was for 1,000. In the spring of 1939, the Air Ministry was wondering whether to order further Spitfires from Supermarine at Woolston; the company's 510th was due to be delivered in March 1940. It had been proposed that Supermarine would switch to production of the Bristol Beaufighter, since Bristol needed additional production facilities. All this changed with the outbreak of war, with further large orders placed with Supermarine, starting with an additional 450

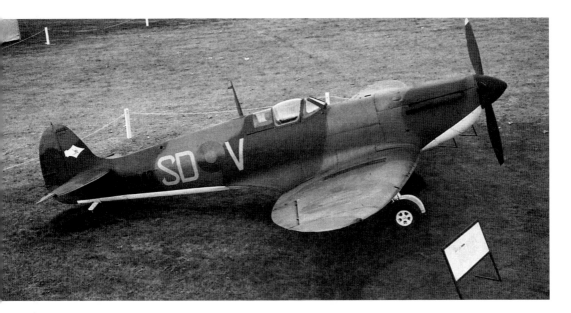

One of Woolston's early production Spitfire Is – K9942 – in an early 1940 camouflage scheme with the markings of 72 Squadron. It survived the Battle of Britain and, after further active service, was set aside for preservation.

A view showing the final layout of the Woolston works in 1938, with a Walrus on the slipway. The lack of any further building space at Woolston led to the construction of the Itchen works further upstream in 1938.

A landside view of the office block built at Woolston in 1937. This housed the design office, which was busy turning the prototype Spitfire drawings into an aircraft for mass production. In addition, it was working on the Sea Otter and Type 317 bomber.

in August 1939. Unflown Spitfire Is N3296, N3298 and N3299 were dispatched from Woolston to Castle Bromwich early in 1940 to act as pattern aircraft for the new production line. Problems in getting Castle Bromwich up and running saw it taken over by Supermarine management in the spring of 1940. The Castle Bromwich aircraft were Spitfire IIs – virtually the same as the Mk I – with the first delivered to the RAF in August 1940.

In February 1939, Joe Smith improved the Spitfire I design by beefing up the airframe. A prototype 'Superpriority Spitfire' was ordered and the rebuilt Mk I N3297 first flew in March 1940 as the Spitfire III, followed by the W3237. The Air Ministry agreed that this was an improvement and the intention was that the final 200 Mk Is be completed as Mk IIIs. A further 120 were ordered in October 1940, but they were cancelled the following April due to the success of the Mk V. This had been developed quickly, being a Mk I fitted with a more powerful 1,440 hp Merlin and greater firepower. It proved to be the main production version of the Merlin Spitfire. Rolls-Royce had also developed a new engine – the Griffon – which was suitable for the Spitfire. Initial work on a Griffon-powered Spitfire design was undertaken in 1940, but delays meant that there was no official interest until May 1941. These various proposals had to be put on the back burner due to the Battle of Britain in the summer of 1940 and the events that overtook the factory in September.

Towards the end of 1939, Smith proposed a hooked Spitfire for the Royal Navy, with a wing that folded back against the fuselage. A potential order for fifty – to be available in 1940 – was not taken up and was cancelled in March 1940 in favour of the existing Fairey Fulmar. To meet Specification N8/39, a new two-seat naval fighter was designed, but it was not ordered. Early in 1940, the Air Ministry desperately needed a floatplane fighter for use in the Norwegian Campaign. Spitfire R6722 was set aside for this purpose in April 1940, along with a set of Blackburn Roc floats. These were passed to Folland at Hamble for assembly and delivery. However, the project was cancelled by the Air Ministry in June, as it now favoured float-equipped Hurricanes.

Supermarine's production facilities were centred on Southampton and after a few months of the Second World War these were looking vulnerable to enemy attack. Spitfires and Walruses were flowing off the production lines of the adjoining sites at Woolston and Itchen, with Eastleigh busy assembling Spitfires. To counter any production disruption, a dispersal plan was drawn up in the late spring of 1940 so that aircraft could be built at a number of sites elsewhere. Locally, fuselages would be produced by Hendy's Garage in Southampton with wings from the Hants & Dorset Bus Garage, then they would be taken to Eastleigh for assembly. Production jigs were moved to these sites in early September. Spitfires would also be built all around Wessex, coming together

With the Spitfire dispersal programme of 1940, many premises around Southampton were commandeered. One of the main works was Seawards Garage in the centre of town. Unlike similar views of the time, the majority of workers here are men.

Different premises around Southampton undertook different roles in the Spitfire production process. Here, local women use their sewing skills in the completion of tailplane control surfaces. There would have been similar scenes in many towns.

for final assembly at new facilities at Henley, High Post and Keevil airfields. In addition, production was undertaken by Westland at Yeovil. Further Walrus production was undertaken by Saunders-Roe in Cowes, who later built the Sea Otter.

The benefit of this planning was realised sooner than anticipated as on 26 September 1940 both the Woolston and Itchen factories were destroyed by Luftwaffe bombing attacks. Only a few Spitfires were lost, as was the second prototype Sea Otter. The two 317 bomber fuselages at Itchen were both badly damaged, and further work on their development was given up. Under advice from Lord Beaverbrook, the Minister of Aircraft Production, Supermarine agreed to abandon the two factories and concentrate on speeding up the delivery of Spitfires from the recently set up dispersal sites. Supermarine's advance planning paid off, as deliveries of Spitfires to the RAF were not severely affected. Future design and development was undertaken from Supermarine's new headquarters at Hursley Park.

Following its destruction, the famous Woolston factory was never rebuilt by Supermarine. In 1943, part of the office block was used by the Admiralty for wartime planning. Post-war, the site was redeveloped for other industrial purposes. A reminder of the past is the old slipway, which is still to be seen alongside the Itchen Bridge. A number of memorials mark Supermarine's presence at Woolston. These include a mosaic set in the ground, best viewed from the Itchen Bridge.

SIMMONDS AIRCRAFT LTD

In July 1928, Oliver Simmonds left Supermarine Aviation so that he could concentrate on his idea of a two-seat biplane designed for ease of maintenance and repair. The wings were interchangeable, as were the tail sections. This also helped reduce manufacturing costs. Built at his home in Woolston and registered G-EBYU, the first Simmonds Spartan was assembled at nearby Weston and flown from a field at Netley at the beginning of July 1928. G-EBYU then took part in the King's Cup Race later in the month. The early promise of the Spartan design led to the formation of Simmonds Aircraft in September 1928 and the move to premises at Weston for future production of the Spartan. This was underway by the end of the year.

Worthy Down

Worthy Down was an RAF airfield, built towards end of the First World War to the north of Winchester. It only had grass runways and was used by the Navy from April 1938, with formal transfer made in May 1939 as HMS *Kestrel*. Worthy Down closed as an airfield in January 1950 and is currently in use by the Army.

VICKERS-SUPERMARINE

Due to the possibility of enemy attacks on Eastleigh, Supermarine moved its development flight-testing to Worthy Down in December 1940. Two new hangars were erected for this purpose, but they were also used for the conversion of a number of Spitfire and Seafire prototype/development aircraft. Other prototypes arrived from Hursley Park for their maiden flights.

Production flight-testing of Spitfire Is and Vs built in the Southampton area was undertaken from early 1941. More interesting work was provided by Hursley Park. The Griffon-powered Spitfire IV DP845 first flew in November 1941, followed by DP851. Further Griffon development flying was undertaken in the summer of 1942, leading to the Spitfire XII. DP851 was converted into the prototype Spitfire XX and flew again in August 1942. This tested a new mark of Griffon that powered the F21 – which first flew in December 1942.

Worthy Down was also involved in early Seafire developments. The first three hooked Spitfires, AB205, AD371 and BL676, were converted at the end of 1941. AB205 became the Seafire I; AD371 became the prototype Seafire IIC in February 1942; BL676 undertook carrier trials in the spring of 1942. The first production Seafire IIC, MA970, was fitted with folding wings in October 1942, and so became the prototype Seafire III. This was the main wartime production version, and was built by Cunliffe-Owen and Westland.

The prototype Supermarine 322 R1810 arrived from Hursley Park early in 1943 and was first flown on 6 February, with R1815 following later in the summer. The type did not enter production. Supermarine moved its flight-testing to High Post in March 1944.

Supermarine used Worthy Down for the flight-testing of production Spitfires. They also assembled a number of Spitfire and Seafire prototypes built at Hursley Park. JF318 was one of the Spitfire XIV prototypes tested in the summer of 1943.

Supermarine 322 prototype R1810 was built at Hursley Park in the winter of 1943/43 and first flown from Worthy Down in February 1943. All flight-testing was transferred to High Post in the spring of 1944.

Bibliography

BOOKS

Air-Britain, various publications.

Blake, John, and Mike Hooks, *40 Years at Farnborough: SBAC's International Aviation Showcase* (1990).

Bingham, Victor, *Folland Gnat* (2000).

Cruddas, Colin, *In Cobham's Company* (1994).

Ellis, Ken, *Wrecks & Relics* (2010).

Endres, Gunter, *British Aircraft Manufacturers* (1995).

Holmes, Harry, *Avro: The History* (1994).

Morgan, Eric B, and Edward Shacklady, *Spitfire: The History* (2000).

Payne, Richard, Stuck on the Drawing Board (2004).

Putnam Aeronautical Books, various publications.

Robertson, Bruce, *British Military Aircraft Serials* (1987).

Skinner, Stephen, *British Airliner Prototypes* (2008).

Smith, Ron, *British-Built Aircraft* (2003).

Sturtivant, Ray, *British Prototype Aircraft* (1990).

Walpole, Nigel, *Swift Justice* (2004).

Wright, Alan J., and A. B. Clancey, *Islander 96* (1996).

MAGAZINES

Aeroplane
Air-Britain News
Aircraft Illustrated
Flight
FlyPast

WEBSITES

Chilton Aircraft, *www.chilton-aircraft.co.uk* (Roy Nerou).
Flightglobal, *www.flightglobal.com*.
Hampshire Airfields, *daveg4otu.tripod.com/h.html* (Dave Fagan).
Spitfire Aircraft Production, *www.spitfires.ukf.net/*.

Airspeed Ambassadors produced at Christchurch.

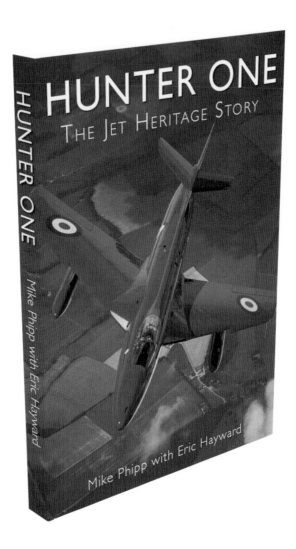

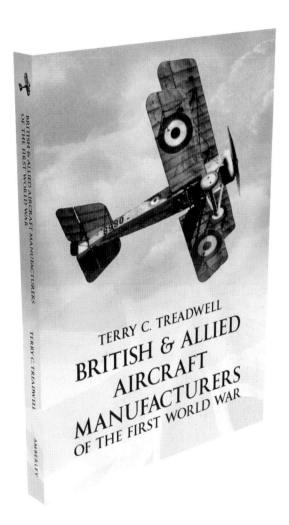

British & Allied Aircraft Manufacturers of the First World War
Terry C. Treadwell

The British air forces started the war with barely 150 aircraft but ended it with thousands. Terry Treadwell takes us through the various types in this profusely illustrated book.

978-1-4456-0101-4
224 pages, 300 b&w illustrations, RRP £17.99

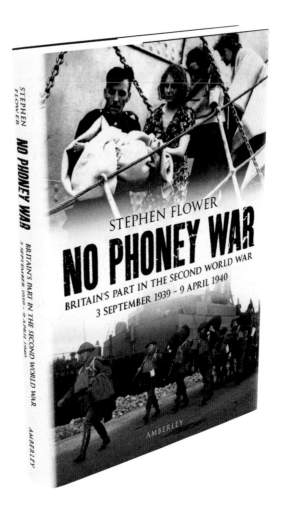